P9-DDI-371

TRUE-LIFE CRIME

☐ **THE SHOEMAKER: Anatomy of a Psychotic by Flora Rheta Schreiber.** The shocking true story of a split personality, Joseph Kallinger, and his horrifying secret life of rape and murder ... "Chilling fascination."— *Library Journal* (160320—$4.95)

☐ **BLIND FAITH by Joe McGinniss.** A galvanizing work of investigative journalism that chronicles the shocking murder of a Tom's River, New Jersey woman by her husband, while exposing the horror and growing disillusionment the couple's three sons experienced in the aftermath of the tragedy. "Remarkable ... fascinating ... a relentlessly true picture of social values gone hellishly wrong."—*Newsday* (162188—$5.95)

☐ **TWO OF A KIND: THE HILLSIDE STRANGLERS: by Darcy O'Brien.** With shocking information never before released to the public and 8-pages of chilling photographs, this is the inside story of a series of rapes, tortures, slayings and nightmares in Los Angeles. Kenneth Bianci and his cousin Angelo Buono, in the longest criminal trial in history, very nearly get away with murder.... "Vivid ... Horrifying"—*People* (163028—$4.95)

☐ **RICHIE by Thomas Thompson.** The heart-rending and powerful true crime story of a normal, strong-valued American family whose lives turn tragic when their son is drawn deeper and deeper into the nightmare world of drugs. "A powerful book.... It ought to be read by every parent and teenager."—*Los Angeles Times* (161297—$3.95)

☐ **BAD BLOOD: A Murder in Marin County by Richard M. Levine.** 1975, Marin County, a couple were savagely slain by their 16-year-old daughter and her 20-year-old lover. This is the story of that murder, and the appalling events that caused it. "A frightening, disturbing book that illuminates the breakdown of the subur-ban American family ..."—*Los Angeles Times* (155033—$4.50)

Prices slightly higher in Canada.

BLIND FAITH

Joe McGinniss

A SIGNET BOOK

NEW AMERICAN LIBRARY

A DIVISION OF PENGUIN BOOKS USA INC.

Copyright © 1989 by Joe McGinniss

The author gratefully acknowledges permission from the following
sources to reprint material in their control:

Almo Music Corp. and Delicate Music for lyrics from
"Take the Long Way Home" by Roger Hodgson and Rick Davies
© 1979 Almo Music Corp. and Delicate Music (ASCAP).
International copyright secured. All rights reserved.

All photographs courtesy of Roby and Chris Marshall.

First Signet Printing, October, 1989

1 2 3 4 5 6 7 8 9

ACKNOWLEDGMENTS

I would like to thank my former student and research assistant, Karen Houppert, for her inquiries into the history of Toms River and Ocean County and for her insights into the social mores of the area today.

I would also like to thank my lawyer and friend, Dan Kornstein, for helping me through the period of time that encompassed the writing of this book. Mr. Kornstein is a man of high principle, great compassion and profound intelligence who has elevated the practice of law to the level of moral statement. He has the personal integrity to stand up for people, books and causes he believes in, even when others do not, and for that I am more grateful than I can adequately express.

For
MATTHEW
and
JAMES

EXPLANATORY NOTE

While much of the dialogue in this book is taken directly from court transcripts, there are numerous instances in which it has been reconstructed on the basis of the author's interviews with relevant individuals. In addition, certain scenes have been dramatically re-created in order to portray more effectively the personalities of those most intimately involved in this story and the atmosphere surrounding the events upon which this book is based.

It should be recognized that a trial produces conflicting versions of events. Where such conflict exists in testimony or recollection, the author has sought to provide that version which in his opinion is the most plausible.

Except for Robert Marshall, Maria Marshall, the three sons, Roby, Chris and John, the parents of Maria Marshall, Judge Manuel Greenberg, assistant prosecutor Kevin Kelly and a few other minor characters, the author has chosen to change the names and to otherwise disguise the identities of the people involved in this story. This has been done to preserve privacy. Any similarity between the fictitious names used and those of living persons is, of course, entirely coincidental.

There is no steady unretracing progress in this life; we do not advance through fixed gradations, and at the last one pause: through infancy's unconscious spell, boyhood's thoughtless faith, adolescence's doubt (the common doom), then skepticism, then disbelief, resting at last in manhood's pondering repose of If. But once gone through, we trace the round again; and are infants, boys, and men, and Ifs eternally. Where lies the final harbor, whence we unmoor no more?

—HERMAN MELVILLE
Moby-Dick

Part One

THE
BOYS

1

At eleven o'clock on the morning of September 6, 1984, Roby Marshall was awakened by his mother. This was unusual. Most days he'd been sleeping past noon.

Where he should have been was back at Villanova for his sophomore year, getting up at eight o'clock in the morning and going to class. But there had been a difficulty in the dorm the previous spring, just before final exams. The difficulty had involved beer, half a dozen other male freshmen, and the kicking down of a resident assistant's door. Roby Marshall, along with others, had been instructed to spend the fall semester of his sophomore year elsewhere, awaiting January readmission. He'd enrolled at Stockton State College near Atlantic City, forty minutes down the parkway from his home in Toms River, New Jersey, but classes there did not begin for another week, and so late on this Thursday morning, as on most other mornings since his job as an Ortley Beach lifeguard had ended, Roby Marshall was still in bed.

"Roby, honey," his mother said. "Your father and I are having lunch at the club. Do you want to come?"

Roby's relationship with his father had been a little rocky through the summer. Rob Senior, a Villanova graduate (class of '63) and the most prominent insurance salesman in Toms River, had not been pleased by Roby's suspension. He had, in fact, refused to give Roby the new Mustang convertible he had promised upon completion of Roby's freshman year. That had been a blow—having to drive the crappy old yellow Mustang to the beach all summer—but even worse had been his father's short temper and cold silences for the past three months.

Since he was going to be living at home through Christmas, commuting (in the old yellow Mustang) to classes at Stockton State, Roby figured he'd better try to mend fences, even if it did mean, on this occasion, getting up before noon.

He told his mother he would join them, then got up, showered, blow-dried his curly blond hair, put on a pair of freshly pressed designer jeans and a freshly laundered shirt from Grog's Surf Palace in Seaside Park (Roby's parents took great pride in how well their children dressed), and went downstairs to the kitchen.

The Marshall house was located on Crest Ridge Drive in the Brookside section of Toms River. Brookside was the neighborhood that people in Toms River moved to when they wanted to show others how well they were doing. The Marshalls had lived there since 1971. Since then, in addition to their country club membership, they'd acquired an in-ground swimming pool, a time share in a Florida condo, an ivory Cadillac, a station wagon, Roby's yellow Mustang, and a new Jeep for his younger brother Chris, who had just begun his freshman year at Lehigh. John, who at thirteen was the youngest of the three boys, had already been promised a Porsche.

Roby kissed his mother and sat at the kitchen counter. She handed him a glass of orange juice. Now that he was up, he was eager to move. "So let's go," he said. "Where's Dad?"

He noticed a sudden tenseness in his mother's expression. "God knows where your father is these days," she said. Then she turned and walked quickly from the kitchen. That was unusual. Most days—though usually it was early afternoon instead of morning—Maria Marshall would be waiting in the kitchen when Roby came down. After giving him juice she'd make him pancakes and then sit at the table and engage him in conversation while he ate. Roby had found this one of the few good things about getting tossed out of school temporarily—the chance to spend more time with his mother.

He'd always been close to her, as had his brothers. She was not only his Mom, he liked to say, but his best friend. Most guys his age—Roby was nineteen— would be embarrassed if told they looked like their mothers. Roby was proud. He had always thought his mother was the most beautiful woman in Toms River.

Roby was six one and broad shouldered and had been a record-setting swimmer in high school, but in his open, round, still slightly babyish face, he did bear an unmistakable resemblance to Maria. At forty-two, with striking blond hair, soft blue eyes, unwrinkled skin, a trim, athletic figure and one of the most extensive—and expensive—wardrobes in Ocean County, she was a woman always noticed and often envied. For Roby, lunch at the club with her would be a treat.

Shortly after noon, his father got home—late, as always; and, as usual these days, irritable and in a hurry. Rob Marshall, at forty-five, was the same height as his oldest son, with a hairline that was receding gracefully, if rapidly, above eyes that were just as flinty as Maria's were soft. His lips were so thin and colorless as to seem almost transparent and his jaw jutted forward hard as the prow of a ship. Until quite recently, the jaw, and Rob overall, had been padded by a beefy layer of middle-age fat, but he'd lost a lot of weight in recent months so that it was now the herky-jerky, nervous energy that one first noticed about him.

Just as the three of them started down the front steps toward the Cadillac, another car pulled up and a man Roby did not know got out.

"Just be a minute," Roby's father said, and he walked quickly with the man back through the living room and into his first-floor office.

"What's that all about?" Roby asked his mother.

"These days," Maria said, "who knows?"

Whatever it was, it didn't take long. In less than five minutes, Rob and the man emerged from the office. Again, they started down the front walk, this time accompanied by the man, whom Rob introduced simply as "Mr. Girard."

When they reached their cars, Rob said goodbye to Mr. Girard.

"Have a nice vacation," Mr. Girard said.

In the car, Roby asked his father what that had meant, since there was no vacation coming up.

"I don't know," Rob said impatiently. "Maybe he was just trying to be funny."

"Ha ha," Maria said, in a voice that betrayed no amusement.

Have a nice vacation. That was one of the little things that didn't mean anything at the time that Roby remembered later, when everything seemed to mean a great deal.

Another occurred on the way home from the club, after lunch, when his mother pulled a cassette out of the tape deck and then picked up the plastic box on which the names of the songs had been written. From the back seat, Roby could see his mother reading the names of the songs.

"Don't you have any that remind you of me?" she asked Rob.

Keeping one hand on the wheel, and driving slightly faster than normal, Roby's father reached down and rummaged through the clutter of cassette boxes beneath the front seat. He kept glancing back and forth, from the road to the tapes. Finally, he found what he was looking for. Roby couldn't see what it was, but it didn't really matter anyway. What he remembered, later, was the ice-cold tone in which his father said the word "there," as he held the box out to Maria.

In the afternoon, Roby's girlfriend, Susan Salzman, came over to the house and they played Trivial Pursuit with Maria. Trivial Pursuit had been the hot game all over Brookside that summer. Rob and Maria Marshall had played it avidly, often with Roby and Chris and their friends, often until 2 or 3 A.M., Rob chugalugging Coca-Cola, the boys swigging Pepsi, Rob and Maria always a team and always the winners, kissing each other after each correct answer as if they were teenagers themselves.

Even playing the Baby Boomer edition, Roby was no match for his mother. There were just too many things—*Where is Kruger National Park? What were the first names of the Maverick brothers? What's known as the universal solvent?*—that his Toms River East high school education had not covered. And Susan Salzman, just starting her senior year at East, was not much help.

In late afternoon, Maria went upstairs to dress for the evening. She and Rob were going to Atlantic City for dinner at the Meadows, the most expensive of the six restaurants at Harrah's Marina, followed by an hour or two of blackjack.

The trip to Harrah's had become a weekly ritual for the Marshalls. In this they were no different from most of their Toms River friends. Since the coming of the gambling casinos in the late 1970s, Atlantic City had become the hub of Toms River social life. Just forty quick miles down the Garden State Parkway, the glittery towers that now lined the boardwalk had suddenly brought to life for the residents of an undistinguished small town along the central New Jersey shore a chrome-plated, free-spending world that had previously existed only on television.

The casino lifestyle did not simply fill a recreational void for the country club set of Toms River: it became the ultimate status symbol. To get "comped"—that is, given a free meal and tickets to a show—at an Atlantic City gambling casino was something you could brag about for weeks. To let it be known that Atlantic City had become the center of your social life ("Dinner Saturday? Gee, we'd love to, but we've got reservations at the Nugget.") was to inform your peers that you had really begun to move in the express lane.

And no one cared more about that sort of thing than Rob Marshall. He didn't just go to a casino, he ran casino bus tours out of his house (in return for which he was "comped" extravagantly). He didn't just play blackjack, he cofounded an instructional club called the Winner's Circle. When he bought a boat—and in Toms River a boat was as necessary a symbol of affluence as a Cadillac—he named it after a type of blackjack bet, the "Double Down."

If Maria was not quite so enthralled by the lifestyle, she certainly didn't find it objectionable. The fact was that the casinos and their most expensive restaurants gave her an arena in which to display the clothes she had purchased in Short Hills or on Fifth Avenue. And there is no question but that she enjoyed the attention lavished upon her by the headwaiters and maître d's to whom she had become such a familiar presence.

When she came downstairs at six o'clock, the smell of her perfume preceding her, Roby whistled. His mother's loveliness was something he just never got used to. People still told her that even at forty-two she looked more like his big sister than his mother, and Roby agreed.

Tonight, though, she did not seem her usual tranquil, cheerful self. All day, Roby thought, she had seemed edgy. And now his father was late again and Roby didn't feel like asking where he was.

Instead, he grabbed a box of Trivial Pursuit cards—the pink questions, Entertainment. Those were the ones his mother knew best.

"What film featured the characters Charlie Allnut and Rosey Sayer?" he called out.

"The African Queen," Maria said.

"Who called himself 'The Errol Flynn of B Movies'?"

She didn't know. "Ronald Reagan," he told her.

"What had one eye, one horn and flew in the 1958 hit by Sheb Wooley?"

She smiled. "The Flying Purple People Eater, of course."

This went on for another fifteen minutes. Then he heard his father calling, telling Maria to hurry, they were late.

Roby kissed her goodbye, the way he did every time either he or she left the house. The night was chilly, unusual for that early in September. Roby spent much of it in front of the television set, doing sit-ups while watching the movie *The World According to Garp.* It wound up as such a bloody mess he didn't like it. Also, it was completely unrealistic. There was no way that intelligent, middle-class parents could ever be so violent and weird.

After talking to Susan Salzman on the phone, he went to bed around midnight, which was early for him.

What woke him, about three hours later, was the sound of a hand fumbling in the darkness, reaching for the light switch on his wall.

Then the light came on and he saw his father in the doorway, crying, and he saw the blood that stained his father's shirt.

The last time Chris Marshall saw his mother was on Friday, August 24, when she and his father left him on the campus of Lehigh University in Bethlehem, Pennsylvania, for the start of his freshman year.

It was not a scene that the Marshalls had ever expected would be played out in Bethlehem, Pennsylvania. What they'd envisioned, all through Chris's career at Toms River East, where he had ranked in the top ten percent of his class, been editor of his yearbook, a member of the National Honor Society and possessor of six different county swim records, was Princeton.

For Roby, who had always been drawn more to parties than to schoolwork, even Villanova had been stretching. He would have been content with Lycoming or East Stroudsburg or any of the other northern Pennsylvania colleges that had proven themselves easy to get into. For Chris, however, the standard had been set higher, which was exactly the way he'd wanted it. He didn't drink, he didn't smoke, he studied until after midnight, and all his teachers remembered him as one of the brightest and nicest students they'd ever encountered.

By his junior year, selecting the right college for him and then making sure he got admitted had become his mother's major project. He'd entered all of his vital statistics, as well as his desire for a career in

architecture, into a computer at the guidance office at
Toms River East. The computer had produced a list of
colleges. His mother had taken the list and a Barron's
college guidebook, and had sat up nights working things
out. Then she'd met with the high school guidance
counselor. Then she'd phoned the colleges' admissions
offices. Then she'd planned the trips to the various
campuses. Then she'd prepared a three-page brochure
that called attention to his merits (including all his
awards and every activity in which he'd ever partici-
pated, as well as a color photograph just because she
thought he was so handsome) and had mailed it to the
colleges at the top of her list. And then, when it came
time to fill out the applications, she'd done it all, even
a bit of rewriting of the essays. (The only mistake that
Chris ever spotted was that she'd left the *i* out of
architecture in every one.) And finally, when it became clear that Princeton was at the top of the list,
she'd actually walked up to U.S. Senator (and Princeton
alumnus) Bill Bradley at a reception and had asked
him to recommend Chris.

Thus, for Maria, it was not just a shock but a
personal rejection when Princeton informed Chris that
he had not been admitted.

Still, there was nothing wrong with Lehigh, especially when they offered a partial scholarship for swimming. Lehigh was a fine school. Very strong in
engineering, as everyone knew. Chris was happy about
it from the start, and before long, so was Maria. It
wouldn't be *quite* the same to talk at the club about
how well Chris was doing at Lehigh as opposed to
Princeton, but the club, after all, was not exactly steeped
in Ivy League tradition.

Chris and his parents had driven to the campus at
the beginning of August to talk with the swimming
coach about what kind of year they could expect.

Maria had asked most of the questions—how would Chris do his laundry (for the first time, she wouldn't be there to do it for him), whether it was customary for parents to attend the home meets (at Toms River East, not only had the Marshalls attended, but Maria had led the cheering section and Rob had videotaped every meet), and which hotel was recommended. What the coach had noticed most about Chris's father was how terribly nervous he seemed.

Three weeks later, they came back for the start of the term, arriving early in the day so Chris would be first in the room and thus able to get the best bed, the best drawer space, the desk near the window. While he and his father went off to go through the registration procedures, Maria stayed in the room to put all his clothes away and to make his bed with brand-new sheets.

After that they'd walked down the hill (the campus was set on a steep hill overlooking the town) to eat lunch at a restaurant called the Bridge Works. All through the meal, Maria had cried. Chris had never seen his mother cry so hard. Sure, she was going to miss him, just as he would miss her acutely—if anything, he'd been even closer to his mother than had Roby, and much more obviously dependent on her—but Lehigh was only two and a half hours from Toms River and he'd undoubtedly be seeing her at least two or three times a month.

He couldn't figure out why his mother had cried so much, but very soon he was too busy to spend time thinking about it. Also, Maria seemed to regain her customary cheerfulness quickly. On Saturday, August 25, a gorgeous late-summer day, she sent him a note saying, "What a great weekend you have for starting school. I'm only concerned you don't have enough clothes. HA!" Enclosed were laundry instructions: "¼ cup detergent. Separate light colors from dark. Warmwater wash the light colors. Cold-water wash the dark." Chris considered that a good sign. If his mother was focusing on laundry she was clearly herself again.

Two days later she sent him another note, saying, "I took Mrs. A out to lunch today. She leaves Wednesday for Florida. I'm going to miss her a lot." That was Andrea Alfonso, perhaps his mother's closest friend. She had recently been divorced and had almost immediately discovered one of the basic facts of life among the Toms River Country Club set: the wives had no social life without the husbands. The husbands had created the social-business network that made whatever happened in Toms River happen. Except for their domestic functions, the wives were strictly ornamental. The system had no place in it for ex-wives. Women—especially those over forty—whose husbands had walked out on them vanished from the scene so quickly and absolutely it was as if they'd been kidnapped in Lebanon. Leaving town was really the only option.

The last letter Chris received from his mother was written on Labor Day, September 3, just after he'd told her about his election as dorm president.

Dearest Chris—

Hi, sweet. It was so good to hear your voice last night. You sound great. Once again, congratulations, Mr. President. I'm *so* proud of you.

Then Maria went on to describe her weekend, which had featured a quick trip to Columbus, Ohio, with Rob to visit friends and attend an Ohio State football game.

We got to the stadium an hour and a half before it began. Your father was *thrilled*. (HA!) We saw all the football players get off the bus (we got there ahead of the team).

Pete Finley has a new Mercedes 450 SLE, brown with a tan interior. He has an alarm system in it that's so sensitive that it goes off even when a car door next to it is slammed! They really gave us the red carpet.

Last night, we took Grandma and Grandpop to dinner at PJ's in Bayville. We all pigged out. When you come home we'll take you guys there. I think you'll like it.

Knock 'em dead at Lehigh. You've got the "Right Stuff." We all miss you mucho.

> Love ya,

At ten o'clock on Thursday night, September 6, he was in his room studying when the phone rang. It was his parents, calling from their table at the Meadows restaurant at Harrah's Marina. Chris could just picture his father sitting there, feeling so important because he'd had a phone brought to the table.

They were calling to say how much they missed him and to urge him to come home for the weekend. But Chris figured that if he was ever going to learn to live on his own he'd better actually do it, and so he told them that he had too much work to do and would be staying on campus for the weekend.

At two o'clock the next afternoon, Chris was sitting on the top half of a bunk bed in his dorm room, talking with his roommate and another friend. Physically, Chris bore more of a resemblance to his father than to his mother (though most who knew the family said the reverse was true in terms of personality).

He was just under six feet tall, with a dark-blond crewcut, stronger, more fully formed facial features than those of his brother, and the well-muscled body of the competitive athlete. Of the two older boys, Chris had always seemed the more mature in many

ways, the more conscientious and responsible, the one
more eager to please adults. He was the one of whom
teachers said, "I've never had another kid I liked as
much."

The door to the room opened and Chris saw his
father standing there. Right away, just from the expression on his father's face, Chris knew that something was wrong. He looked over his father's shoulder
for his mother, expecting her to be standing in the
doorway, because all his life he'd been used to seeing
the two of them together, and because if something
was so wrong that his father had had to drive all the
way out to Lehigh to see him, then surely his mother
must have come, too.

"Where's Mom?" he said.

Chris's father didn't answer. Instead, he motioned
to the two other freshmen in the room.

"Guys," he said. "Get out." Then he pulled a chair
away from a desk and took a seat. Chris jumped down
from the bunk bed and stepped toward him.

Rob Marshall looked up at his son. The two of them
were now alone in the room.

"Something terrible has happened," Chris's father
said.

2

AS soon as Roby came awake enough to see the priest from St. Joseph's, Father Mulcahy, standing at his father's side, he knew that his mother was dead.

What was strange was that nobody said anything. Once they saw that Roby was awake, the two men left the room and walked down the hall to the bedroom of his younger brother John. They were back in what seemed like less than a minute, with John, who looked very sleepy and confused.

Then Rob sat on Roby's bed and John sat on the foot of the bed, next to him, and Rob put his head on Roby's chest, crying harder. He was trying to talk through his sobs. Trying to tell Roby what had happened. Something about pulling into a picnic area to change a flat tire. Being followed. Getting hit on the head. Maria shot. Maria dead. Roby's mother. *Murdered!*

Roby had been sitting up to listen. Now he lay down again, on his back, feeling that he was about to throw up. Later, he remembered thinking, *"This* is a stupid dream, buddy," and knowing that he had to wake up. He was crying. He knew he was crying. But over his own sobs he heard the sound of his brother. John was *bawling.*

Poor John. Only thirteen. He would need help.

Roby sat up again and made himself stop crying and then actually made himself talk.

"You know that Mom's happier than we are right now," he said. "She's in heaven." Then he reached across the bed and took his younger brother in his arms and hugged him tight. All the while, he could hear his father's voice. Saying, "I wish it was me, I wish it was me," through his tears.

What time was all this? Three A.M.? Four A.M.? It didn't matter. Time had stopped. His mother was dead. His brother was hysterical. His father had blood all over his shirt and also, Roby could see, stitches to close a cut on his head. The priest didn't seem to know what to do, what to say. Who could blame him? Nobody could know what to do. Except his mother. She always knew just what to do, just what to say, to comfort her sons. He remembered the smell of her perfume. He remembered how great she had looked dressed for dinner. And the delighted way she had laughed when she'd said, "Purple People Eater."

He didn't throw up. But he didn't really stop crying, either, even though he knew he had to be strong because his brother John was going to need a lot of help. He didn't feel strong. He felt sick. The terror was locked into the pit of his stomach and he was a little boy again, crying because he'd lost his mother, except that this time he'd never find her and it wasn't a dream, like the dreams he'd often had of his parents being killed in an automobile accident, and it wasn't a movie, either, like *Garp*. His mother had been murdered by a man with a gun in the Oyster Creek picnic area off the Garden State Parkway, ten miles south of Toms River.

At some point his father put on a clean shirt. Then the police came. That pissed him off. He needed time. He needed to talk more to his father. He needed to find out exactly what had happened. He needed to figure out why. He needed to know if his mother had suffered. He needed somebody to tell him what to do next.

The police said they had to take his father to the Bass River state police barracks in order for him to make a formal statement. Roby got more pissed. He started yelling at one of the cops, some smart-ass detective named O'Brien, a guy with a mustache who had the kind of 1890s face that made him look like a cop from a silent movie. Bass River was more than a half hour away. It was on the parkway, well south of Oyster Creek. That meant his father would be driven right past the picnic area where it had happened. This seemed so unnecessary, so unfair, after all that had already happened.

"Relax, son," O'Brien said. "I pride myself on being a fast driver. We'll have him back to you in no time."

Then his father was gone. It was just Roby and John and the priest, and the priest looked as if he wanted to get out of there, too. Who could blame him?

Roby went to the phone. It was now 6 A.M. Susan Salzman would be getting up for school. Roby called her, told her that his mother had been murdered. Within twenty minutes, she and her own mother were at the house.

Some time after it was light out, Rob got back from the state police. Before long the phone started ringing. News of the murder apparently had been broadcast on the radio. By 8:30, friends were already arriving at the house. Joe Moore, who'd been Rob's boss when he'd worked for Prudential. Sal and Paula Coccaro, who were friends from the club. Sal owned a restaurant-supply business on Route 37.

"She loved you two so much," Rob said. "You know

she loved you. You know she loved you." Paula
Coccaro could barely walk. She looked as if she was
about to faint. Sal just looked stunned. He hugged
Roby and John a lot. Roby found it hard to move
around. His limbs felt overwhelmingly heavy, as if he
were standing underwater. He also knew how much
new horror still lay ahead. Chris hadn't even been told
yet. Neither had Grandma and Grandpop, his mother's parents, who lived in Philadelphia. His Uncle
Gene, a lawyer—the husband of one of his father's
three sisters—was said to be on his way to the house
from Wilmington, Delaware.

Somebody had followed them, his father kept saying.
A car had followed them into the picnic area when
he'd turned in there to check a tire that had felt like it
was going flat. It must have been someone who'd
followed them all the way from the casino. Someone
who'd seen them win money at blackjack. It was a
robbery. He'd been knocked unconscious as he knelt
at the rear of the car to check the tire. When he
awoke he found his head bleeding, more than two
thousand dollars in cash missing from his pants pocket
and Maria sprawled facedown across the front seat of
the car in a puddle of blood.

Roby was amazed at how quickly his father had
become functional again. He'd already been on the
phone making funeral arrangements. There was to be
no viewing. Maria's body would be cremated. They'd
have a memorial mass at St. Joseph's on Monday,
followed by a reception back at the house. That was
the way Maria would have done it, Rob kept saying.

At some point, Roby went back upstairs and lay on
his bed. Images of his mother flooded his mind. She
was so real, so warm, so loving, so alive . . . she
couldn't be dead. She had always been so *there* for
him, she couldn't all of a sudden be not there. He kept

telling himself it still might be a bad dream. Worse than bad. The worst and longest dream he'd ever had. But then he heard the sound of his brother John crying down the hall. It wasn't a dream. It was real. But how could it be real when it seemed so unreal?

The worst of it was that every other time in his life when he'd felt sad, alone, threatened, despondent or unfairly maligned, his mother had been there to help. She was the one person he'd always been able to turn to, the one person who would always understand and who would know just the right words to say to make things better. Even at nineteen, Roby had still had that kind of relationship with his mother. He'd known it was unusual but that had made it all the more valuable. His mother's love and concern and understanding were the most precious gifts that Roby had ever received and there had not been a day he could remember when he hadn't, at least once, told himself how lucky he was because of her. He'd never taken her for granted. On the other hand, he'd known that she would always be there. He'd often thought that he'd like to get married young—he didn't know to whom yet, Susan Salzman wasn't *that* big a romance— just so he could watch his mother's face as she held her first grandchild in her arms.

It was images like that—dreams that now would never become reality—that filled his mind. He knew he needed to keep thinking about good things. Otherwise, some of the other images might creep in. His mother lying facedown on the front seat of the Cadillac, all the blood and warmth and love draining from her. His mother looking out the car window and seeing somebody coming at her with a gun. Did she yell? Why didn't she run? Why hadn't they shot his father, too?

The phone kept ringing. Sal Coccaro had volunteered for the job of answering it. Paula Coccaro was trying to comfort John. His father had retreated to his office, where he had a separate phone line. Roby made himself get up and go back downstairs. In early afternoon, his Uncle Gene arrived. Being a lawyer, he knew how to act calm, he knew how to be organized. It was good to know that someone was now in charge. That Roby wouldn't have to be a full-fledged grown-up quite yet. For a few more hours, at least, he could still be a little boy who missed his mother.

Gene and Roby's father assembled two groups to bear the bad tidings. Gene and Roby and John would go to Philadelphia to break the news to Grandpop and Grandma, Dr. and Mrs. Puszynski, and then bring them back to Toms River. Rob and Joe Moore and Chris's ex-girlfriend, Melissa Merrill, would go to Lehigh to tell Chris and to bring him home. Poor Joe. He had just walked in for a previously scheduled business meeting, having no idea that Maria had been murdered.

Sal and Paula would stay in the house to answer the phone. Rob talked to Sal just as he would talk to a secretary. "I want you to write down every call," he said. "And whoever it is, be sure to find out if they want a return call. Keep a separate list of those, so I'll know who I have to call back." Paula just couldn't stop crying, which was starting to get on Roby's nerves. He dreaded the trip to Philadelphia (actually, what he really dreaded was the trip back, with his aged, unwell grandparents in the car), but it would be good to get out of the house.

Maria's parents lived in a row house in Philadelphia's old Polish neighborhood of Port Richmond. It was one of those neighborhoods that look like a foreign country, with narrow, cobblestoned streets and low, brick-front buildings and signs in store windows in Polish. Old people in dark clothing walked the streets slowly. Old people who had been through a lot. Casimir's Barber Shop and the Polish Army Veterans were across the street from the Puszynski home, and the Syrenka Restaurant was a couple of doors down, enshrouded by the smell of steaming cabbage. Vincent Puszynski, Maria's father, had been born in Port Richmond and had never found reason to leave. For forty years he'd practiced medicine from an office attached to his house. He'd been one of those doctors who, if a patient was unable to come up with cash, would be happy to accept a crock of soup or some freshly baked bread for services rendered.

In the late 1970s, with the coming of Medicare and all its paperwork and what he felt was government interference in private enterprise, Vincent Puszynski retired. Since then, he'd had a heart attack. He was in his midseventies, as was Maria's mother, who in recent years had begun the slow slide into senility.

The two of them had been rock-solid Catholics all their lives, their values those of the old country. Maria had been their only child. They worshipped her just as ardently as they did the Blessed Virgin. The two of them—Maria their daughter and Mary the mother of Jesus—accounted for ninety percent of the pictures that hung in the Puszynski home. Photos of their three grandchildren and an oil painting of the Last Supper that hung above the dinner table and was almost as large as the table itself made up the other ten percent.

Maria, of course, had gone to Catholic schools: St. Adalbert's for elementary school and high school and then Chestnut Hill College. She'd commuted to it by trolley along Germantown Avenue. Going away to school had not even been considered. Young women away from home were subject to bad influences. The

Puszynskis were not the kind of parents to subject their only child to that sort of pressure. In addition, Vincent Puszynski had never forgotten what had happened to his mother.

In 1917, when he was nine years old, his mother had become one of the first residents of Philadelphia to die in a plane crash. His mother and brother, right out there on Roosevelt Boulevard on a Sunday afternoon. There was a pilot with a Flying Jenny, charging five dollars a ride. It was always a treat to go to the Boulevard on Sundays, it put people in a festive mood. Sure, his mother had said, she'd go up. His brother made such a fuss she took him with her. Vincent Puszynski and his father watched the plane go up, his mother smiling and waving, his brother looking grim, a little scared. He watched it in the air, watched it start to fall, watched it drop like a rock a mile up the Boulevard from where he stood. But for years he refused to admit she was dead. He kept saying, "She's hiding somewhere. She'll be back."

With Maria, his only child, he took no chances. Even when she was in college he would not schedule patients for late afternoon on school days. Instead, he would drive up to the intersection of Germantown and Allegheny and meet her trolley. Just to assure himself: she had come back.

But now she'd never be back again. And even the worst of his nightmare fantasies about something terrible happening to her—a car accident, a problem during childbirth, breast cancer—had not included murder. Maria Marshall, faithful only daughter and classic, archetypal suburban mother, existed in a carefully shielded universe where random acts of violence did not occur.

Roby couldn't tell who took it worse, Grandma or Grandpop. Grandma had started weeping the minute

Uncle Gene had said what happened and she hadn't
even tried to make herself stop. She was already so
senile, so out of it, so locked into her old Polish dream-
world, that this tragedy might well turn out to be a
mortal blow. Grandpop didn't cry. He didn't speak.
After the first five minutes, he didn't even ask any
questions. All the way back to Toms River he just
stared out the window of the car. It was as if Roby and
John weren't even there. No way that Roby could play
the radio. Just silence thick as quicksand except for his
grandmother's steady weeping. What made it even
worse was the traffic. Friday afternoon commuter traffic. They must have sat at the Cherry Hill circle for
half an hour. Roby could hear his Uncle Gene, who
was driving, start breathing harder, as if he needed to
decompress lest he explode. This was a new, painful
twist to Roby's agony: being stuck in traffic with his
grandmother's sobs. It made him want to shatter the
car windows with his fists. Roby had always grown
angry and impatient in heavy traffic. But that was
because there was always somewhere he wanted to go.
Surprising, in a way, that it was even worse when you
didn't want to get where you were going.

The traffic stayed heavy all the way. If Roby were
driving he would have floored it and whipped around
most of those cars. But Uncle Gene apparently did not
want to add fear to the Puszynskis' sorrow. They stayed
in line, creeping slowly along Route 70. This was only
the first weekend after Labor Day and Friday evening
traffic to the shore was still like summer's.

It was eight o'clock before they pulled into the
driveway. Then, before they were even out of the car,
Rob, in the station wagon, pulled in behind them.
There was just enough light from the open car doors
so that Roby could see that his brother Chris was still
crying.

They embraced in the driveway and then Roby, too, began to cry again.

"Dad, what is it? Where's Mom?" Chris had said.

His father looked him squarely in the eye. "We were driving home from Atlantic City, Chris, and somebody followed us and she was shot. She's dead."

Chris and Rob were both sitting backward on their chairs, their toes almost touching. Rob leaned forward and put his head down on Chris's chest. As if he were the one who needed comforting.

In that first moment, Chris was so stunned—*this can't be happening, this can't be real, nobody could ever shoot my mother, I love her too much for her to die*—that the only thought he was able to recall clearly when finally he was able to talk about it was the worst thought he could have had: *Dad, if you had something to do with this, I'll never forgive you.*

Why would he think such a thing? How could such a truly vile and horrible idea occur? He didn't know, not then or later, and the thought was gone as quickly as it had come.

Chris rode in the back seat going home. He kept falling asleep. It was the only escape open to him. He didn't know why his father had brought Melissa Merrill. He'd broken up with her back in June. It was good of her to come and he was still friends with her, but he didn't want to have to talk to her now. Nor to Joe Moore, either. Joe Moore was someone he barely knew. Why hadn't his father come alone, so the two of them could have talked?

Every time he woke up he asked a question. "What did she say? Did she suffer? Was she afraid?" It was those moments between the time his father was knocked unconscious and the time his mother was shot that tormented him most. His father's answers were vague.

Trying to picture the scene kept Chris awake for a while. How much time had elapsed between his father's being hit and the shooting? His mother must have been going crazy. Chris had an extremely logical mind and tried to fit the pieces into a pattern that made sense. It didn't work. Why hadn't she jumped out of the car, tried to run? He couldn't imagine her, having just seen his father get knocked out, simply lying facedown on the front seat to wait for whatever happened next. He knew the Oyster Creek picnic area. It sat right between the parkway's northbound and southbound lanes. Just twenty yards in either direction and she could have been out on the road. Even at one o'clock in the morning there was traffic—especially northbound, heading back from Atlantic City. Sure, they might have shot her as she ran, but why not try it? Anything was better than just lying down and waiting to die.

Then he considered how terrified she must have been. Nothing in the highly polished, well-organized suburban Catholic life she'd always led could have remotely prepared her for dealing with a gunman in the woods in the dark. She would have instinctively reached out to Rob to solve the problem. But Rob was lying unconscious by the trunk of the car. And the gunman was now coming toward her, making it clear that this was not a problem that could be solved. Yes, it was possible that she had simply been paralyzed by her fear. That she'd lain down and shut her eyes in a desperate, pathetic attempt to pretend that it wasn't really happening.

It was just too awful to contemplate. Chris stopped asking questions. He fell asleep again as the car reached the eastern end of the Pennsylvania Turnpike and crossed the Delaware River and entered New Jersey. At least, thank God, they could take the Jersey Turnpike north to 195. They wouldn't have to go near the Garden State.

When he awoke the next time, he kept his eyes closed. He didn't say anything to anybody. He just thought about his mother. If he thought hard enough, and remembered clearly enough, it might be a way of keeping her alive.

He thought about swimming. That had been the biggest thing in Chris's life since fourth grade, and his mother had been so involved she'd done everything but jump in the pool with him. Before each meet, she would decorate the whole house with banners and crepe paper in school colors and she'd have corsages made up for the mother of every swimmer on the team, passing them out at poolside as Rob set up his video equipment to tape the meet. Rob's equipment, of course, was the newest and best and most expensive available, and he insisted on setting it up in exactly the same spot every time, as if he were ABC covering the Olympics. That became a little annoying to some people, but Maria's enthusiasm never did.

She was easy to spot at a swim meet: the blond lady in the expensive clothes (though sometimes she would show up in a red cowboy hat and cowboy boots) cheering the loudest. And after each Friday home meet, win or lose (usually it was win because Roby and especially Chris, who set nine school records and was named Ocean County Swimmer of the Year as a senior, made Toms River East conference champions three years in a row), it was back to the Marshall house for a party. Sometimes eighty or ninety parents and kids. They'd send out to Antonio's for pizzas— twenty large pizzas, or twenty-five—and watch the videotapes Rob had made at the meet, or play with the fancy new video games and pinball machine in the basement rec room. No surprise that when Chris was a senior, his mother was voted the swim team Mother of the Year.

Chris knew he owed a great deal to his mother. When he was nine years old and didn't even feel like getting wet, she'd made him join the country club swim team. That had been the start of what was turning out to be a career. As a senior, he'd broken almost every record in the county: the 200 individual medley, the 50 freestyle, the 100 butterfly, the 100 freestyle, the 500 freestyle, the 100 backstroke, just about all of them except for diving. His name had been in the headlines every week. His coach had gotten calls from dozens of colleges. In Toms River he was even mentioned as a 1988 Olympic candidate.

And all of it, Chris felt, was because of his mother. On one wall of his room he had a cartoon torn from a swimming magazine. It depicted the ultimate "swimming parents." The mother was wearing a school jacket with prize ribbons pinned all over it. She was holding extra bathing suits, extra goggles, extra nose plugs and several stopwatches. The father stood next to her with his video camera. To Chris, it didn't even seem like a caricature. His parents were exactly like that.

No matter how early he had to get up for an away meet on a Saturday morning, 6 A.M., even 5:30, Maria would be up before him, making pancakes, packing his bag, preparing his lunch. After her death, when trying to explain what a wonderful mother she had been, it was the pancakes that Chris remembered first. "She always used fresh butter for every batch," he said, "and each pancake always had a crisp little 'butter edge' around the outside. She made the best pancakes in the world."

She would also do things like this: if East had a meet against archrival North, nicknamed the Mariners, Maria would put a sign over the toilet in the boys' bathroom saying "Flush the Mariners." And she'd put notes inside the cookie jar, where she knew Chris would be sure to find them. "Go East. Beat North." Things like that. At the meets, she'd pass out not only corsages for the mothers, but straw boaters for all the fans, festooned with ribbons in the school colors and with signs saying "East Is #1." She'd also bring oversized foam-rubber fingers that rooters could put on their hands and wave in the air to indicate further that East was Number One.

But it wasn't just swimming. In elementary school, she would go over his homework with him every night. She would get more excited than he did when he got a good grade on a test. Every night before going to bed, she'd set the table for breakfast and every morning when he came downstairs she'd already be there, making sure that whatever he wanted for breakfast was ready for him.

Chris remembered when he'd turned sixteen and had started working as a pool boy at the club in the summer. He'd have to be there at 8 A.M., which meant that most mornings he raced out of the house without having eaten. An hour later she'd be there, driving up with egg and bacon on a bagel and fresh orange juice. It seemed to him that that had happened *hundreds* of times.

He had always been less adventurous, more dutiful, even more of a momma's boy than Rob. But why not, with a mother like that? He remembered her telling him, months after it happened, how on his first day of work at the club, when he'd had to ride his bike across Route 37 and down Washington Street to get there, she had followed him in her car to make sure he got there all right, but being very careful that he didn't see her, because she hadn't wanted to embarrass him.

Until he had started falling in love with appropriate

regularity, there was no one he'd rather spend time with than his mother. She cared so much about everything he did, about his feelings, about his accomplishments and infrequent setbacks. She would wait up for him when he was out late at away swim meets and then ask him questions for an hour afterward. Who won such-and-such? How did so-and-so do? What did the coach say?

Most nights during high school, he had stayed home to study. Sometimes he'd take a break and watch TV with her. They'd sit on the couch and scratch each other's back for half an hour. Then he'd head back to the books and she, most likely, would fall asleep on the couch, wearing her favorite blue bathrobe. He'd still be up working at one or two in the morning (just like his father, who invariably worked in his den after midnight), and she'd come upstairs and tell him to go to sleep, tell him he was a perfectionist, a workaholic. But he knew how proud of him she was and her joy in his development gave him the happiest feelings he'd ever known.

Chris had a particularly vivid memory of the last race he'd ever swum in high school. It was the 100-yard backstroke, his specialty, and he was up against a swimmer who had beaten him the previous year by touching the edge of the pool just a fraction of a second before him, setting a new county record in the process. For a whole year, often joined by his mother, Chris had watched the videotape of that race, his most galling defeat.

At the final meet of his high school career he'd already won two gold medals. Then, in the 100 backstroke, he swam the best race of his life, not only winning by a wide margin but also cutting two full seconds from the record. That victory earned him his third gold medal of the day and, as soon as it was presented to him, he'd walked over to his mother and put the medal and its ribbon around her neck. The expression on her face was something he would never forget.

Actually, in Chris's presence, Maria's expression had almost always reflected happiness. So had her voice. The sound of her singing or humming to herself as she went about her daily household tasks was something else that Chris knew he would carry with him as long as he lived.

He couldn't tell whether it was hours or days or only minutes later that his father turned onto Brookside Avenue and then left up the hill and left again and up Crest Ridge and then into the driveway. The odd thing was that they arrived just as his brothers and grandparents were starting to climb out of his Uncle Gene's car.

As Chris got out of the station wagon, he saw his brother Roby hurrying toward him. Then they were hugging and then, literally, crying on each other's shoulder. This caused Chris to feel closer to Roby than he ever had before, and then he thought how happy that would make his mother, and with that he began to cry so hard that his knees buckled and Roby had to help him into the house.

3

THE way you can tell when you've reached Toms River is that all the FM stations you set in the city suddenly fade from your car radio.

It doesn't matter which way you come—sixty miles down the Garden State Parkway from New York or fifty miles east from Philadelphia, along old two-lane Route 70, past the fruit stands and cornfields and the billboards for the retirement communities—when the music stops is when you're there.

There really isn't any other way to tell. It's on the New Jersey road map, near the shore, about halfway down, between Asbury Park and Atlantic City, but no sign says "Entering Toms River" when you get there and there's no Toms River Police Department or Toms River City Hall.

What there is, officially, is Dover Township, which is sort of the same as Toms River, but not quite. The Toms River School District, for instance, includes areas which are not part of Dover Township, and sections of the township, such as Ortley Beach, certainly would not be considered Toms River.

What it really comes down to, as much as anything, is that Toms River is an attitude, a state of mind, and the longer you've lived there the smaller you're inclined to think it is.

Some people who have lived there all their lives still insist that it's only the village downtown, and maybe a mile up Main Street to the Office Lounge, and maybe a mile out Washington Street to the country club. Newcomers, on the other hand, consider Toms River to extend to at least wherever it is that they live, no matter how far west of the parkway or north of Route 37 it happens to be. This is because to the newcomers, the name Toms River suggests prestige.

Its history and geography are very simple: there was no Tom and there isn't any river. Actually, there were a couple of Toms, one of them an Indian who spied for the British during the Revolutionary War, but who would also spy against them if the price was right (thereby establishing the profit motive as the governing principle of Toms River society), but the town was named after a British Army officer named William Toms, which is why there's no apostrophe.

As for the river, it's really just an estuary, extending four miles inland from Barnegat Bay.

The first settlers were pirates, the banished sons of wealthy Monmouth County families to the north. They would lie in wait behind a thin strip of sand that separated the bay from the Atlantic Ocean, and when they saw a passing merchant ship they would sail out through an inlet and attack. The goods thus acquired were then auctioned off in the center of town. By the early 1800s, Toms River was notorious for its illicit commercial activity.

In 1812, however, a storm closed the inlet, putting the pirates out of business and creating an unbroken barrier between ocean and bay that stretched forty miles down the New Jersey coast, with the village of Toms River stuck in the middle.

For the next hundred years, Toms River existed as a
sleepy little trading post at the edge of the Pine Barrens, notable mostly for humidity and mosquitoes and
populated almost exclusively by those whose chief char-
acteristic was that they lacked the energy or imagination to leave.

Even as late as 1920, land in the area was so cheap
and plentiful that it was given away with newspaper
subscriptions. "Subscribe to the New York *Tribune*,"
said one ad, "and secure a lot at beautiful Beachwood."
People wrote in, asking if they could have the newspaper
without being obligated to take the land.

But then came the automobile and with it, tourists.
Those bound from New York to Atlantic City had to
drive straight down the main street of Toms River.
Many turned left instead, and traveled five miles along
tree-shaded Locust Street and crossed the wooden
bridge over Barnegat Bay to the thin strip of sand that
separated the bay from the ocean. There, they vaca-
tioned at temperance resorts in such communities as
Seaside Heights and Seaside Park, which were described in brochures of the era as being "free from the
blighting influence of immorality, drunkenness, and
Sabbath desecration."

Enough chose to stay in Toms River itself that, for a
time, the village became a thriving resort, "sought
each year," said one tourists' guidebook, "by throngs
of visitors, principally of a well-to-do class, who seek
health and quiet recreation rather than to engage in
the more exacting social life of the fashionable water-
ing places."

From Memorial Day to Labor Day, tranquil visitors
rocked slowly back and forth on the long wooden
porches of grand old hotels like the Riverview and the
Ocean House and the Marian Inn. In September they
departed, and Toms River went back to being a lazy

little Jersey shore town that wasn't even quite on the shore.

It stayed that way right through the thirties and forties. There were only two movie theaters and one of them closed for the winter. Of the town's three policemen, one still wore his World War II Army uniform, dyed blue. The only new arrivals were a few Jewish poultry farmers who settled on the scrubby, sandy land to the north and west of the village and who had the good sense to keep to themselves.

Every store on Main Street was run by a graduate of Toms River High. Your school classmates would surround you all your life. If you were born in Toms River, chances were you would die there. If you were born anyplace else, chances were you'd never even know the place existed.

In 1950, Toms River had a population of just over seven thousand, not counting the chickens. True, it was the county seat of Ocean County, but that was not much to brag about, since Ocean County was the most sparsely populated and second poorest county in New Jersey.

Things began to change in 1952 when the Cincinnati Chemical Company came to town, looking for an inconspicuous body of moving water—preferably close to an ocean.

There had apparently been some difficulties with the authorities regarding the peculiar color of the Ohio River in the vicinity of the chemical company's plant. So the company set up shop on several hundred acres west of town, behind high metal fences, with very tight security around the plant, and changed its name to the Toms River Chemical Company.

Soon the Toms River turned the color of blood. It began to give off an odor. Fish died. A foul-smelling

foam covered its surface. The chemical company said
not to worry, the river was going to be fine.

The company's executives, of course, needed a nice
neighborhood in which to live. Not finding any in
Toms River, they made their own. Twenty-eight of
them purchased fifty-five acres north of Locust Street
in an undistinguished and previously uninhabited area
known as Long Swamp. They subdivided the land into
seventy-eight lots and took the best ones for themselves. Then they built the sort of ranch houses that
everybody was building in the fifties.

It occurred to the executives that people so highly
stationed in life ought not to live in an area called
Long Swamp, so they changed the name of Long
Swamp to Brookside. Immediately, their property values increased by fifty percent. Townspeople began to
snap up the leftover lots. Nobody in Toms River had
ever considered building a house in Long Swamp before, but Brookside, with all those vice presidents,
soon became the town's first ritzy neighborhood.

Next, the executives decided that they needed a
country club. They acquired a nine-hole golf course on
Washington Street and named it the Toms River Country Club. For a stiff initiation fee, townspeople were
permitted to join.

All at once, dozens of Toms River natives discovered how deprived they'd always been. The country
club: why, one simply *had* to join the country club.
This was especially true if you had just built a new
home in Brookside. After all, if you didn't join the
club it might look like you couldn't afford to.

In 1955, the Garden State Parkway opened and
made Toms River suddenly accessible to the rest of
New Jersey. The parkway stretched 172 miles, from
the state's northern edge to its southern tip at Cape
May. From Asbury Park south it ran parallel to the

coast and only ten miles inland. For the first time, everybody in north Jersey could get to the shore without spending half the day in the car. And everybody did.

They poured into Toms River by the thousands, turning off the parkway at Exit 82, hitting the first stoplight on Locust Street and clamoring for directions to the beach. The traffic got so bad on weekends that high school girls in bathing suits stood in front of gas stations, selling hand-drawn maps for a dollar that showed the back roads to the bridge.

Each year, a few more of the tourists did not go home. Now that it was so easy to get to, Toms River began to seem like the sort of place where a person might actually want to live. By 1960, the population had grown to seventeen thousand, the color of the river notwithstanding.

In 1967, a Toms River poultry farm was turned into a sort of ghetto for old people called a "retirement community." That first one was given the name Holiday City. It consisted of 1,600 nearly identical houses on fifty-by-hundred-foot lots. In less than a mile of driving down freshly paved streets with names like St. Moritz Place, Parisian Drive, Yellowstone Road and Kilimanjaro Lane, one passed 150 such houses, each with a plot of gravel in front of it instead of grass. The only way to tell them apart was that some had ceramic deer on the gravel while others had pink flamingos or smiling ceramic rabbits pushing wheelbarrows.

And Holiday City was only the start. Almost overnight, it seemed, where only chicken coop or pine barren had stood before (on the largest tracts of the cheapest land, so far from the ocean that you might as well have been in Kansas), there came Leisure Village, Silver Ridge Park, Crestwood Village, Holiday City South, Leisure Village East, Silver Ridge Park

West, Cedar Glen Lakes, Cedar Glen West, Pine Ridge
at Crestwood and on and on, until there were more
old people in Ocean County than chickens. It was as if
everybody's grandparents had come for a visit and
decided to stay.

In 1967, there also occurred an event which, in the
history of modern Toms River, is the equivalent of
the arrival of the Pilgrims at Plymouth Rock. This was
the rioting of black people in Newark.

Even before the tear-gas fumes had dissipated, the
whites of north Jersey by the thousands had jumped in
their cars and sped down the parkway until they found
an exit where they didn't see any black faces. Then
they looked around for a house. Sociologists came to
call this white flight. In Toms River they called it a
boom.

These new immigrants—actually, they were more
like refugees—were almost exclusively blue-collar apartment dwellers from cities like Newark, Jersey City,
Union City and Elizabeth—places where the old neighborhoods were collapsing. The ones with money moved
to the established suburban communities of northern
New Jersey. The ones without it rushed south.

Housing was cheap because land was cheap, and
land was cheap because Ocean County was in the
middle of nowhere. But the apartment dwellers from
the north didn't care how far away it was. They were
willing to commute fifty miles up the parkway to work
every day, as long as they did not see any black faces
at night.

The population of Toms River had jumped to 43,000
by 1970. The county around it was growing just as
fast. In 1950, there had been only about 50,000 people
in Ocean County. By 1970, there were more than
200,000 and they were streaming down the parkway so
fast that increases were measured in arrivals per min-

ute. In the 1950s, one person had moved into Ocean County every ten minutes. In the 1960s, the rate jumped to one every five.

Traffic congestion was no longer just a summer phenomenon. Suddenly, there seemed to be nothing but strangers on the streets, and lines at the supermarket checkout counters when a few years before there hadn't even been supermarkets. But nobody in Toms River was complaining. This was progress, after all. The people of Toms River had heard a lot about progress, but except for the arrival of the chemical company, they had not experienced much of it before.

In 1971, when Locust Street was widened from two lanes to six—which meant the end of locust trees on Locust Street—nobody complained. It was progress. Likewise, when overcrowding forced the Toms River schools to go on double session, it was deemed a sign of progress and became an immediate source of civic pride.

The chemical company was making progress, too. By now, it was polluting the Atlantic Ocean, pumping four million gallons of waste every day through a pipeline that ran under the streets of Toms River and emptied into the ocean half a mile offshore at Ortley Beach.

In 1972, the chemical company was actually indicted, which didn't happen often in New Jersey. A 206-count federal indictment charged the company with polluting both the river and the ocean with toxic substances believed to cause cancer and genetic mutations.

But that was not the big news of 1972. The big news was the opening of the mall. Suddenly, right out there on Hooper Avenue, just a mile and a half from downtown, there was a real live fully enclosed shopping mall, with Bamberger's, Sears, J. C. Penney and more

than forty other stores—just like they had in the
suburbs.

A suburb, in fact, was what Toms River was becoming. The only peculiar thing was that there wasn't any
"urb." Toms River was sixty miles from anywhere,
not part of the social or cultural or economic orbit of
either New York or Philadelphia. It was a town with
no connection to anyplace else; the sort of place that
one always had to apologize for being from.

But now, with the mall, all that was different. Toms
River had arrived. Toms River was big league. At
long last, the people of Toms River could shop at
stores that issued credit cards.

The boom continued throughout the 1970s. All over
Toms River and around it, bulldozers advanced like
battalions of tanks, uprooting anything green. Swampy
meadows were drained faster than bathtubs and sold
as "lagoon property." It was the alchemy of Long
Swamp to Brookside repeating itself on the grandest
scale Toms River had ever seen.

During the 1970s, the county population increased
at a rate of one person every four minutes. In the
entire United States, only Orange County, California,
grew as fast.

Such growth, of course, had its cost. The Marian
Inn became a parking lot, the Riverview gave way to a
Travelodge, and the Ocean House, which once had
graced the town's main intersection, was replaced by
the largest 7-Eleven in Ocean County.

Out on Route 37, which nobody called Locust Street
anymore, the growth of fast-food outlets, car dealer-
ships and discount department stores was as dense as a
tropical rain forest. K mart, Caldor, Zayre's, 7-Eleven,
Cumberland Farms, Pizza Hut, McDonald's, Burger
King, Howard Johnson's, Holiday Inn, Lum's, Taco
Bell, a new one, it seemed, every week: if it was

franchised, Toms River had it. Even the chemical company became part of the multinational Ciba-Geigy corporation, with headquarters in Basel, Switzerland (where the river that got polluted was the Rhine).

By 1980 there were more than 65,000 people in Toms River, 99.6 percent of them white. Ocean County's population had jumped from 200,000 in 1970 to 350,000 ten years later, with more than twice as many residents over sixty-five as in their forties and almost as many chiropractors as blacks.

These new arrivals were no more affluent, individually, than had been their predecessors in the sixties, but there were so many of them that, for the first time, there seemed to be a lot of money in Toms River. Enough, anyway, so that the First National Bank of Toms River replaced the chemical company as the county's leading private employer, and shopping—especially at the Ocean County Mall—became the area's most popular recreational activity.

Each weekday morning the shuttle buses from the various retirement communities would file slowly into the mall's vast parking lot to discharge their cargo of the stooped and frail, come to wander, dazed, among the altars of consumerism. *I shop, therefore I am.*

Younger residents would arrive by private car (more than 55 percent of Ocean County households possessed two or more automobiles and, in Toms River, more traffic accidents occurred in the parking lots of shopping centers than on the roads). They would come on Friday night, all day Saturday, all day Sunday. It was the primary source of diversion for teenagers and housewives as well as for the elderly.

So normal had shopping as a form of recreation come to seem that when the newspapers wrote their summer holiday roundup stories ("The beaches were crowded, boat traffic on the bay was lighter than ex-

pected, state parks reported heavy turnout"), they
would include activity at the major shopping centers
("The Ocean County mall was filled to capacity this
holiday weekend as avid buyers with no better way to
occupy their spare time once again made thousands of
unnecessary purchases").

There seemed to be an emptiness at the core of
their lives—these tens of thousands of new arrivals
who found themselves stranded in a land without character or style, trapped in a vacuum that only possessions could fill.

There was nothing unique about that. Hollowness at
the core of American middle-class life has engaged the
attention of social commentators for a quarter century
or more. It's just that in Toms River you got a highly
concentrated dose.

Part of the problem was that, in the Toms River of
the 1980s, almost everyone had come from someplace
else. Nobody knew who anybody was anymore. And
because you didn't know who they were or where they
had come from or what sort of lives they were living, it
was hard to know how to feel about them.

Thus, the acquisition of objects that would make it
appear that their owner was affluent, and therefore
successful and desirable, became an important task.
Shopping was much more than the town's number-one
recreation: it was the only means available for Toms
River's upper middle class to make a statement about
who they thought they were and what they wanted to
be.

In Toms River you were what you drove, you were
what you wore, you were where you lived—no matter
how heavily mortgaged it was.

The members of this new acquisitive class worked
hard at stamping out their blue-collar roots, at forgetting where it was they had come from. They built a

wall of credit cards to shield their past from view. A lot of Cadillacs were bought, a lot of wives drove all the way to Short Hills so they could shop at Bloomingdale's instead of Bamberger's, and a lot of backyards found room for swimming pools even though the ocean was less than ten miles away.

It became, in fact, a mark of status to brag about how long it had been since one had actually gone to the beach. It was an even bigger mark of status to own a home in Brookside, which was now populated largely by people who didn't even know (or pretended they didn't) that Brookside had once been called Long Swamp.

There were people who bought houses in Brookside and then discovered that they had no money left with which to furnish them. This meant that for months or even years they could not invite anyone to dinner. They couldn't invite people from their old neighborhood because those were the kind of people that Brookside residents no longer spent time with, and they couldn't invite their new neighbors because they could not let it be learned that they couldn't afford proper furniture.

So instead they joined the country club, which they couldn't afford either, because at the country club they would be able to socialize with the kind of people they were trying to become.

The country club crowd took itself very seriously, even though the building looked as if it had been made from LEGOS and even though its members had only a nine-hole golf course to play on and even though they had only each other to try to impress on Saturday night.

They were, for the most part, middle-aged, restless and bored. They were too far from the cities to be hip, but not far enough away to be oblivious. They turned their backs on New York and Philadelphia because they felt threatened: by the standards of those cities their own quarrels and aspirations were laughable. But, facing inward, they saw only reflections of themselves.

It was neither an easy nor a rewarding way to live: that barrenness, that *abyss* covered only by a thin veneer of apparent affluence which they had to strive desperately to maintain.

Cocaine helped. (Besides, it was expensive enough to be a status symbol.) So did the surface glitter of the Atlantic City gambling casinos. So did spending the night with a spouse who was not your own.

They laughed when they heard their town called Peyton Place. Each new item of gossip or scandal would bring a clucking and chuckling and shaking of heads. "Imagine that," they'd say. "Right here in River City."

But it was okay. No harm done. We're all grown-ups. Nobody gets hurt. This is what life in the fast lane is all about. This is what it means to be successful. This is the way they do it on TV.

The fact is, life in Toms River—at least life as lived by certain members of the Toms River Country Club—was lived at the miniseries level. Only it was a miniseries without an event.

Until the night Maria Marshall was murdered.

4

ONCE inside the house, Rob headed straight for Sal Coccaro. He seemed less concerned with the emotional state of his sons or in-laws than he did with Sal's list of phone calls received. He stood in the living room, scanning the fifteen or twenty names.

"David Rosenberg? At two P.M.?"

"That's right," Sal said.

"Where did he call from?"

"I don't know, Rob. Probably the office. I wasn't asking people where they were calling from." David Rosenberg, husband of Felice Rosenberg and formerly a pharmacist, was the manager of Fred Frankel Motors on Route 37, a car dealership owned by Felice's father, Fred Frankel.

"Well, what did he say? What did he say?" Both Roby and Chris noticed that their father seemed extremely agitated.

"Rob, he didn't say anything. He just asked for you and I said you weren't here but I'd tell you he called."

Rob began to pace back and forth across the living room. Without seeming aware that he was doing so, he slowly crumpled the paper on which Sal had written the names.

"Sal," he said. "This is very important. How did David seem?"

"Rob, I don't understand." Sal glanced around the room at his wife, Paula, and Dr. and Mrs. Puszynski, all sitting on the same couch, silently weeping.

"How did he *seem*, Sal? Was he warm, was he cold, was he friendly, was he hostile?" Rob's voice had acquired a new edge of impatience.

"Well, to tell you the truth, Rob, not that I have the faintest idea why you're so concerned about it, David seemed very cold. He just asked if you were here and when I said no, he asked what time you'd be back."

"What did you tell him?"

"I told him about six or seven o'clock. I should have known better, Rob. I should have known you'd be late, as usual." Sal, too, had turned his voice up a notch.

"Did he say he was going to call back?"

"No, he didn't."

"Did he say he expected me to call him?"

"No, he didn't."

"All right." Rob sighed and looked around the room. For the first time since entering the house, he seemed aware of the presence of other people. "All right, how about a drink, how about a drink? I think everybody could use a drink."

Rob made himself a rum and Coke. Coca-Cola, even without rum, was by far Rob's favorite drink. Indeed, he seemed addicted to it, drinking, at a minimum, a six-pack a day and often more as he worked in his office until the early hours of the morning.

"All right," Rob said. "Sal, Gene, I want the two of you to handle any calls. I'm just not available to talk to anyone."

"Not even David?" Sal asked.

"That's right, Sal," Rob said, glaring at him. "Especially not even David." Then he turned and walked into his office and closed the door.

The phone continued to ring until almost midnight. Tom Kenyon, the lawyer, who with his wife, Madge, had come by during the afternoon when Rob was gone, called back to ask Sal to look for Rob's phone directory. He said it should have Andrea Alfonso's new number in Florida. He said Maria would want her to know what had happened, which did not strike Sal as strange, since he knew Maria and Andrea had been friends.

Other friends of Maria's came to the house. Friends from the neighborhood and country club, like Anne Peck, who was married to Burton, a lawyer, and her sister-in-law, Kathy Peck, who was married to Benjamin, a high school principal, and Diane Critelli, who was married to Pete, who owned a car dealership.

An odd thing about Maria was that while she had many acquaintances and even a number of women who would have described themselves as her friends, she didn't have any close friends. It was widely agreed that she was an exceptionally warm and caring mother and avidly interested in everything her boys did and that, unlike her husband, who was viewed as testy, pretentious and overly aggressive in both business and social situations, Maria was easy to get along with and seemed to have a genuine interest in other people. (At least in other people who seemed pretty much like herself.)

But with her, according to the country club consensus, the surface of things, the appearance, mattered most. Intimacy seemed to make her uncomfortable. Emotion was untidy, and Maria had never permitted a hair out of place. It was as if there had been an invisible screen around Maria. You could get only so

close and no closer. Too close and you might see a
wart. People who had known her for twenty years
could not remember ever having seen her perspire. If
she'd had a motto, it would have been: "Looking
Perfect Is the Best Revenge." She had always appeared to be the perfect wife, the perfect mother. She
and her family had been a symbol of what the good
life in Toms River was all about.

That was what made her murder so upsetting on so
many levels. If it could happen to her, despite all her
expensive insulation from the less pleasant aspects of
reality, then it could happen to any of them, despite
their husbands' incomes and their lifestyle. Thus, whoever had shot Maria Marshall had taken not only a
human life but a talisman that, unconsciously, all of
them had looked to for protection.

After giving Sal Coccaro the new number for Andrea
Alfonso, Rob emerged from his office and began to
play the role of the perfect host, making sure everyone's drinks were freshened, offering cold cuts, trying
to carry on the sort of conversation that might have
occurred if Maria had simply been in bed with the flu
and friends had stopped by for a drink.

The only obvious signs that the mother of the house
was not just sick but suddenly dead were Chris, curled
up on one couch in fetal position, crying uncontrolla-
bly; the Puszynskis on the other couch, so dazed and
shaken that they might have been survivors of a plane
crash; Roby in the kitchen with his hands covering his
face, refusing to speak to anyone; and John, the
thirteen-year-old, following his father around the living room, hugging him constantly, as if the hugs could
bring his mother back.

Eventually, it became obvious that there was no
more that any friends or neighbors could do that night

and, in small groups, they departed. Then, one by one, the Puszynskis and the Marshalls went to bed. All three boys lay awake in their separate bedrooms for hours, unable even to cry themselves to sleep.

Downstairs, Gene Leahy—Uncle Gene, the lawyer who was thirty-eight years old, drove a Mercedes, smoked big cigars and enjoyed a beer or two in the evenings, especially along with a good story, and who could have passed for a ward leader in any Irish neighborhood in Boston, New York or Philadelphia but who, in fact, was senior partner of his own eight-lawyer firm in Wilmington—sat alone in the darkened living room. He was the only person in the house, he knew, who realized why Rob had asked so many questions about David Rosenberg's phone call.

Now the question that he sat up asking himself until nearly dawn on September 8 was, what could or should he do about it?

The Philadelphia *Inquirer* for Saturday morning ran a brief item in its regional news section under the headline WOMAN SLAIN AT REST AREA ON N.J. PARKWAY. The story described how Maria Marshall had been shot twice and her husband knocked unconscious after they'd pulled into the picnic area to change a flat tire. The story also said Marshall had told investigators he'd been robbed of an undetermined amount of money and mentioned that a spokeswoman for the Ocean County prosecutor's office had said robbery was the motive in the attack.

The Asbury Park *Press,* which paid considerably more attention to doings in Toms River, ran a three-column headline on page one: WOMAN SHOT TO DEATH AT PARKWAY PICNIC SITE. The story quoted the Ocean County prosecutor as saying that while robbery appeared to be a possible motive, he wasn't yet ruling out others. "We never settle on any one motive in the early part of an investigation," the prosecutor said. He added that while bullet shell-casings had been found in the front seat of the car, there were not yet any suspects.

The story went on to say that the Oyster Creek picnic area was unlighted and heavily wooded with scrub oak and pine and that there was a sign at the entrance that forbade parking after dark.

A spokesman for the New Jersey State Police, whose jurisdiction included the entire length of the parkway, as well as the New Jersey Turnpike and all interstate highways within the state, said that Marshall's 1981 ivory Eldorado had been impounded for forensic testing and that underwater recovery teams wearing wet suits and snorkels were searching for a weapon or other evidence in the waters of Oyster Creek itself. Anyone who had been traveling the parkway at the time of the murder and who had seen anything unusual was asked to contact the Bass River state police barracks.

The story concluded by saying that Rob Marshall, in addition to operating an insurance and estate-planning business in Toms River, had served as 1982–83 fund-raising chairman for United Way of Ocean County.

He was up early on Saturday morning, which was extremely unusual. Normally, Rob worked in his den until 1 or 2 A.M. and then slept until nearly noon. Maria had always said it was the caffeine in all the Coca-Cola he drank that kept him up. He said it was just that he often got his best ideas after midnight. Even when he finally went to bed he would be apt to sit up suddenly and turn on the light so he could write down something he'd just thought of. Eventually, on one of his birthdays, Maria had given him a combination pen and flashlight to make it easier for him to

write in bed at night. Like many of the other possessions he'd acquired, it seemed to please him mostly
because nobody else in Toms River had one.

By 7:30, Rob was out the door. It might have been
the earliest he'd ever left his house, if one did not
count the day before, when the police had come for
him at 5 A.M.

An hour later, Chris emerged. He got in his brother's yellow Mustang and headed north to Newark Airport to meet Jennifer, his girlfriend, who was arriving
from her college in Atlanta. He turned on the car
radio and heard a news broadcast describing the death
of his mother. He pushed a button to change the
station. "Toms River socialite slain on parkway," an
announcer said. "Back in sixty seconds with details."

Chris pushed another button, but even as he did so,
he heard himself laugh. "Toms River socialite." His
mother would have found that hilarious. When the
third station he'd turned to also began to broadcast an
update concerning the "parkway slaying," Chris simply turned the radio off.

In the silence that enveloped the remainder of his
trip, Chris was plagued by the one thought that he
least wanted to have: "What if my father was involved?"

Why was he thinking that? How could he be so
disloyal? He knew there was something irrational, even
dangerous, and quite possibly unforgivable about such
an idea. Chris had never taken a serious psychology
course and knew little about the murky and treacher-
ous world of the unconscious, but he had some vague
awareness of a Freudian idea concerning a son wanting to sleep with the mother and developing hatred for
the father who prevented fulfillment of the child's
desire.

But that was crap. Chris was a logical, disciplined,
rigorously controlled young man (he had never, for

example, drunk so much as a can of beer and would not even remain in a room where marijuana was being used). If there were no rational basis for a thought, it was invalid and should therefore be suppressed. The thought that his father might have somehow been involved in the murder of his mother was like the worst, sickest fantasy that some really lame and screwed-up loser might succumb to.

Chris knew that it was a notion he could never talk about. Not to Roby, not to his Uncle Gene, not to Sal Coccaro, who was really a great guy to have around in bad times, not even to Jennifer. He just knew the way they'd look at him: like the whole thing had proven too much, like he was losing it, like they'd better quickly take him to a doctor. And what if his poor father ever heard? Maybe the only thing worse than finding your wife of twenty years shot to death on the front seat of your car (though perhaps the death of a child would prove equally traumatic) was hearing three days later that one of your sons suspected you of involvement in the crime.

Back at the Marshall house on Crest Ridge Drive, a bleary-eyed and slack-faced Gene Leahy, having just endured his first entirely sleepless night since law school fifteen years earlier, carried a cup of black coffee to the patio that overlooked the backyard pool.

He knew so much and yet he didn't know anything. And one of the things he didn't know was what to do about the things that he did know.

He was still sitting there an hour later, his first cup of coffee finished, his second forgotten and gone cold, when Rob returned to the house. Rob seemed paler than normal and his typical blend of confidence and arrogance was not evident. He took a seat next to Gene.

"There's something I've got to tell you," he said.

"Good," Gene said. "And when you're done, there are a few things I'm going to tell you."

Rob blinked twice in quick succession. "What are they?" he said.

"No," Gene said. "You go first."

Rob, in blue blazer, rep tie, neatly pressed chinos and brown loafers, looked out of place by the pool. Gene, still in the same clothes he'd put on in Wilmington more than twenty-four hours earlier, looked as if he wanted to dive in.

"Gene, I've been having an affair."

"I know," Gene said. This was not the response Rob had been expecting. He seemed to turn just one shade paler.

"You know?"

"Yes, Rob, I know. You've been having an affair with Felice Rosenberg, who lives right down there, about two blocks away, and it's been going on for at least the past year."

Rob jerked forward so quickly that his lawn chair almost tipped over. "How did you know that?"

"Maria told me."

"*Maria* told you?! What the hell are you talking about?"

"Rob, do you remember back in June when Sally and I were down in Annapolis for the weekend looking at boats, and I saw that ad in the *Inquirer* for the sailboat up here?"

"Of course."

"And you went down and made a five-hundred-dollar deposit on it for me and it turned out to be a such a piece of shit that I couldn't believe you'd actually put down the money?"

Rob nodded.

"Well, that day, Rob—it was a Monday when we

came up to look at the boat—afterwards, we stopped over here to say thanks, anyway, before we went home. You were out and Maria was here alone and she looked like she was about to tear her hair out."

"Maria didn't know about the affair," Rob said softly, but the remark seemed directed as much at the swimming pool as at Gene.

"It was so obvious that she was in distress that I asked her what the trouble was and that's when she told me. She brought me right out here on this deck and showed me a folder filled with American Express receipts that she'd come across in the spring while she was pulling your tax stuff together. I don't remember the names of all the motels, Rob, but there were two or three on Long Beach Island and one, over and over again—the Best Western in Lakewood."

"Those were dinners with clients," Rob said.

"Hey," Gene said. "I'm not Maria. Don't bother lying to me."

"Dinners with clients," Rob repeated, "and it was none of her business, she had no business snooping through my desk."

"Right, and that's apparently what you told her when she confronted you. In fact, Maria said you blew up. Said you scared the hell out of her, the way you started screaming. But she wasn't stupid, Rob. Maria might have been naive, she might have led a sheltered and overprotected life, but Maria was not a stupid woman."

Rob kept glancing over his shoulder, as if afraid that someone was eavesdropping on their conversation.

"She also showed me the phone bills, Rob. Forty, fifty calls a month to the same number down in Peterboro, which happens to be the number of Seaview Regional High School, where your friend Mrs. Rosenberg just happens to be assistant principal. Rob, she was not a stupid woman."

"Why did she tell you all this?"

"Because she loved you, Rob. And she was afraid she was losing you. And she wanted me to try to help her save her marriage."

Gene stood up. He walked to the edge of the deck and pointed toward the driveway. "You know your little closets, those little cubbyhole things right there by the back door, that you use for storing boating gear and all that crap?"

Rob was nodding, but absently, as if his mind already were elsewhere.

"She showed me what you'd stashed in there, Rob. An extra toiletries kit, toothbrush, toothpaste, the whole bit. Plus a little cologne for you and a little perfume, I guess, for Mrs. Rosenberg? And tapes, Rob. Cassettes with love songs on them. But not songs Maria had ever heard you play."

Rob stood up, too. "This was none of your business," he said, almost indignantly. "Maria had no right to discuss any of this with you."

"Rob, every time she tried to bring it up with you, you told her she was losing her mind, you told her she should get psychiatric help, you told her she was having a nervous breakdown."

"I suppose she told you that, too?"

"Yes, Rob, she did. Do you remember when I came back here in August, just after you got back from that little family vacation in Michigan?"

"Yes. You and I went out on the bay."

"And then we docked at that restaurant, PJ's. And we spent the afternoon boozing. Rob, I was trying to get you loose enough to where you'd admit to me that you were having the affair. Maria thought, if you'd only admit it to *someone* then maybe she could get

you to talk to her. But it didn't work. You were
stonewalling. In fact, it seemed to me—and I told
Maria this the next day—that you weren't even there,
mentally. You were someplace far away."

"I did talk to you," Rob said. "I told you I was
depressed, bored with my work. I remember saying
that I just didn't see any challenges left in my life.
And I also admitted that we were having financial
difficulties.

Gene laughed. " 'Financial difficulties'? You told
me, to use your exact phrase, that you were 'in debt
up to your eyeballs and sinking fast.' And you blamed
it on Maria's spending."

"It's true, Gene. She had to have everything. She
spent money in the *most* irresponsible ways."

"Don't start, Rob. Don't even start in about Maria.
In fact, why don't you sit down again? I've got a few
more things to tell you."

Rob sat. Gene walked back across the deck until he
was standing almost directly in front of Rob. He looked
down. He said, "Rob. You signed Maria's name on a
one-hundred-thousand-dollar home equity loan application."

Rob looked up. "What are you talking about?" His
voice was almost a whisper.

"Maria found those loan documents in your desk.
She saw that you had signed her name."

Rob stood again. "Listen, Gene, I can explain that
very easily. I had a remarkable opportunity to buy
stock in our local cable television company. It could
have been an extremely lucrative proposition. But I
knew Maria wouldn't understand. She'd get nervous,
be afraid we could somehow lose the house. You
know, Gene, Maria was completely unsophisticated in
matters of finance."

"Yeah, but she knew her own signature when she saw it."

"We also had a number of outstanding loans. Maria had been overspending and I had been trying to keep up. The home equity loan allowed us to consolidate the others at a much more favorable interest rate, but that's not the kind of thing Maria could understand either."

"Listen, Rob. Maria knew all about your debts and she was just as worried as you were. The overdue bills, the installment loans, the personal loans you'd taken out, then you signing her name on the home equity loan. Maria was scared to death. She didn't know where all the money was going. You're making a hundred and twenty-five, a hundred and thirty thousand a year and there's not a damned thing to show for it except debt."

Gene motioned to the deck chairs. "Let's both sit down again. I'm not quite finished yet."

They sat. But Rob's physical movements had suddenly become awkward and disjointed, almost as if he were a life-sized marionette.

"Maria called me on Tuesday," Gene said quietly, leaning forward now. "She sounded more upset than I'd ever heard her before. She said everything was coming to a head and that she was, to use her phrase, 'truly worried.' I asked her about what, and she wouldn't say."

"This is preposterous!" Rob said. "The woman was having a nervous breakdown."

"She said she was finally ready to confront you but she was afraid to do it alone. She asked me to be with her and I agreed. I was planning to come over Monday morning, Rob. Maria and I were going to sit down with you and she was going to tell you everything she knew.

"Then I was going to remind you of all you'd be losing if you kept on the way you were going. Your reputation, Rob, which seems to concern you so much. That civic status that's such a big deal to you. Your precious country club. If Maria divorced you, or if you left her because of Felice, they'd either throw you out or laugh you out and it wouldn't really matter which.

"Not to mention, of course, your three sons. I was going to remind you of how much their happiness and well-being depended upon you and what you did.

"But it didn't happen, Rob. We never got there. So we're having this little meeting instead."

"I don't believe this," Rob said. He was shaking his head. "I don't believe any of this."

"Maria loved you, Rob. She was willing to do anything to save the marriage. But she'd gotten to the point where she knew she had to do something to save herself. And, as I've mentioned, Rob, she wasn't stupid. She'd hired a private detective. To follow you."

"What? What did you say?"

"I don't know how long she'd had him, Rob, but on Tuesday she told me that he had full documentation of the affair. This was what she was going to confront you with on Monday morning."

But Rob did not even seem to be listening. Beads of perspiration had popped out on his forehead. He spoke audibly, but slowly and softly, as if to himself. "Maria had a private detective. Following me . . ."

He looked at Gene. "Was this detective still working this week?"

"I don't know, Rob. She didn't say."

"Who was it?"

"I don't know that either. She didn't mention his name."

Rob put his head in his hands. "Gene, Gene," he said. "Why didn't you tell me?"

"We were going to tell you everything on Monday morning."

"But you don't understand, Gene." Rob's voice seemed suddenly hoarse with tension. "If you had told me about Maria's detective, then none of this would have happened."

For the first time all morning, Gene looked startled. "What's that supposed to mean?" he said.

"Oh. Oh, yes," Rob said. "I see your point." He looked around uneasily and licked his lips. "What I mean," he said, "is that if I had known Maria already knew about the affair, then I would have left her sooner and we wouldn't have been in Atlantic City Thursday night.

"You see, Gene, what I guess you don't know, and Maria didn't either, was that Felice and I were planning to move in together. We'd already put down a deposit on a little beach house in Manahawkin. We've opened a checking account and a safe deposit box. But we thought it would be easier on the kids if they were all back in school before we made it official. Felice has two children, you know, and they both go away to boarding school. And I wanted Chris to get started at Lehigh without having to be upset by something like this. As you know, he's always been particularly close to Maria."

Gene Leahy lit a cigar. A thick billow of smoke rose into the warming September air. He leaned forward and slid an extra deck chair into a position that would enable him to rest his feet upon it. Then, when all was arranged, he sat back in his own deck chair and looked at Rob, for the first time, less like a brother-in-law and more like a lawyer. Rob had loosened his tie, which was something he rarely did because he thought it looked vulgar and sloppy.

"Question, Rob," Gene said.

"What is it?" Rob had seemed slightly dazed since Gene had told him about the detective.

"You have any life insurance on Maria?"

"Of course," Rob said. "Of course I did. Listen, Gene, I believe in insurance. I'm in the insurance business."

Gene nodded. He slowly blew a stream of cigar smoke into the air. "How much?" he asked.

"I believe," Rob said, "that the exact figure at the time of her death was slightly in excess of one point five million dollars."

Gene nodded slowly, almost absently, as if Rob had just remarked that it looked like it was going to be a nice day.

"I know it sounds high, Gene," Rob said quickly, "but you have to understand. I used it as a sales tool. You see, a lot of times when I'm selling a policy to a doctor or lawyer or executive in town I make it a point to also sell one on his wife. But they always resist. They don't realize how much economic impact the death of a spouse can have on the wage-earner in a family. The child-care expense, the reduced working hours, not to mention the temporary emotional dislocation. But they always say, 'Come on, I bet you don't have any insurance on your own wife.' And I need to be able to say, 'I certainly do. In fact, her life is insured for as much as my own.' It's a marvelous sales tool, Gene, it really is. It almost always breaks down resistance."

"One point five million," Gene said.

"That's right," Rob said impatiently. "I don't see anything peculiar about that. What's your point?"

"Well, Rob, I'm sitting here, out by the pool, lovely morning like this, after I lie awake on your couch all night wondering just what the hell is going on, and, you know, the thought just occurred to me that maybe I should ask that little question about insurance. You remember, Rob, before I went into private practice, how I used to work for the attorney general's office down in Delaware?"

"Yes, I remember, Gene."

"Well," Gene said, exhaling one more long plume of smoke, then studying, for a moment, the ash that was forming on his cigar, "I was just thinking: suppose I still worked in law enforcement, only it was here in Ocean County where Maria Marshall was murdered. I learn (a) that the husband is having an affair; (b) that the husband is planning to leave the wife; (c) that the husband is in desperate financial straits; and (d) that the wife has a million five in life insurance riding with her when she gets shot to death in the front seat of the husband's car. Sometime after midnight. In a thickly wooded picnic area. Where the husband has pulled in to check a tire. And the husband only gets hit on the head."

Gene swung his legs to the deck and stood up. "Rob, my friend," he said, gesturing with the cigar, "when the husband wakes up from his little tap on the head, what has he got, besides the lump?"

Rob was staring straight up at Gene, his face so pale he looked embalmed.

"What he's got," Gene said, "is one point five million coming instead of a wife who won't give him a divorce."

Gene studied the cigar for a moment, then looked down at Rob. "That," he said, "is my point."

It took a moment, but then Rob awkwardly got to his feet. "Gene," he said, "that was a very effective and even chilling little performance. But there's something which, not being a resident of this community, you have failed to take into account. There is no way that the authorities could possibly suspect me of any involvement in Maria's death."

"Why's that?" Gene asked.

"I am, quite simply, far too prominent. In Toms River, I'm much too high up the civic ladder. My reputation within the community, in fact, places me beyond reproach."

"Okay," Gene said. "In that case, I'll go back to being your brother-in-law and stop pretending to be a lawyer. Now, as your brother-in-law, let me give you some advice."

"Of course," Rob said.

"Knowing Toms River to the limited extent that I do, I am willing to make just one prediction: this is going to be all *over* town by Monday morning. Everything you've told me and everything I've told you. A lot of it isn't going to sound very nice, Rob; I don't care how high up the flagpole or the ladder you think you are.

"What you want to do, Rob, and you want to do this as soon as possible, is sit yourself down with Sal and Jack Rogers, and anybody else you think needs to hear about the affair, the financial problems, your plans to leave, the insurance, Maria's detective. Let them hear it from you and not from the newspapers or the radio or the bartender at the country club.

"Then you want to sit yourself down with Roby and Chris and John and tell them the whole goddamned story, too, so they hear it from you first and no one else. And don't expect them to be particularly thrilled when you get to the part about Felice."

"They're mature kids," Rob said. "They can handle it."

"Swell. I'm glad you're so confident. But the third thing, Rob, and in fact, the more I think about it the more I think this ought to be first, is, since I'm just your brother-in-law, you've got to get yourself a lawyer."

For the first time all morning, Rob looked relieved, even a little pleased with himself. "I've already taken care of that," he said. "I've already retained a lawyer. In fact, that's where I was this morning, meeting with him."

"Good. Who is it? Somebody experienced? Somebody you trust?"

"Absolutely," Rob said. "He's the best, the very best. His name is Ray DiOrio, and he's not merely an attorney, he's one of the most influential political figures in the state. There's certainly not a more powerful man in Ocean County. So don't you worry about that, Gene. I am in the very best of hands."

5

ROBY slept late on Saturday. Even when he woke up he didn't get up. His mother was dead. Somebody had shot her. She'd never hug him or smile at him or look at him with love and understanding. He'd never smell her perfume again or hear her sing. But at least he was nineteen. Poor John, down the hall, was only thirteen. What would his life be like without his mother? It was going to be up to himself, Roby knew, and to his father and to Chris, to grow enough, to be strong enough, to love enough to fill at least part of the terrible void.

That afternoon, more friends of his mother's came to the house. He assumed they had come to console his father. But after watching them head straight for his mother's closets he began to wonder if they had not instead come to visit his mother's clothes. And it turned out to be more than a visit. It was, he said later, "a panty raid." Roby, who was quite conscious of the labels inside articles of clothing, had the distinct impression that everything that said Gucci or Polo disappeared.

By late afternoon, Chris was back from the airport with Jennifer, lying on one of the couches with his head in her lap, and Sal and Paula Coccaro were there again, along with Jack and Barbara Rogers (he had his own engineering firm), and there seemed to be a limitless stream of other visitors, many of whom brought food and almost all of whom were in tears.

The visitor whom Roby remembered most vividly was Jerry Mitchell, a loan officer at one of the banks, and it was because he didn't seem sad, he seemed angry. He and his wife had come by with Les Perilli and his wife (Les was an orthodontist), and Jerry had stood right in front of the piano and demanded, in what was very nearly a belligerent tone, that Rob tell him exactly what had happened. Then, as Rob tried to, he kept interrupting.

"What the fuck did you pull in *there* for?"

"The tire felt a little wishy-washy," Rob said, going on to explain about a doctor from Toms River who had been struck by a car and killed a few years earlier while changing a flat tire on the parkway. Then he described how he'd said, "Honey, pop the trunk," and how, as he bent down at the rear of the car to inspect the mushy tire, he'd noticed that another car, with headlights off, had pulled into the picnic area behind him. The other car came to a stop a few yards away and killed its engine.

"Wait a minute, wait a minute," Jerry Mitchell said. "Rob, I *know* you—competitive you. What do you mean, 'a car pulled in'?"

Roby noticed that his father seemed ill at ease.

"I'm just explaining what happened, Jerry," Rob said.

"Wait a minute, Marshall. You're trying to tell me you're crouching down there in the pitch darkness with Maria in the front seat and a couple grand of the casino's money in your pocket and you don't even get back in your own car when somebody pulls in right behind you with his lights off and then he shuts his *engine* off?"

"That's what happened, Jerry."

"No, no," Jerry Mitchell said loudly. "I don't buy it."

At that point, Sal Coccaro had heard enough. "Jerry, for Christ's sake, back off."

And that had been the end of it, at least for then.

Not long after the Mitchells and the Perillis had left the house, Rob asked Sal Coccaro and Jack Rogers to come into his office. He shut the door firmly and took a seat behind his desk, acting very businesslike, as though he were about to go over the fine print in a policy.

"I've been speaking with Gene," he began, " . . . Gene thinks you should hear . . . it may sound worse than it is . . ." His voice was so low that Sal had trouble hearing. " . . . been having an affair, a torrid affair . . . Felice . . . year and a half . . ." Now he raised his voice and looked his two friends straight in the eye.

"I love her," he said. "As difficult as this is to say, I'd fallen out of love with Maria. I'd had every intention of confronting her, telling her that Felice and I had rented a little bungalow in Manahawkin, that we were going to be moving in together."

Then he began to talk about the fact that he'd been having "severe" financial problems. He did not go into any detail about how they had arisen, other than to complain that Maria had spent money recklessly, nor did he mention anything about insurance. He did, however, admit that he'd signed Maria's name on the $100,000 loan application.

As he'd spoken of Felice, Rob had sounded defiant and proud. But Sal noticed that now, as he talked about money, and not having enough, he sounded for the first time as if he were confessing to something

shameful. Given the value system that held sway in
Toms River, this wasn't surprising.

When he finished, Rob sat back, awaiting some
response. Sal and Jack looked at each other, but neither spoke. Jack was a handsome man in his late
fifties, with distinguished gray hair. He was polite,
reserved, almost courtly in manner. Sal, who was still
in his thirties and who lifted weights every morning at
a health club, was almost entirely bald. Thus, when he
became angry, which he did with some regularity,
being emotional, expressive, opinionated and fiercely
loyal, not only his face but most of his scalp quickly
reddened. It reddened now.

"Well, say something," Rob said. "What do you
think?"

"I think you're a fucking hypocrite," Sal said.

When Sal and Paula had moved down from north
Jersey three years before, Rob and Maria had been
among the first to befriend them. Later, Sal had learned
that the Marshalls made it a practice to "tutor" a
younger couple socially, to be the benefactors who
would enable the new arrivals to win acceptance at the
country club and in the civic organizations that dominated Toms River social life—groups such as Rotary
and the Businessman's Association and the Twigs, the
women's volunteer group (but very much by invitation
only and the invitations were seldom mailed to ad-
dresses beyond Brookside) that sponsored fundraising
events for the local hospital.

The Coccaros, like the Perillis and the Mitchells and
a number of others before them, had been lavished
with attention from Rob and Maria. Usually, what
happened was that the younger couple came to find
Rob overbearing, arrogant, egocentric, slightly crude,
and concerned (even more than the rest of the town)
with status symbols and appearances. Then the friend-

ship would fade, as the younger couple made its own way. But that had not yet happened with Sal and Paula. The four of them were frequent companions at the club and in Atlantic City, as well as regular visitors in each other's homes.

Sal and Paula, in fact, had been to the Marshalls' for dinner only ten days before the murder and they'd all dined and gambled at Harrah's Marina together three days later. A few points from the dinner conversation stood out in Sal's mind. He remembered a long talk about cremation, during which Rob had said several times that he and Maria had decided that they wanted to be cremated after death, though in her case Maria's strict Catholic parents would not approve. Rob had also discussed with Sal how much insurance he carried on Paula. He'd said that as a selling point he always kept at least a million dollars, worth on Maria.

But the discussion that had dominated most of the conversation in the Marshall home had concerned Rob's practice of taking every Friday off from work and devoting the time to his family. It was the least a man could do, Rob said, to repay his wife for all that she did for him. Since he'd begun to do it, the enduring love that he and Maria shared had blossomed again into romance. Rob went on and on about it—how he carefully budgeted his time to be sure that he had accomplished his week's work by Thursday night, how it would be the greatest thing in the world for Paula, how Sal could do it without strain if he would only impose the same sort of self-discipline as Rob, and that how not doing it was really just an act of selfishness.

Rob's unctuous, self-congratulatory and patronizing tone had irked Sal at the time, but now, having just learned of Rob's affair and his plans to divorce Maria, the memory of it infuriated him.

"I think you're a fucking hypocrite," he repeated.

"And I resent having been preached to to follow your example."

Rob didn't respond. He turned to Jack Rogers and said, "Jack, you understand. You know what it's like to fall out of love." This was a reference, apparently, to the fact that once, many years earlier, Jack had been divorced.

Jack just shook his head and looked back at Sal.

"You have to understand," Rob said to both of them. "I *love* Felice. With her, I've found the true meaning of happiness. Of joy, Of ecstasy. Feelings I had never even dreamed of. Physically—the sexual part—it's so far beyond anything that Maria could even comprehend. But the relationship is much more than that. It's not just our bodies. We're *soulmates.*"

He stared across the table as if he'd just completed a sales presentation. His next move might be to hand pens to Sal and Jack and point to where they should sign.

Had he done so, Sal, at least, might have broken the pen in two. He could not believe what he'd just heard. An affair—it was bad enough that Rob was confessing to an affair within two days of the murder of Maria—but an affair with *Felice!* That was the news that Sal could not absorb.

Even in the few years he'd lived in the town, Sal had heard more stories about Felice than about all other women (or men, for that matter) in Toms River combined.

He knew she'd moved down from north Jersey in the late 1950s, just about at the start of her high school years. Her father, Fred Frankel, had opened a car dealership on Locust Street, long before it grew into Route 37. The way Sal had heard it, the town had not known what to make of her then, and despite the passage of twenty-five years, Toms River still hadn't figured her out.

Was she threatening, or merely amusing? Scandalous, or merely entertaining? Was she serious or was her whole life a put-on, designed to poke fun at a town that took itself very seriously? About one point there was no debate: life without her would have been more comfortable for a lot of people, but duller for nearly all.

Felice did things that other women in Toms River only talked about (and there were quite a few who wouldn't even talk—they just fantasized). Whatever was new, whatever was "in," whatever bordered on being outrageous, Felice would try it. The list ranged from roller-skating to Club Med vacations to Transcendental Meditation, although Sal knew that the whispered rumors extended well beyond that. A regular Madame Bovary of the Pine Barrens was what she seemed to be, and in Toms River that was no compliment.

But it was not so much her actions, Sal knew, that bothered the other women of Toms River (except when she flirted with their husbands), it was her attitude. How she thought she was better than anyone else. How she thought she was too good for the town. If she didn't like it, they asked—if it was too tame for her—why didn't she just go elsewhere, to New York, or Los Angeles, or even Bergen County, leaving the rest of them in peace?

The same people who asked the question had the answer. Felice stayed because she needed to be the center of attention, and in any town a little bigger or a little more sophisticated than Toms River, she might just get lost in the crowd.

Her most garish display, in Sal's view, had been her fortieth birthday party the previous fall, which had already achieved legendary status as the most notorious public event in the history of Toms River society. It had been billed as a surprise, but most who attended (and Sal was not among them—his information, like most information in Toms River, was secondhand) were convinced Felice not only had known about it in advance but had helped to plan it. There were just too many details that involved Felice's distinctive touch.

The invitations had been accompanied by cards that said, "Frisky Felice Turns 40!" The party was held at a beachfront disco that most of the country club crowd stayed away from. A billboard outside had proclaimed: LORDY, LORDY, FELICE IS 40!

As Sal had heard the story, the first thing that happened was that somebody dressed up like a policeman had come to Felice's house saying he had a warrant for her arrest. He led her outside, where two men dressed in leather jumpsuits and carrying whips "abducted" her. They put a blindfold on her and led her to a Rolls-Royce. When they got to the disco they placed her on a litter, which was decorated with red and black and silver balloons. (Those were the colors she favored in clothing and jewelry.) Amid cheering and shouting and the blare of loud music they paraded her around the room. Then the blindfold was removed and Felice, for the first time, saw the guests. And that, Sal imagined, was quite a sight.

All the women were dressed like Felice in red and silver and black. Some wore black wigs and fake silver necklaces made up of paper clips, and purple exercise suits (another of Felice's favorite outfits). It was a whole chorus line of fake Felices. They called themselves the "Felicettes." They wore name tags that said, "Hi. My name is Felice." Even the waitresses were dressed like Felice. And all female party guests

received a party favor of Frosty Red nail polish wrapped
in red and black, with a note saying, "A touch of
Felice."

In addition to the male strippers, the party featured
makeup artists who painted the faces, and in some
cases bodies, of the guests, and then added sparkles
and feathers for decoration. There was also a professional videotape crew to record the whole thing.

The party made the society page of the Asbury Park
Press, which delighted those in attendance, especially
those whose names were mentioned, though most
feigned embarrassment. The names included Rob and
Maria Marshall. Rob had gone barechested under his
tuxedo in recognition of the festive nature of the occasion, but Maria (somewhat churlishly, many thought)
had refused to dress as a Felicette.

The thought of the whole thing made Sal sick. He
stood up. His face had colored like an autumn leaf.
"I've heard enough," he said. "Less than forty-eight
hours ago, the woman you've been married to for
twenty years was murdered. The loveliest woman in
all of Toms River. Murdered! Nobody has a fucking
clue yet about who did it or why. And you sit here—"

"Robbery," Rob said.

"What?"

"Robbery. The motive was definitely robbery. They
must have followed us up from the casino."

"Rob. Stop talking and *listen* for just a minute.
Right now, I don't give a fuck what the motive was.
And I don't even give a fuck yet who did it. Don't
worry. I will. That'll come. But right now I am grieving, I'm filled with sorrow. The few hours I haven't
been here since I heard about it, I've been down the
street crying in my pillow.

"You know why? Because I loved Maria. So did
Paula. And so did Jack and Barbara. And so did the

Pecks, and the other Pecks, and the Critellis, and the Kenyons, and the Mitchells, and the Perillis and about five hundred other people in this town. Maria was a very special person. She made you feel good about yourself. She made you feel like how happy you were was the most important thing in her life. And you know what? She wasn't faking. She didn't bullshit. It was real. She was real. And now she's gone, and all of us are the poorer for it, and her three sons are basket cases.

"You've seen them out there. Walking around hugging anything that moves. They'll be outside hugging the fucking *trees* in a minute. And you know why? Because their whole *universe* has been destroyed. And you call us in here to talk. Do we hear one word about those boys and how we can help them survive this? No. Not one fucking word about the boys. Do we hear one word about Maria? Yes. We hear you've 'fallen out of love' with her.

"Well, tough shit. What you did is, you got hot pants for Felice. Big deal. Probably every guy in the country club has had hot pants for Felice. But you, Rob Marshall, the biggest fucking showoff in the county, what do you do? You toss over twenty years of marriage. Jesus Christ! What are those boys going to think now? First, their mother gets murdered, and then they hear—and I presume you're going to tell them before they read it in the *Observer* or the *Press*—that you were about to leave her anyway. To run off with Felice. *Felice!*"

"I love her, Sal."

"Knock it off. Just stop with that love shit. I know what you loved about her. So does Jack. So would anybody who's reached the age of puberty. And I'll tell you this—it ain't her fucking intellect. But I don't want to talk about Felice. David is a friend of mine, too, and I don't talk about friends' wives behind their backs."

"But you don't understand. The depth—"

"Don't start with that depth shit either. The only thing deep about banging Felice is how deep your pockets had better be to buy her all that silver jewelry and the Day-Glo jumpsuits and the Club Med vacations. I mean it, Rob. I'm your friend and I'm here to help you, but I don't want to hear another fucking word about Felice."

Rob was nodding and pursing his lips. "All right, Sal," he said. "All right. I only wanted you to know the facts. And I wanted you to hear them from me. But I won't push it. There's just one more thing."

Sal sat down again, the color receding slowly from his face. "What's that?" he said.

"You do remember—in case you start hearing anything about insurance—that I told you, at least ten days ago, that I carried a lot of insurance on Maria. It was no secret. You remember I told you it was a selling tool. I just want to be sure, Sal. You do remember that, don't you?"

"Yeah, Rob. I do." Then Sal stood and walked to the door and left the room. Jack Rogers followed, leaving Rob alone at his desk.

When he told the boys, a few hours later, there were no harsh words or recriminations, only tears. He said, "I have to be honest with you. There is somebody else in my life. I'm sure you have no idea who it could be."

"Mrs. Rosenberg," Roby said. Rob's knuckles turned white as he gripped the edge of his desk.

"You knew?" he said. But Roby had not known, he'd only guessed. He could never figure out why he had been so quick to guess Felice, but oldest sons sometimes have extremely sensitive antennae.

"I'm so sorry," Rob continued, after getting assurances that Roby had never been told anything specific by either Maria or her private investigator. "But there's nothing I can do about it now. If only I had it to do over again it never would have happened."

But then, in almost the same breath, he added, "Felice and I are so good together. You should just see us together. And you will. I know she'll never replace Mom, but she can be your friend, and she wants to be. She'll be spending a lot of time here now and you'll all get to know her very well."

"Hey, Dad?" Roby said.

"Yes?"

"The minute she walks in the door, I'm walking out."

"Me, too," said Chris. John just cried.

"Don't worry, boys, nobody's going to do anything that will make you uncomfortable. Felice is a very sensitive and caring person. We both know it's going to take time. But I must tell you, she's the most important person in the world to me, now that your mother is gone, and I need her for my happiness. I hope you can all understand that and I hope you'll support me in this."

The three boys were staring at the floor, arms folded, all crying now.

"Will you? Will you promise me you'll try to understand? I'm devastated, boys. The loss of your mother is a terrible blow. Felice's love and your understanding are all that I'll have to get me through this. Will you promise me I can count on you?"

Neither Roby nor Chris could quite believe it. But in the past day and a half they'd lost their capacity for disbelief. Things just happened. Unreal things. But nothing mattered. They'd already lost everything and knew they'd never have anything again. All they could

do was cry and hug each other. And Roby could hug
Susan Salzman and Chris could hug Jennifer. John just
kept trying to hug his father.

Because nothing mattered, the boys would say anything; words had lost all meaning and importance.

"Sure, Dad," Roby said. "Whatever makes you
happy's fine with us."

Chris just nodded and sobbed.

John looked at Roby and then he nodded, too,
mumbling something that no one could hear.

Rob grinned. Then he got up and came around the
desk and hugged each of them firmly. "I knew I could
count on you. You're fine young men. I'm very proud
of you all."

Don't say it, Dad, don't say it, Chris thought. But he
did. He said, "And your mother would be proud of
you, too."

He kept talking for another ten minutes, but none
of them heard much that he said. There was some
mention of financial difficulties, some talk about insurance, and something that seemed quite peculiar (except to Chris, who had never shaken loose from his
feeling).

Rob said, "The worst thing is, some people may
think I was involved. The police might even suspect
me. But if you ever hear anything like that, don't
worry about it. That's very common where the wife is
killed. They always look to the husband first."

That night, Chris started remembering things that hadn't
seemed important at the time. Like the night of his
senior prom, in May, when he and Roby, who was
also attending, were dressed up in their tuxedos and
their father, after taking the usual pictures, walked
over to them and murmured that he wanted them to

stop by the Rosenbergs' on their way, so Mrs. Rosenberg could see how nice they looked.

This had struck the two of them as odd at the time, especially when they rang the Rosenbergs' bell and Felice came to the door all sweaty and still in a purple jogging suit and they saw her husband in the background, just out of the shower, with a towel wrapped around his waist. It was obvious they had not been expected. It was equally obvious that Felice was not impressed.

"Oh, look," she said to David. "How cute. Trick-or-treaters."

Later that night, when Chris came back to the house to get the keys to the boat so he could take some friends out on the bay, Rob, who earlier had given his approval, said he'd changed his mind. He thought it might be dangerous. Chris got angry. In fact, he got so angry that with both of his parents standing together, he yelled, "Hey, Dad. Why not tell Mom how you made us go to Mrs. Rosenberg's before the prom."

Though, consciously at least, he didn't even suspect an affair, he knew how much his mother disliked Felice and knew this would get her angry at his father. But he didn't know, until now, how sensitive a nerve he must have struck. Now he knew why, when his father had come down to the rec room hours later (Chris never did get permission to use the boat), he was so upset, saying, "Why the hell did you have to tell your mother that?"

He also remembered another night in early summer. Robin Rosenberg, Felice's daughter, had just returned from her boarding school in France and had given Chris a sweater she'd bought for him in Europe.

It was a cool night and Chris started out of the house with the sweater on. His parents were in the family room, playing Trivial Pursuit with the Rogerses and Burton and Ann Peck.

"Don't wear that sweater," his mother had called. "Felice is a bitch. Who knows where she got the money to pay for it?"

Chris was embarrassed. Such an outburst was so uncharacteristic. "Mom, I'm going to wear it," he'd said. "It's not from Mrs. Rosenberg, anyway. It's from Robin."

"I don't care!" Maria responded, angry now. "Take it off. You are not going out of this house wearing clothing given to you by the Rosenbergs."

"Hey, Mom, you're really being a jerk. There's nothing wrong with this sweater and I'm going to wear it."

"You're not going to wear it! And I'm going to *burn* it!"

"Forget it, Mom," Chris said, and left the house before his father could get involved and start yelling at him for being disrespectful to his mother.

But later, in fact, less than an hour later, over on the boardwalk in Seaside Heights, he took it off, feeling sorry that he'd done something to make his mother so upset. Not until now, though, did he realize why she'd been upset.

Now, on Saturday night, Chris said to Jennifer, "What if my father was involved? What if he had something to do with all this?" Oh, it was a terrible thing to say. A shameful thing even to think. But Chris was now plagued by it and he hoped Jennifer could drive it away.

She said, of course, what he knew she would say, which was also what he wanted her to say. "Oh, no!" she said. "That couldn't be. What a terrible thing to think. Chris, you'd better not say that to anyone else. It sounds *awful.*"

He agreed. And so, of course, he didn't mention it again to anyone. But still the ugly notion haunted him.

Roby didn't know how he had known that Felice was the woman with whom his father had been having an affair. He had just blurted out her name without thinking. Now, a he did think, he recalled the same sort of incidents as had Chris. In particular, he remembered the day after the prom, his mother telling him that no matter what his father said he was not to go to the Rosenbergs' house.

"I don't want you to have anything to do with that woman," Maria had said. "She's poison. She's *fire.*" But the notion of an affair with his father had never entered Roby's mind.

He also remembered how, over the summer, he had several times observed his mother listening at his father's office door. He had even kidded her about it, telling her how insecure she was, and saying she'd better watch out, if Dad was in there talking about insurance she'd get so bored she'd fall asleep on her feet.

But now he considered how secretive and mistrustful his father had seemed throughout the summer. Especially regarding the den. It was the first door one came to from the driveway and the boys had always used it as a shortcut to the rest of the house. Over the summer, however, his father had started locking the door and telling the boys that even if it were unlocked they should *absolutely* not walk through there when entering or leaving the house. No matter that they'd done it for years. It was to stop.

Now Roby thought he understood why. It was because his father had been whispering sweet nothings to Felice on the telephone. Whatever it was, it didn't matter now. The whole thing was so disgusting he couldn't believe it. And how could his father seriously ask the boys to start thinking of Felice as a new friend, some sort of special fairy godmother? That bitch. If she ever came into the house again, he'd spit on her.

Angry, troubled, grieving, stunned, torn by what now seemed almost conflicting loyalties—to his newly dead mother and to his living, but newly unmasked father—Roby closed the door to his room and let himself cry.

What all three of them wanted, the only thing they wanted, was the one thing they'd never have again: their mother, to hug them, to soothe them, to understand their pain.

It had been more than twenty-four hours since they had lost her. And now, on top of that, was this horrible new awareness that in a sense they'd also lost at least a part of the father they'd always known. He wasn't who they thought he had been. By having the affair, he'd hurt their mother, and he'd been about to hurt her worse—to hurt all of them worse—by leaving her.

And so, all three of them, Roby, Chris and John, lay awake through the darkest hours of the night.

6

THEIR father, Robert Oakley Marshall, had been born on December 16, 1939, in the borough of Queens, in New York City, to Howard Marshall of New York, and Oakleigh Valentine Weeks of Grand Rapids, Michigan, whose parents had lost everything in the Depression.

Howard Marshall had dropped out of St. John's University in New York after two years and was employed as a sporting goods salesman at the Wanamaker's department store in Manhattan. In his spare time, he gave tennis lessons to earn extra money.

Rob's first years were spent in a rented house in the Elmhurst section of Queens. Then, so abruptly that they could not even rent a house or apartment but had to live in a less-than-luxurious hotel, the family moved to Chicago. Two years later, they moved to Kiel, Wisconsin. Then there were other towns, in Wisconsin and Michigan and throughout the Midwest. Always, they lived in rented houses. Howard Marshall died without ever having owned a home, which—or so went the joke among friends and family—caused Rob to grow up wanting to own everything he saw.

One might have said that Rob's father was a traveling salesman who actually traveled. The truth was, he was an alcoholic, which was why none of his jobs lasted long. Oakleigh prayed every day that her husband, a non-Catholic, would convert. Instead, he drank. But not only did her religion prevent her from leaving him, it prevented her from not having children. She wound up with five, of whom Rob was the oldest.

By the time Rob was a teenager, the family was living in Thomaston, Connecticut, where his father was employed by the Seth Thomas clock company. After that job was lost, they moved to Havertown, Pennsylvania, where Rob (who, like the other children, was being raised as a Catholic) was enrolled in Monsignor Bonner High School.

He'd always felt like an outsider wherever he'd lived. By the age of sixteen, he felt like an outsider even at home (this new home, at least the tenth of his life). He spent a lot of time in the basement of the rented house in Havertown, playing the drums and feeling superior to his parents. Soon, he put up partitions and brought down a cot and created his own basement apartment, in which he lived, except for meals.

In school, he had problems. English was the worst. He flunked it his junior year and had to go to summer school. But that turned out to be fortuitous. He made friends with a boy who was forming a dance band. Rob volunteered to play drums. Another member of the band had an older brother who was leaving home to join the Air Force. The dance band played at the going-away party, which was how Rob met Maria. She was a cousin of the friend of the friend's.

Maria: a doctor's daughter with blond hair so long and beautiful that if you were her father you would want to lock her in a tower. What better way to prove yourself superior to the rest of your family than to acquire a girlfriend like that?

She went to St. Adalbert's, a Polish Catholic school in the city. With her long blond hair, her lovely singing voice (especially when she sang hymns) and her sweet and tender disposition, Maria was an overwheming favorite among the nuns. Also, being a doctor's daughter didn't hurt.

The terrible thing about a child like that, of course, is you cannot really lock her in a tower. You cannot even keep her a child. You can keep her out of Flying Jennies on Roosevelt Boulevard, but you cannot stop her from growing up. Boys, being boys, will come around. Even so, in the Puszynski home they were not welcomed.

Maria was only fifteen when she first met Rob and began (secretly) to date him. But she waited until she was in college before she discussed him at home. By then, Rob was in college, too—a Catholic college—and she hoped this would make him more acceptable to her parents.

Rob's goal had been Annapolis. On his eighteenth birthday he joined the Naval Reserve and then spent an entire year of post–high school prep boning up for the SATs. Still, he did very poorly. Not only did he not make Annapolis, he barely managed acceptance at Villanova, which, particularly in those days, was not one of the country's more rigorous academic institutions. But at least it was college. And Rob was Navy ROTC.

And so, when at last he presented himself in Port Richmond, he felt it was with proper credentials. Dr. Puszynski, however, was less than charmed. Maybe it would have been the same with any suitor, but he didn't like Rob and he liked him even less after he'd met the rest of the Marshall family. A no-class outfit if he'd ever seen one, the doctor grumbled later to his wife. "A bunch of gypsies," he said. "First one up in the morning is best dressed for the day in that house."

At the same time, they struck him as phony, putting

on airs, pretending to be better than they were. "A deficit spender," he said of Rob's father. "Just like the government." From Dr. Puszynski, these were not words of praise. And when he looked at Rob he saw an apple falling close to the tree.

Life would have been simpler if Rob had failed to graduate from Villanova, as almost happened. After three and a half years, he had only a 1.9 grade point average, with a 2.0 required for graduation. If he fell short, he would not receive his commission as a naval officer, he would not be accepted for flight school, he would not be permitted to marry Maria.

When he got a second-semester D in marketing, all seemed lost (or won, from Dr. Puszynski's point of view). Instead, that was when Rob discovered the one true talent he possessed: salesmanship. He persuaded his instructor to change the grade to a C, and in June of 1963, just barely, Rob graduated. Now there were no grounds on which Dr. Puszynski could base further opposition to the marriage of Rob and Maria.

Rob went to Pensacola for Navy flight training, completing the course on November 22, 1963, the day of the first Kennedy assassination. Then, having been accepted for helicopter training, he returned to Philadelphia in triumph to claim his bride.

They were married three days after Christmas, but no more reluctant father than Vincent Puszynski had ever walked more stiffly or slowly up the aisle of St. Adalbert's to give a daughter away.

And such a daughter! No bridal magazine had ever had a better cover girl than the beautiful, blond, sweet Maria on her wedding day. And Rob, of course, tall and handsome, eyes piercing, jaw jutting—all the clichés. He was resplendent in his dress uniform, a regular recruiting poster of a man.

On the wedding invitation, next to his name, he'd

insisted on gold wings and an embossed *U.S.N.*, indi-
cating he was already a Navy pilot, though in reality
he was still a trainee. This was somewhat improper,
but Rob had a tendency not to let propriety stand in
the way of appearances. The gold wings were just part
of the image. He had escaped from his own private
ghetto. He had acquired the possession he'd wanted
most. The doctor's daughter, the beautiful blonde,
was now his wife.

After a year spent in Florida and overseas, Rob was
assigned to the Naval Air Station in Lakehurst, New
Jersey, and got his first look at Toms River. He liked
what he saw. Houses were cheap and available. The
town was near the base and near the beach. And just
the right distance from Philadelphia to assure that his
wife could have access to her parents but that they
would not be in his hair all the time.

But there was something else: some flickering nerve
deep within the unconscious that enabled Rob Marshall to recognize that Toms River was his kind of
town.

He and Maria moved into their ranch house two
months before Roby was born. A year after Roby
came Chris. By then, Rob was no longer in the Navy.
He was a homeowner, the father of two, the husband
of a beautiful wife. All around him, a boom town was
springing up. New neighborhoods were being born
overnight, filled with new people, just like him, just
starting out in life, from backgrounds that did not
include wealth, but now with their own families and
first homes, and all of them wanting to be prudent and
responsible.

Rob Marshall did the obvious thing. He became a
life insurance salesman. He sold the policies of Provident Mutual Life of Philadelphia. In his first year he
sold more than two million dollars' worth, which made

him one of the company's top fifty salesmen in the country. The next year he did it again. The Marshalls moved to a bigger house, three blocks away. Their third son, John, was born in 1971.

Every Sunday you would see them at St. Joseph's Church. Rob, by then, had a new red Cadillac convertible with a white top and he would park it directly in front of the church, as if that special place had been reserved for him.

Then the family would march straight up the center aisle to the front pew, as if that had been reserved for them also. Rob, stern, unsmiling, intense; Maria beaming warmly at everyone, so elegantly dressed, her long blond hair flowing; the boys dressed in neckties and suits, their hair freshly cut: such fine little men, so clean-cut and well scrubbed; just like their mother.

It was almost as if Rob and Maria were royalty: a young king and queen on a visit to a remote outpost of the empire. This was not the sort of attitude that Toms River had seen much of before and there were some who found it slightly unsettling. But after all, Rob had been a naval officer. And Maria, so everyone said, was from a very wealthy Main Line family. And really, the fact that people like that would have chosen to settle in Toms River at all was, in its way, a very nice compliment to the town.

So Toms River tended to admire the Marshalls, and even to envy them a bit: their good looks, their lovely children, the fact that Rob was so obviously successful, the fact that they were always buying something new.

They moved to Brookside in 1973, to a brand-new house which Rob had hired an architect to design. They joined the country club. Rob played tennis. The boys swam. Maria was invited to join the Laurel Twigs, an organization whose ostensible purpose was to raise money for the hospital, but whose real function seemed to be to provide a goal toward which a Toms River housewife with an interest in social climbing could aspire.

Those were the boom years, in which a life insurance salesman found himself surrounded by hundreds of new potential clients every week. In order to prosper, all you had to do was get out of bed in the morning and answer the phone when it rang. But Rob Marshall did a lot more than that.

He was, to put it bluntly, the most aggressive salesman Toms River had ever seen. If he viewed you as a prospect (and unless you'd just had your second coronary or were suffering from an obvious malignancy, Rob Marshall viewed you as a prospect), he'd come at you with all the social grace of a wolverine. Buying a policy from him was the only way to get him out of your hair, if not your life. Finally, you gave in and did it. Finally, it seemed, everyone in Toms River gave in and did it.

Rob became a very successful businessman, and because he was successful—and because he made it so obvious he was successful—he became a big man in town. A power in the Rotary Club (though he quit in a fit of pique and founded a competing organization when he was passed over for president), a leader of United Way, men's singles tennis champion (and doubles partner of both Ray DiOrio and David Rosenberg) at the country club.

And, as he made it glaringly apparent, a figure to be reckoned with at the Atlantic City gambling casinos. The deference shown him at the fifty- and one-hundred-dollar blackjack tables was something Rob seemed to take a great deal of pride in and something he spent a lot of time talking about.

What he seemed to take the most pride in, however

and spend the most time talking about, was his wife, Maria; or, as he consistently referred to her, "the beautiful Maria." He talked about how much he loved her, how good to her he was, how proud he was to be married to such a fine-looking woman who always knew just where to go to buy the best clothes and then how to wear them so well.

"Look at her," he'd say, practically every Saturday night at the club (or, in her final years, at a lavish casino restaurant in Atlantic City), "isn't she gorgeous? Isn't she just absolutely beautiful?" He seemed even more proud of her than of his Cadillac, and she, it must be said, appeared quite flattered to be treated as an ornament.

Actually, even for Toms River, Rob and Maria were extreme. Around the country club they were referred to (in their absence) as Ken and Barbie. But it wasn't until later—until too late—that people looked back and realized that maybe she'd become a slave to his vision of her and to the image she was trying to project. That her obsession with appearances might have cost her her life.

Until then, in a town where one's possessions were viewed as a mirror of one's soul, Rob Marshall seemed to have it all and Maria seemed his ultimate possession. Not a sex object, despite her attractiveness, but something which, in Toms River, was even more to be cherished: a status object.

Which might have been why the town was so quick to turn against Rob after her death. In Toms River, you're supposed to take better care of your possessions.

7

On Sunday morning, the Asbury Park *Press* quoted the county prosecutor as saying, "The investigation is continuing."

Friends of Rob's were quoted as saying such things as, "He's a very organized person, very energetic, personable. He makes people feel very confident in him," and, "Rob is a very giving person. Anything he takes up to do he gets totally involved in. It's the same with his job, his tennis, his family. He always gives one hundred percent." Another friend said, "He and Maria are very close."

An aerobic-dance instructor said, "They took workouts together, exercises to music. They were definitely a happy couple."

Another aerobic-dance instructor said, "People admired her because she seemed to have the ideal family and lifestyle. You know, like you'd see on TV."

A housewife from the neighborhood said, "She really enjoyed life and being with her husband. She was a super-perfect type of wife. I don't know why anyone would want to kill her."

The press, however, was getting tired of talking to neighbors. Reporters had been camped outside the Marshalls' house for forty-eight hours, watching the

steady stream of relatives, neighbors and friends come
and go. The county prosecutor and state police still
said only that the investigation was continuing but
there was no progress to report. The press wanted
more. The press wanted access to the family, preferably to Rob himself. This was the message relayed by
visitor after visitor throughout Sunday morning and
afternoon.

Rob would have been happy to talk, but Ray DiOrio
had been adamant about that. Do not talk to *anyone*,
DiOrio had said the day before, during the breakfast
meeting at a diner on Route 37. Say *nothing*, DiOrio
had told him. Not one word to anyone about anything.

That had been the first rule. The second concerned
Felice. DiOrio instructed Rob to have absolutely no
contact of any kind with her. No meetings, no phone
calls, no letters, no tapes. Pretend she didn't exist.
And Ray DiOrio was the sort of man whose admoni-
tions one heeded. Especially when one's wife had just
been murdered and when the police were already acting (as they had at the Bass River barracks early
Friday morning) distinctly unfriendly.

But it was hard for Rob, just when he was, for the
first time, revealing his love for Felice to close friends
and family, to cut himself off from her suddenly. For
the past year, the two of them had averaged three or
four encounters per week, had exchanged cassette tapes
into which they'd murmured words of love (Rob had
even rented a Toms River post office box to facilitate
the tape exchanges) and had spoken on the phone at
least daily and often several times a day.

Now, at the most stressful moment of his life, at the
time when he needed her most, he could not have her.
He was not even permitted to hear her voice. To make
it worse, Rob had been told by Brookside friends that
police had stopped Felice's car on the Garden State

Parkway Friday afternoon and had taken her in for questioning. He'd also heard that David had become so furious when he'd learned of the affair that he'd banished her from the house.

No matter. Ray DiOrio had said stay away. And keep your mouth shut. So Rob was determined to do both.

By midafternoon, however, he'd decided that it would not look good for the whole family to remain in seclusion. He did not want it to appear that they had anything to hide. He told Roby that it was his duty as the oldest son to go out to the front lawn and speak to the press. He instructed Roby to tell them what a wonderful person Maria had been and to inform them that he, Rob, was still too grief-stricken to appear.

Roby walked tentatively down the driveway and spoke in a somber and hesitant voice. Despite his lifeguard's build and curly blond hair, there seemed something vulnerable and almost waiflike about him as he began to talk about his mother.

"She wanted everyone to like her," Roby said, "and they all did. You really didn't have to know my mom to love her, you just had to know of her. She's one of a kind. How can I put it into words? We have friends in and out all day and it's like, even though my mom is gone, she's taking care of us through her friends, because they loved her, too. She was just a classy, beautiful lady.

"My father's still trying to get over the shock. So my brothers and I have decided we're going to be tough. For him. He needs it now. We're going to do as much as we can and just take care of everything my mom would have."

As Roby stood in front of the house, eyes red-rimmed from tears and exhaustion, explaining how the boys were going to try to help their father deal with the pain of his loss, Gene Leahy and Sal Coccaro were sitting on the rear deck, gazing out over the pool.

All day, friends had been calling Sal aside and speaking to him in low and worried tones, passing on some of the rumors which already were sweeping the town.

"What do you think?" Gene said.

Sal sighed and shook his head. He looked ten years older than he had when he'd arrived at the house Friday morning. "I don't know," he said. "I don't know what to think. But I can tell you what a lot of other people think. A lot of other people think he's involved."

"Nice town," Gene said.

"What do you mean?"

"Where your friends and neighbors are so quick to think the worst of you."

"Hey, go easy," Sal said. "People got reasons."

"Such as?"

Sal scratched his bald head. "Look, I can talk to you, right? I mean, I don't really know you very well, but you seem like a good guy to me. A straight shooter. Not full of bullshit."

Gene nodded and grinned. "So far, so good. You want to quit while you're ahead?"

"The thing is," Sal said, not grinning, "I'm hearing so much stuff I just need somebody to talk to. You know, somebody who can maybe help me put it in perspective."

"Well, I'll try," Gene said, "but I'd better tell you up front that there are a few things I'm having trouble with perspective on myself."

"Just sit here a minute," Sal said. "I'm going to go get us a couple of beers. You like beer?"

"Beer's fine," Gene said.

When he returned, Sal leaned forward and began to

talk almost immediately. "One thing I'm hearing," he said, "is that Rob was familiar with that site. That Oyster Creek. I'm hearing he'd been there a couple of times with Felice. They used it as a place to make out when they didn't have time to get to a motel. I hear the troopers chased them out of there a couple of times. Rob had his pants down, or her pants down, or something. Trooper said you can't do that sort of thing along the parkway. Said next time he'd arrest the both of them."

Gene nodded.

"So, you're a lawyer," Sal said. "What do you think?"

"I think it's better if you can get to a motel," Gene said, "but you don't have to be a lawyer to think that."

"No, I mean, is it bad? Is it suspicious? That he was already familiar with the site? That he'd been there with *Felice,* for Christ's sake?"

"Frankly, if you're talking strictly in terms of whether or not it tends to cast more or less suspicion on him, I might think less, in that if it was a site he was already familiar with, it's not quite so strange that he'd pull in there to check a flat tire."

"All right," Sal said. "You want something that's strange? How about this? *How about his whole fucking story?* You think anybody's gonna watch some turkey rake in ten thousand bucks at a blackjack table at Harrah's and they want to take it off him, so what they do is they let him get into his car and they follow him forty miles up the parkway in the middle of the night, hoping that maybe, just *maybe* his tire would go flat and that he'd be dumb enough to pull into the Black fucking Forest to change it?"

Gene nodded. "The story has problems," he said. "I've already told Rob that they'll be apparent to a prosecutor. So, what else?"

"The tire," Sal said. "At least six people have already told me they know for a fact—don't even ask how everybody knows everything for a fact when the cops haven't said word one to anybody, that's just the way Toms River works—they know for a fact that the tire wasn't 'mushy' or 'wishy-washy' or any of the other words Rob's been using. The tire was slashed with a knife. There's some kind of big, raggedy tear halfway across it. The condition of that tire, you couldn't drive from here to the pool."

"Not good," Gene said.

"You bet your ass, not good. And the other thing, which even my kids have figured out for Chrissakes, is that that picnic area is only a couple of miles beyond the toll plaza, and only about four miles before you hit the Roy Rogers, which is open twenty-four hours a day.

"You got a mushy, wishy-washy tire, what're you going to do at half past midnight? You're going to stop at the goddamned toll plaza, which is lit up like Giants Stadium for a night game, and you're going to say to one of the guys, 'Hey, my tire's a little soft, I'm going to pull over to the side here and change it.' Christ, you're probably going to have three state cops fighting over who gets to hold your hubcap for you while you do it, and they'll be serving Maria fucking demitasse. That's what you're going to do.

"And if for some reason, like maybe you had a couple extra rum and Cokes while you were supposedly winning all that money at the casino, and you don't want the assistance of the state police, you drive your mushy, wishy-washy tire another four miles to the fucking Roy Rogers. There, you can take your wife inside and buy her a plate of week-old french fries while some minimum-wage gas pumper changes it for you. And then you can tip him ten bucks out of all those thousands you got in your pocket and you feel like a big shot again.

"Gene—you know as well as I do, probably better, that Rob Marshall never changed a tire in his life. This is a guy who insists on fresh ice cubes every time somebody offers him another drink. He wouldn't know which end of the jack was up. You get your hands dirty changing a tire and Rob don't like dirty hands. Especially at half past midnight in the woods.

"And Maria, for Chrissakes, that woman was more scared of the dark than a two-year-old. She used to jump out of her skin every time she walked into a movie theater. She's sure as hell not going to sit there like little Mrs. Goodwife while Rob pretends his Eldorado is an ATV and he takes her into the forest like Little Red Riding Hood to visit grandmother."

"He says she was asleep," Gene said.

"Yeah. I know. He says a lot of things. Which is why Ray DiOrio told him to keep his mouth shut. But I'm not telling you what *he* says. I'm telling you what everybody else is saying *about* him already and they haven't even had the mass yet for Maria."

"It's not good," Gene repeated.

"Don't misunderstand, Gene, I love Rob like a brother and—"

"You're one up on me, then."

"Huh?"

"I only love him like a brother-in-law. Besides which, I used to work in the attorney general's office in Delaware. And I can guarantee you this much—Ray DiOrio or no Ray DiOrio, these Ocean County guys are going to cut him a new asshole before they're done."

The next day, Monday, was the day on which the memorial mass was said for Maria at St. Joseph's

Church. It was not a funeral because, within hours of the murder, Rob had ordered her body cremated and cremation had occurred before anyone from the state police or prosecutor's office had thought to prevent it.

Rob was up early again, this time making sure that Jack Rogers and Sal Coccaro had arranged everything with the caterer for the big reception he planned to have back at the house after the service. Rob said he wanted the house filled with people—Maria's friends—because "that was the way she would want it."

Upstairs, at 10 A.M., Roby walked down the hall to wake up Chris. One of their mother's friends was downstairs, waiting to take the three boys out to buy new suits for the service. Maria had always been especially proud of how well her sons had dressed for church.

Chris was lying on his back, staring blankly at the ceiling, wondering how he would ever get through the day. "I can't do it," he said to Roby.

"Chris, come *on*. Mrs. Fallon is waiting."

"I can't do it. I just can't. I can't even get out of bed. I just can't make myself. I want to stay here forever."

"Goddamn it, Chris, pull yourself together."

Chris suddenly sat upright. "Why the hell should I?" he shouted.

"Why the hell should any of us?" He leaned forward, put his head in his hands and started to cry.

"What are you going to say next? You want your mommy?"

"Yes. Yes! What's wrong with that?! I *do* want my mommy. And you want her, too. And so does John. But none of us will ever have her again. Has that really sunk in yet, Roby? This isn't just a bad dream. We're not going to wake up from this. This is the way it's going to be for the rest of our lives."

"Yeah, that's right, Chris. This is the way it's going to be. So maybe it's time you started growing up so you can deal with it."

"Oh, give me a break. I'm not some reporter. You don't have to feed me that let's-be-tough-for-Dad bullshit."

For a moment Roby felt himself getting angry. But it passed as he looked at his brother's anguished face. "Hey, Chris," he said in a new and softer tone of voice.

"What?"

"You know Mom would want us looking good to-day. Let's go buy a couple of suits."

Chris lay back down, as if his own outburst had used up his quota of energy for the day. "Nope," he said. "I can't do it, Roby. The first time I tried something on I'd remember why I was doing it and you'd have to scrape me up off the floor. Besides, Mom's not here anymore. So there's no sense trying to make her happy. All she is is ashes, Roby, and that's all she's ever going to be. There isn't any Mom anymore, so why give a damn how we look?"

Now it was Roby who started to cry. As he did, he leaned over Chris and hugged him tight.

What people remembered most about the memorial service was the reception back at the house afterward, how much like a party it seemed. Not that it was a party that the boys enjoyed much, but Rob himself seemed almost ebullient. He bustled from room to room, freshening drinks, urging food upon the guests, shaking hands heartily and saying repeatedly, "Don't you think Maria would have loved this? Don't you think this is just the way she'd want it done?"

So inappropriate was his apparent enthusiasm for the event that later many would say it was that behav-

ior that first caused them to suspect that the rumors of
his involvement in the murder might have some basis
in fact.

Certainly, by Monday afternoon, the rumors were
everywhere. Rather odd, actually: to attend a memorial service for such a well-known and well-liked member of the community, who had been murdered in
such shocking fashion, and to hear murmuring throughout the church (and louder murmuring back at the
house) that the police considered her husband a suspect.

And then to have him standing right there, beaming
at you and waiting to be congratulated on the lavish-
ness of the food and drink (the way Maria would have
wanted it—she loved to travel first class).

There was at least one guest at the reception who
was not content to murmur. This was Madge Kenyon,
wife of the lawyer Tom Kenyon. Both Roby and Chris,
who were in separate parts of the house at the time,
heard the sound of voices suddenly raised. Or at least
one voice. Madge Kenyon was shouting.

Even though she was standing right in front of Rob,
she was shouting and waving a finger in his face.
"You'd better not have had anything to do with this!"

There was more, but that was the sentence both
Roby and Chris remembered. Roby was shocked, then
angered. What right did Madge Kenyon or anyone
else have to walk up to his father within an hour of the
memorial service and start yelling crap like that at
him?

Chris, however, just stood there staring at the scene.
So somebody else feels the way I do, he said to himself.
He didn't know why she would, just as he didn't know
why he did, and he didn't think he should ask her. But
in a strange way Mrs. Kenyon's outburst made him
feel a little better about himself. At least, if he was

crazy or sick or just plain bad for having had thoughts
like he'd had, he wasn't the only one who'd had them.

Roby stood by the pool looking at all the people
milling about (there were at least 150, maybe 200 at
the reception) and thinking, *pretty soon they'll all be
gone and I'll be alone.*

And by evening they were gone, and so was Chris,
driven back to Lehigh by Uncle Gene. Rob stepped
onto the deck and motioned for Roby to join him. He
was holding a glass that might have contained rum and
Coke to start with but seemed now to be mostly melted
ice. From the look on his face, Roby could tell he
wanted to have one of his "man-to-man" talks.

"Roby," he said, "I think I'd better tell you something. Man to man."

"What is it, Dad?"

"The atmosphere, ah, the ah, climate, so to speak,
is turning pretty negative around town. A lot of people seem to think I'm—that I'm involved."

"Yeah, I heard Mrs. Kenyon. But that's crazy, Dad.
That's really crazy. And it pisses me off."

"Yes, but you know the people in this town. A
bunch of phonies. Shallow, materialistic phonies. All
they care about is the size of your bank account. Now
that there are rumors that we were having financial
difficulties they're eager to walk all over me."

"Yeah, but thinking you—that you had something
to do with—you know, with Mom—Mom's death . . .
What kind of bullshit is that?"

"That's just what it is, son. It's bullshit. And I know
you know it. Just never forget it, whatever you may
hear in the days ahead."

"What am I going to hear in the days ahead?"

"I don't know. More of the same, I guess. More
crazy, ugly stories by people who have to titillate
themselves by trying to pile scandal on top of tragedy."

"Well, if I hear much more of it, Dad, whoever I hear it from is going to find himself flat on his back looking up."

Rob frowned. "Don't talk like that, Roby. It's not polite. Remember, especially at a time of stress like this, you're a Marshall. That means a great deal in Toms River. You have a lot to be proud of and a lot to live up to. Just stay tough, for my sake. And hold your head high, whatever happens."

"Okay, Dad. But nothing much better happen. Nothing bad, I mean. I don't think, as it is, that I'm going to be handling all this very well."

"Sure you will. You're tough. You're strong. You're my son." He put his glass down and reached out to squeeze Roby's shoulder. "And always remember— Felice and I will be there for you, to help you over the rough spots."

Roby could feel his cheeks color. Involuntarily, his fists clenched. "Listen, Dad," he said. "I'll be strong and tough and proud and all that. But there's just one thing you'd better know. Man to man."

Rob smiled at his son benignly, if just a trifle blearily. "What's that?" he said.

"From now on," Roby said, "I don't ever want to hear the name of that bitch spoken in this house again."

On his way to bed that night—*what was it, the third night since Mom was killed? The fourth? The thousandth?* —Roby was walking through the kitchen when a business card tacked to the bulletin board caught his eye.

The name on the card was that of the director of admissions at Stockton State College, where Maria had taken Roby in late August to preregister for fall semester classes.

It had been a difficult summer for Roby, after the

trouble at Villanova. His father had seemed pissed at him for three straight months. As if his one-semester suspension was the worst disgrace in Marshall family history. Even if it was, there was nothing he could do about it.

Now, he realized that there had been other sources of stress contributing to his father's irritability. Like an affair. And planning to split. And being however deeply in debt he really was. But at the time, which was all summer long—until Friday morning at 3 A.M., which was the start of an entirely different, and much longer, season—his father had been cold and unforgiving. It was his mother's love and understanding that had sustained him.

Roby took the card down from the board. To attend classes at Stockton State he would have to drive, twice a day, past the Oyster Creek picnic area on the parkway. Roby knew he would not be able to do that. He dropped the card in a wastebasket. As it fell, he saw handwriting on the other side. His mother's handwriting.

He bent down and retrieved the card. He read the writing. It was a message from his mother to him. It said:

Our greatest glory consists not in never falling but in rising every time we fall.

Crying once again, Roby Marshall went to bed. Wondering if his mother had somehow known that by the time classes started she would not be there to offer inspiration in person.

8

AT noon the next day, Sal Coccaro got a call from Rob, asking him to come to the house right away.

"I'm in trouble, buddy," Rob said. "I need you."

Sal left his office immediately and drove to Crest Ridge Drive. He didn't know what it might be and he didn't want to think too much about it in advance.

He found Rob bleary-eyed from sleeplessness and apparently only a few minutes past a recent episode of crying.

"Come in, Sal, come in. Let's go into my office. We've got to talk."

Sal almost said no. Whatever was coming, he didn't want to be the one to hear it. Especially not when it was just he and Rob alone.

But he did follow Rob into the office and took a seat. Rob, as usual, seated himself behind his desk, though it struck Sal that the attempt to maintain a business-as-usual façade was pathetic.

"I don't know what to do," Rob said. "I just had to talk to somebody. I'm going crazy." He began to cry again. "Sal," he said, "Sal. You've got to help me. I just can't go on this way. Sal, Sal, I miss her so much." Then the crying overcame him and he could no longer speak.

Sal got up and moved behind the desk and put his hands on Rob's shoulders.

"Oh, Rob," he said, "I know it must be so hard for you. To lose her so suddenly like this. And in such a horrible way. And now to have to deal not only with your own pain but with the boys', too. I feel for you, Rob, believe me. Maria was one of a kind."

Rob's crying subsided. He shifted in his chair so that Sal's hands were no longer touching his shoulders. Then he looked up.

"Sal," he said. "I'm not talking about Maria. I'm talking about Felice."

"You son of a bitch," Sal said softly, backing away from the desk.

"There's no way I can get through this without her," Rob said. "I need her. I need her right now. Sal, if only there was some way for me to let you know the depth, the beauty of our love. Someday, maybe you'll be able to appreciate how unique, how glorious it is."

"You son of a bitch," Sal repeated, this time not quite so softly.

"Sal, I *physically ache* from missing her."

For Sal, this proved too much. He looked Rob squarely in the eye and made a suggestion.

"Try jerking off," he said, and walked out of Rob's office, slamming the door behind him.

Roby left the house in early afternoon. As he stepped toward the yellow Mustang in the driveway he was approached by several reporters, who, again, had been waiting at curbside all day.

"Do you have any comment?" one of them asked.

"About what?"

"About the rumor that your father is about to be arrested."

"That's bullshit," Roby said.

"How do you know?"

"No comment. I believe in my father. That's all I have to say."

"Did you know your father was having an affair?"

"What about his gambling?" another called. "Was he deeply in debt to the casinos?"

"Did your mother know about the affair?"

"Listen," Roby said, the politeness so deeply ingrained by Maria all that stopped him from pushing the reporters out of the way and getting into his car and slamming the door. "Listen. I don't have any comment about anything and I really wish you'd all leave the family alone. But I will tell you one thing. My father didn't have anything to do with my mother's death."

"What makes you so sure?"

"If you met him," Roby said, "you just couldn't think stuff like that." Then he spoke in a softer voice that was less of a plea and more of a recollection. "You just had to see him and my mother together. It was like something out of a story book." He stood in the driveway, gazing off into space. The reporters could see tears in his eyes. The questions stopped.

Late that night, in his office, with the door closed, Rob switched on a tape recorder containing a blank cassette and placed next to it another recorder that was playing a song.

The song was "Lady," sung by John Denver, one of Rob's favorite romantic vocalists. After thirty seconds of music he turned off the song and began to speak, using a low, intimate voice.

"Hi, babe," he said. "I couldn't think of a more appropriate song, or words, than this one. I do still love you so. I wanted you to have some communication from me and I guess, if you feel comfortable, this

might be the only way we'll be able to communicate
for a while.

"I know your attorney has told you not to have any
contact with me, and Ray DiOrio has indicated that
it's best that we not, either. I did ask him about a tape
and he said—the way he puts it is, whenever a question like that is asked, he asks what good can it do and
what harm can it do, and he couldn't think of an
answer on either side. He said, 'I'm not going to tell
you to do it and I'm not going to tell you not to, so
you do what you want.'"

"I felt that I had to communicate to tell you that I
love you—" He sobbed. "So much. And I feel so
terrible—" Here, his voice broke. "About all of this.
What happened to you, being picked up by the police
and confronted with all that evidence that we didn't
even know existed. And the horrible scene that I'm
sure happened at home with David . . .

"The rumors are flying hot and heavy out there, but
you must know, babe, that much as we were going to
hurt Maria by my leaving, I could never hurt her that
way. Never. She had to be around to care for the
boys. No one can do that as well as she could. But I'm
here now by myself, with them, and I'm hoping of
course that *we'll* still have a life together when all the
dust settles.

"I want that more than anything, anything in the
world. I want to care for you and I want your love,
and the most wonderful thing is, on Saturday I guess it
was, I sat Roby and Chris down and I told them about
you and me and I told them that the problem was there
before you and I met—that Mom and I were having
difficulties and that we probably wouldn't have lasted
much longer in any case, and then I told them about
my feelings for you and how they evolved and how

special the relationship was, and they really did understand. They were incredibly supportive.

"Roby said, 'Dad, if that's what you want then that's what we want.' And Chris backed him up. Johnny, I explained it to him from a slightly different angle, without quite so much detail, of course, but Johnny was—of course they all cried."

Here, Rob, too, began to sob again. "It's difficult for them to understand." (Sob.) "I realize that. But they said they did and they said they still loved me and they said they loved me more now than before because I told them. It was unbelievable. You'd be so proud." He sobbed a little longer this time.

"I told them, too, that you would never, ever try to take Mom's place but that you wanted to be a friend, a friend of theirs, and that I hoped that they would be your friend, and they said they would try. And I think that as time goes on that's what will happen, honey, and it will be a good relationship for all of us.

"I won't tell you now, I don't think it's worth any—it needs telling, but you can imagine how difficult it was for me to come home and tell first Roby, and John, and then drive up to Lehigh and tell Chris. It was so horrible. I—but at the same time, of course, I feel anguish for you, too, because of what you went through. And now this separation—our separation—amplifies everything, all the hurt.

"Hearing the rumors that are being spread around, I'm being looked at very carefully, and I'm being implicated. Ray DiOrio and Gene Leahy have said that the fact that we've had an affair for the past year and the fact that there's insurance and that I'm in debt all of course enhance a reason to be involved—provide motive, in other words.

"But it's purely circumstantial. And, assuming that that's all they find—and that's all they could find—

they couldn't, or wouldn't bring it to court. They're digging real hard trying to find more, obviously.

"We're public information now, babe, so we're going to have to grit this one out. I'm truly sorry for that happening but it would have happened anyway in another week. The ironic thing is that I found out that Maria was going to confront me with all the evidence she had, documented evidence. And the ironic thing is that if anybody had told me, none of this would have happened. They didn't. It did. And here we are.

"The purpose of this tape is not to review all of that, though, but to tell you that—how much I love you and how much I'm thinking about you and how terrible, of course, I feel about Maria.

"I want you to know that—I want you to try to think of a way you can respond, either by mailing tapes to the office if you want, or we'll get another post office box—that occurred to me—because the key was in the car, and also the safe deposit key.

"I'm not even going to see the car again. I told Pete Critelli that when they release it to just sell it, get something else. And you have to tell me also what your status is as far as a car. Let me know, and if you need something we'll work that out, too.

"What I plan to do is give Pete the station wagon back and get something smaller for myself, and if you need a car, babe, we'll take the value of the two cars and we'll get something for each of us. Let me know what you want to do.

"If you want to write, or make a tape, you can send that over to the office, or get it to me some other way. I desperately want to talk to you this way, if we can't talk any other way, just to—to hear your voice, to know that I can talk to you this way, which has always been so therapeutic for us, such a release, such a wonderful way to just communicate, just—stream of consciousness, as someone I love said.

"Well, babe . . ." There was a pause. "I'm numb. I just—" A longer pause, and then he whispered, "I hope I get through this."

When he resumed, after another pause, his voice was stronger. "I've gotten closer to God," he said, "closer, and I'm confident that with God's help we can both get through this and see the light at the end of the tunnel soon. I don't want you to forsake God. I want you to ask for help. Let's do that together. I want our lives to be good and rewarding lives and to help people. I've made that commitment when I asked for God's help to get through this. I hope you'll join me in that commitment, babe. I love you with all my heart. But you know that."

A light drizzle was falling and there were still a couple of reporters in front of his house when Roby returned home Tuesday night. One of them, a young female in a raincoat, approached him.

"How're you doing?" she said.

"Okay. Getting by."

"You want to take a walk?"

"What?"

"Take a walk. Just around the block. Look, I know how bad this must be for you. But I'm not like the rest of them. I'm not just trying to get a story. I'd really like to be your friend."

"My friend, huh?" Roby grinned. "Is that because of my rugged good looks or is it more my irresistible charm?"

The reporter smiled back.

"Oh, I don't know," she said. "Maybe a little of both. I just thought maybe you could use somebody sort of your own age to talk to. Not about this, if you don't want to. Just about anything. Or nothing at all."

Roby stepped forward and reached toward her. Her raincoat was unbuttoned and he pulled one side open to reveal the tape recorder that had been partially concealed underneath.

"Careful," he said. "You don't want that to get wet." Then he went into his house.

On Thursday afternoon, September 13, Felice called Sal Coccaro's office while he was out and spoke to his secretary. "Tell him it's very personal," she said. "I need to talk to him. He'll understand. I can't say who I am. I'll call again tomorrow at four."

On Friday at four he was there, waiting for her call just so he could have the pleasure of slamming the phone down in her ear. He was thinking about how good a cold draft beer at the Office Lounge would taste. He planned to go get one as soon as he slammed down the phone.

"Before you hang up," she said, "can I ask you one thing? Will you give Rob a message for me?"

"Felice," he said, "I'm not making any moral judgments on anybody, but I'll tell you the same thing I told Rob. I'm not going to be in the middle. David is a friend of mine, too, and running messages between you and Rob behind his back is not something I'm going to do. Does that answer your question?"

Felice, however, was very persuasive in her dealings with men and soon persuaded Sal "just this once" to pass on "a very quick and simple message" to Rob.

"All right, Felice, all right. What is it?"

"Are you ready?"

"Yes, damnit, I'm ready, Felice. What's the message?"

"Tell him I love him."

There was a pause.

"That's it?" Sal said. "You love him?"

"That's all, Sal. Tell him I love him."

"Jesus Christ, Felice, if that's all it is you could've sent him a fucking Candygram instead of all this cloak-and-dagger shit."

"Sal?"

"What?"

"When can you deliver it?"

"Soon, Felice, soon."

"In person, Sal. It has to be in person. We think your phone is tapped, too." Then she hung up. Well, Christ, Sal Coccaro said to himself, maybe Rob had a cold beer in the icebox.

He got to Crest Ridge Drive at 4:30 P.M. just as Rob and Roby were returning from breakfast at Perkins' Pancakes. Rob had resumed his old schedule of sitting up through the night and sleeping until afternoon.

Roby went inside and Sal and Rob sat on some railroad ties that formed a bench at the edge of the driveway.

"Felice called me," Sal said. "She had a message."

Rob immediately began to shake. His face turned pale. "What's the message?" he whispered.

" 'Tell him I love him,' " Sal articulated loudly and clearly.

"Oh, my God! Oh, my God!" In what was becoming a familiar sight to Sal, Rob put his head in his hands and began to shake with sobs. Sal lit a cigarette and waited.

"I'm so relieved," Rob said, his face tear-streaked. "So relieved."

"What the fuck is she talking in, some kind of code?" Sal said. "Suppose she'd said, 'Have a nice day.' I would have had to call the fucking rescue squad." He stood and tossed his cigarette aside.

"Keep your voice down," Rob said. "I really think the police are watching the house." He looked up at the trees, which were still in full leaf. "At least now I know she hasn't gone back to David."

"Hey, Rob. You ever heard of tranquilizers? You ever heard of maybe going to bed before midnight some night?"

But Rob didn't seem to be listening anymore. Still quivering, and gazing up at the thick green canopy that lined the street, he shouted: *"Wherever you are— listen to this! I didn't fucking kill my wife."*

Upstairs, Roby opened a bedroom window and looked down at his father.

"He'll be okay," Sal called up to him. "Just stick him in a cold shower for a while." Then, wondering just how he had ever gotten to be a friend of Rob Marshall's in the first place, Sal headed for the Office Lounge.

Felice moved into a condominium on the beach and soon found, apparently, that she was as desperate for Rob's company as he was for hers. Disregarding her attorney's instructions, she called him. Disregarding Ray DiOrio's instructions, Rob came running when she called.

Through much of the week that followed, they were inseparable. Much to the displeasure of the boys, she was even spending time at the Marshall house. She was there, in fact, on the afternoon of Friday, September 21, sitting around with Rob and an old college friend of his, Paul Kennedy, who had also become a frequent visitor.

The three of them were having a drink when the phone rang. It was a Detective McGuire from the prosecutor's office. This was Rob's first contact with anyone investigating Maria's murder since the morning it had happened, when they'd taken him to Bass River to give a statement. McGuire said he wanted to come over and speak to Rob.

"We were just on our way out," Rob said.

But McGuire said he was calling from a phone booth only a few blocks away and could be there in five minutes. It wouldn't take long. Just one point had come up on which Rob might be able to assist him.

"Well, all right, Rob said. "Come on over."

As soon as he hung up, he called Paul Kennedy into the kitchen. He told Paul to take Felice for a ride. Go to the mall. Buy something. Anything. But quick. He didn't think it would look good for the police to come and find Felice sitting around the house. But Felice wouldn't budge. "The hell with that," she said. "I've got nothing to hide."

There were two detectives, actually—McGuire, a cheerful, burly young man, and Murray, short, trim, well dressed, also young. Very pleasant men, both of them. McGuire and Felice were already acquainted. He'd been the one who'd brought Felice in for questioning the day of the murder. Still, it was Rob who acted as host, offering drinks (they politely declined while Rob freshened up his Cuba Libre), calling Roby down to meet them, showing them a bit of the house.

Then they stepped into the family room, still very casual and friendly. "Really sorry to bother you on short notice," McGuire said, "but we were in the neighborhood and, ah, certain names have come to light in our investigation and we thought maybe you could assist us in identifying these people."

"Anything at all, gentlemen. I'm as eager to get to the bottom of this as you are."

McGuire took a small notebook from a jacket pocket and flipped through it. "Ah," he said. "Here we go.

Are you familiar with a fellow, or have you ever heard the name Ernest, or Ernie, Grandshaw, from Shreveport, Louisiana?"

Later, in his official report, the way McGuire described it was that Rob seemed "visibly shaken" by mention of this name, "like a fellow who had just heard some very bad news."

He became pale and the hand holding the drink began to tremble. There was a difference in recollection about whether or not he actually spilled it, but, McGuire said, "his hand action was such that I thought he was going to."

In any case, quick as a wink, the gracious-host mask was gone. "As you are probably aware, gentlemen," Rob said, in a much more somber, even officious voice, "I am being represented in this matter by Mr. DiOrio. He has advised me, in fact instructed me, not to answer any questions that might be put to me by anyone. And that, I'm afraid, includes even representatives of the prosecutor's office."

Rob put his drink on the nearest flat surface. His hand was shaking so that the glass rattled as he set it down. He seemed also to have suddenly developed a tic. His thin lips, pursed tightly now that he'd stopped speaking, twitched irregularly to one side.

"How about L'Heureux?" McGuire said. "A Ferlin L'Heureux, also of Shreveport?"

Gentlemen, as I've just stated, my attorney, Raymond DiOrio, has instructed me not to answer any questions concerning any aspect of any of the circumstances surrounding the death of my wife. And I really don't think it's appropriate for you to be here persisting with such questions after I've informed you of this. And before this goes any further, I would need to consult with my attorney. Until such time as I've had that opportunity, I'm afraid I'm going to have to terminate the interview."

McGuire nodded affably. "That's fine," he said. "Just thought we'd ask."

After they'd left, Roby approached his father and asked, "Dad? What was that all about?"

Rob seemed highly agitated, almost frantic. "Nothing. It was nothing. I don't know."

"Why would they be asking you about people in Louisiana?"

"Goddamnit, Roby, I told you—I don't know."

"You don't know them, do you?"

"Of course I don't know them. I've never been to Louisiana in my life. Felice, let's go. Let's get out of here. Let's go over to your place."

The bill that Rob eventually received from Raymond DiOrio—a bill for $4,750—specified September 16, five days before the visit from McGuire, as the last date on which DiOrio had worked in Rob's behalf.

Thus, the morning after he'd been asked about the two names from Louisiana, when Rob decided it would be useful for him to consult with an attorney, it was to the home of a criminal lawyer named Carl Seely that he went. Seely lived in a New Jersey suburb of Philadelphia, and practiced in Pennsylvania as well as in New Jersey. He did considerable work for individuals believed by prosecutorial agencies to be associated with organized crime.

It was, Seely later said, "through mutual friends" that he had been recommended to Rob as DiOrio's successor. Neither Rob nor DiOrio ever spoke with much clarity about the circumstances that had caused them to decide to sever their professional relationship after little more than a week, but in any event, it was to Seely's home that Rob traveled on Saturday morning, September 22, and it was Felice who drove the car.

At the conclusion of a lengthy conference, she drove him back to Toms River. They stopped for dinner at a Mexican restaurant on the way. Then they spent the night together at her condominium on the beach.

They were still at the beach the next afternoon when the phone rang at the Marshall house. Roby answered.

"Robert Marshall, please," said a voice with a thick Southern accent.

"Senior or junior?" Roby asked.

"Senior."

"He's not here," Roby said. "May I take a message?"

"Yeah, you can take it," the man at the other end said, "but you better be sure he gets it damned fast."

"Okay. I think I know where to reach him."

"You tell him to call Ernie Grandshaw in Shreveport right away. Tell him it's urgent. Real urgent." The man left a phone number and hung up.

Roby called Felice's number at the condo but reached only her answering machine. He left a message. *"Dad. This is Roby. A man named Ernie Grandshaw just called from Shreveport, Louisiana. He said you need to call him right away. It's very urgent."* There was a pause. Then Roby continued. *"Dad? What's this all about? You just told the police you didn't know anybody in Louisiana."*

Rob got the message in late afternoon, as he and Felice returned to the condo from a long, hand-holding walk along the beach.

Already, the day had been difficult, for it had been the occasion Rob had chosen to explain to Felice that his financial plight was, in fact, considerably more serious than he had first led her to believe. Debtwise, he confessed, he was in worse shape than he had wanted her to know. *Much* worse shape.

So when he received the phone message, he did not accept it with tranquility. He quickly told Felice a story about having made a big bet on a basketball game with a fellow from Louisiana—damn, it had just slipped his mind when McGuire had questioned him on Friday—and having had to send money down there to pay it off. That, he said, must be what the call was about. Something to do with that silly bet he had made. Then he jumped into his car and drove back across the bridge at high speed.

"Roby? Roby!" he shouted as he ran in the door. "What time did that call come in? What else did he say?"

"Dad. I thought you didn't know any Ernie Grandshaw in Shreveport."

"Never mind that. I just met him once. It's not important. Listen, Roby, I want to know *exactly* what he said and how he said it."

"All he told me was the message I gave you. But, Dad—"

"Listen, Roby, I met this fellow once a long time ago, way back in the spring I think it was, at some big party, some wedding reception or something. He was a big sports fan. Basketball fan. There was a game on the TV over the bar, an NBA game, the playoffs. We made a bet, just to keep it interesting. He won the bet and I wired him the money to pay it, that's all. That's the only time I ever saw the fellow in my life. I really don't know why he was calling or why he'd want me to call back."

Roby was staring at his father, his mouth open. Things weren't making sense. He didn't like it. He felt scared. "Dad," he said. "You've never watched a pro

basketball game in your life. I bet you couldn't even
name two teams in the NBA."

Rob didn't answer. He went to his office and closed
the door. He was on the phone for hours, late into the
night.

Among those he called was Gene Leahy. "You may
be hearing," he said, "that I sent some money to
Louisiana. This was to pay off a bet on a basketball
game—that's all it was. I bet a fellow three thousand
dollars on an NBA game and lost, so I wired him the
money."

That struck Gene as odd. He'd never known Rob to
have any interest in basketball. And even if he had,
why would he bother—in the midst of everything else
that was going on—telling Gene that he'd paid off a
bet to somebody in Louisiana?

The following Wednesday, September 26, it was announced that a grand jury in Ocean County had indicted a Louisiana hardware store clerk on a charge of
conspiracy to commit murder in connection with the
death of Maria Marshall.

The news jolted even those in Toms River who'd
felt themselves to be at the very nerve center of the
gossip network. *Louisiana?* This brought a whole new
dimension to the story. It was a bizarre twist that
suddenly gave the death of the Toms River East swim
team Mother of the Year an exotic allure that her life
had never possessed. *Louisiana?* Roby Marshall said,
"I couldn't even find Louisiana on a map."

Just as startling, to those very few, like Roby, who
had any awareness of the events of the preceding week
and weekend, was the name of the man who'd been
indicted. For it was not Grandshaw and it was not
L'Heureux: the man indicted was named Andrew

Myers, and he was being held in Shreveport on $1.5 million bail.

He was forty-seven years old, the newspapers said, and he lived in a suburb of Shreveport called Bossier City. He worked at the Caddo Hardware Store in Caddo Parish. He lived with his wife, Vivian, and her daughter from a previous marriage in a one-story ranch house with a neatly kept lawn.

As one newspaper reported:

> The bewilderment at the Imperial Lanes bowling alley in Bossier was typical of the reaction of Myers's friends, neighbors and employer when they learned that he had been arrested.
> "It was on the six o'clock news that he'd been arrested, and then that night Vivian was here bowling," recalled Barry Aitken, standing behind the counter at the lanes. "We're all shocked. We don't know what to think."

The news of Myers's indictment was only the latest in the series of shocks suffered during the previous week by Rob Marshall. First had been McGuire with his names. Then had come the call from Louisiana. And then, just two days later, Felice had informed him that their relationship was over, that she never wanted to see him or hear from him or have anything to do with him again. She had said it was obvious that he had lied to her about Louisiana, and about how bad his financial troubles really were, and since she had always felt that their relationship was based upon mutual honesty and trust, she did not feel she could continue it. (She did not specify, at that time, that this was an action she was taking upon the advice of counsel.)

Rob drove to Red Bank Thursday afternoon and sold his boat to Joe Moore for six thousand dollars, so he'd have some money to give to Carl Seely. Later, he called home and spoke to a housekeeper, asking for Seely's telephone number. Then he called each of his sons. And that was the last that anyone who knew him heard from, or of, Rob Marshall until the next morning, Thursday, September 27.

9

Sal Coccaro, an early riser, heard the news on the radio at 6 A.M. Rob was in satisfactory condition at Point Pleasant Hospital following an overdose of sleeping pills. Sal drove immediately to the Marshall house and, for the second time in less than three weeks, found Roby and John stunned and dazed.

"He called me last night," Roby said. "I knew something was wrong. I could tell from the sound of his voice. Jesus Christ, why didn't I do something? This is my fault! I could have stopped him." Roby slammed a fist into the wall.

"Knock it off, Roby," Sal said. "Don't even start with that blame stuff. You've got enough real problems without creating unnecessary ones. Not one thing that's happened since September 7 has been your fault, or Chris's, or John's. That doesn't mean you're not going to suffer the consequences, but for Christ's sake don't make it worse for yourself. Now let's get in the car and drive up there and find out what the hell is going on. What the hell's he doing in Point Pleasant, anyway? How come he's not in Ocean County?"

While John Marshall sat in absolute, frozen silence throughout the fifteen-mile drive, Roby explained that his father had called him at work the night before.

Roby was working nights at Feet First, one of the shoe stores at the mall, while taking classes at Ocean County College.

"He was up in Monmouth County," Roby said. "He was calling from Red Bank. He said he was up there on business and would be spending the night. But he didn't sound right. He was all flat and lifeless. And he said, he said—'I just wanted to hear your voice.' That should have told me something. In fact, it did. It scared the hell out of me. I almost called you. But then I said, no, no, come on, Roby, don't freak out. You know, I didn't want to seem hysterical. See, it was my fault. If I had called you we could have done something!"

"Roby, calm down," Sal said. "If you had called me I would've told you, 'Roby, don't freak out, don't get hysterical.' Listen, I go to bed at ten o'clock at night. I sure as hell wouldn't have gone driving up to Red Bank just because you told me your old man sounded 'flat.' The point is, he's alive. He's in satisfactory condition. And in five minutes we'll be there, so give your brother a hug and give my ears a rest. I can tell I got a long day ahead."

Rob was awake and alert in an emergency room bed. Both Roby and John broke down completely as soon as they saw him. Less than three weeks after losing their mother, now they had somehow to cope with this.

Once he saw that Rob was in no imminent danger of death, Sal Coccaro let his temper rise. "Why, Rob?" he said loudly. "Why? How could you do this? Look what you've done to these boys!" A nurse ran in to tell him to lower his voice.

"I thought it would be easier on them," Rob said weakly. "It would spare them having to go through a trial."

"What do you mean, a trial?" Sal said. "What the hell are you talking about, a trial? Does this have anything to do with that guy they nabbed down in Shreveport?"

"Myers?" Rob said. "Not him. He's not the problem. The problem is Grandshaw. And, Sal? You don't know the worst of it. That night—the night of the murder—Grandshaw was there, in the casino."

"What do you mean, he was there?"

"He's an investigator," Rob said. "A private detective. From Shreveport. Myers is just the guy who recommended him. I hired Grandshaw because there was some money missing. Sal, you know how Maria and I always kept a separate account just for casino winnings? Well, there was three thousand, maybe thirty-five hundred missing from that account and I thought Maria had taken it and she kept denying it, so I hired this Grandshaw to look into it." Rob paused. Sal Coccaro, Roby and John were staring at him expressionlessly.

"He was up there that night. At Harrah's," Rob continued. "And the worst of it is, I gave him eight hundred dollars in cash right there in the casino. Now the prosecutor's office is going to try to build a case that I hired him to—to kill Maria, for some reason."

He paused again. There was silence in the room.

"Of course—" he said. "Of course, that's not true. I loved—I loved Maria." He looked at Sal Coccaro. "She was the mother of my boys, Sal. I could never take her away from them. I could never do a thing like that." Then he began to cry.

A few minutes later, he recounted the details of the suicide attempt. He had been distraught, he said, since Tuesday, when he'd gone to Felice to confess to her that he'd lied on Sunday and that he really did know an Ernie Grandshaw from Shreveport. Ray DiOrio, he said, had told him at their first meeting not to say anything to anyone and so, on what he considered the advice of counsel, he'd lied to her. She had not been willing to forgive him, he said, and had told him she was ending their relationship. This had shaken him deeply, he said, because she was really all he had to live for, except for his sons.

He had gone to Red Bank to sell his boat to Joe Moore for six thousand dollars because he needed the money to pay his new lawyer, Carl Seely. But as the day passed he had grown increasingly morose and eventually had decided to drive to the Best Western in Lakewood, scene of so many passionate trysts with Felice, and check into their special room, room 16.

There, he'd dictated brief, final messages to his three sons and a much longer, more general testament to Gene Leahy, in which he'd explained all that had led up to that moment. After putting the cassette in an envelope and leaving it at the front desk to be mailed, he'd returned to the room and had emptied fifty Restoril sleeping capsules into a glass of Coca-Cola, intending to drink it and end his life. Instead, after stirring the mixture with his finger and then licking his finger and finding the taste unpleasantly bitter, he'd lain back on the motel bed—scene of so much unbridled lust in the past—and had fallen asleep.

At some point thereafter, a rescue squad had arrived in the room, summoned by Ocean County detectives who'd been following him. A detective had explained to him that—fearing he might try to take his own life—they'd phoned his room at 1 A.M. to check on him. When he failed to answer, they'd called for medical assistance.

To Sal, it almost seemed like September 7 all over again. Roby went to one phone to call Chris at Lehigh. Sal went to another to call his wife and ask her

to call Gene Leahy. Somebody had to call Maria's
parents before they heard it on the radio. But this
time, Sal realized, there was a different, scarier edge
to everything. *The police had followed Rob to the
motel.* That meant they must have been following him
everywhere. That meant they weren't fooling around.
That meant the gossip was right again. Rob was a
suspect.

Later in the morning, when Gene Leahy arrived,
Sal stopped him in the hall outside the room to which
Rob had been moved and told him what Rob had said
about giving the Louisiana investigator, Ernie Grandshaw,
a cash payment at the casino.

"Cash?" Gene said. "Rob never paid eight hundred
in cash for anything in his life. But forget that, forget
that. You're telling me Rob hands eight hundred bucks
to some joker from Shreveport, Louisiana, in a gambling casino, and an hour later he pulls off the parkway and somebody murders his wife? Listen, Sal, if
the police know about this they'll grab Rob right here.
Today. This is trouble. We've got to get Roby and
John out of here. We can't let them be here for that."

Roby protested, saying he wanted to stay by his
father's side, but after a conference with Gene and
Sal, Rob himself ordered the boys home. Once they
were gone, Gene Leahy began to question Rob.

"What is this about eight hundred dollars? What the
hell did you pay the guy eight hundred dollars for?"

"I owed him," Rob said.

"For what?"

"An investigation."

"You just told me three days ago you sent him three
thousand. Only then it was supposed to be a bet on a
basketball game."

"That was actually for the same investigation."

"Wait a minute, wait a minute," Sal said. "You told

me you sent Grandshaw twenty-five hundred, not three thousand."

"I did. But that was a different payment."

"What?" Gene said. "You sent the guy money twice?"

"Twenty-five hundred and then three thousand?" Sal said.

"And then you paid him eight hundred cash?" Gene said.

"What the hell was he investigating, the lost continent of Atlantis?" Sal said.

"I told you," Rob said. "There was blackjack money missing."

"What," Sal shouted, "thirty-five hundred? So you pay some clown from Shreveport fucking Louisiana *fifty*-five hundred to try to find it?"

"Sixty-three hundred," Gene said quietly.

The two of them were on opposite sides of Rob's bed now, looking at each other, not at Rob. A doctor stepped into the room, drawn by the noise. "This was an attempted suicide," the doctor said. "This patient should not be disturbed. In fact, only family members are supposed to be in here."

"I'm his brother-in-law," Gene said. "And an attorney."

"And I'm his uncle," Sal said, scowling. "His Uncle Sal."

"All right, gentlemen, but please allow the patient some tranquility."

"This is nothing, Doc." Sal said. "Wait till the cops get here."

The police did not arrive. By evening, it seemed apparent that if they had intended to arrest Rob at the hospital they would already have done so. The boys were called and told they could return. Chris, however, who had just arrived in Toms River from Lehigh, refused to come.

When Roby had first called him to say that their father had attempted suicide, Chris had been so angry he'd just hung up. Instead of driving straight home, as had been expected of him, he'd stayed at Lehigh and had competed in a swim meet, his fury driving him not only to win but to set a new personal record in the 100-yard backstroke.

Once home, he said that was as far as he was going. If their father was selfish and stupid enough to risk putting them through the agony and shock of his own death less than three weeks after the murder of their mother, just because he was afraid that the police were fabricating some charges against him, then he could lie there and rot in his hospital bed for all Chris cared.

"How could he do this to us?" Chris shouted at Roby.

"He did it to himself, Chris, he didn't do it to us," Roby said.

"All it does is prove he doesn't love us."

"Oh, shut up, Chris, you little baby. All you can think about is yourself."

"No, Roby. All Dad thinks about is himself. If he cared about us one bit he could never even think about killing himself."

"You don't have any idea the stress he's been under. You haven't even been here. You've been tucked away safely at school, Chris, you don't have a clue about what things have really been like."

"Sounds to me like the police have a clue," Chris muttered.

"What are you talking about?"

"Nothing," Chris said. "I just don't want to go to the hospital. I don't want to see Dad right now." For two weeks he'd been hoarding his guilty, secret, evil fear. The last thing he wanted to do was blurt it out to Roby in the middle of an argument.

"You're just so selfish, Chris. You're just such a selfish little brat," Roby said.

"Maybe," Chris said. "But I'm also stubborn. And there's no name you could call me that could make me go up to the hospital tonight."

An hour later, however, when Rob himself called and said, "I need you, Chris. I want to see you, why aren't you here?" Chris relented tearfully. And before leaving the house, he took a large photograph of the three boys down from the mantelpiece. At the hospital, he wrote a note that said, "Think about what's important." The three brothers signed it and gave it to their father with the picture. The presentation was followed by hugs and tears.

Chris didn't know what to think or what to believe or what to feel. What he felt mostly was the pain of his mother's death. That had seemed to be getting worse day by day, as the numbness of the initial shock began to fade.

Rob's other visitor that night was his new lawyer, Carl Seely, who had been speaking to his client throughout the day via the car phone in his BMW and who arrived, in slacks and sports shirt, at about 8:30 P.M. Seely was accompanied by a psychiatrist who was prepared to sign Rob out of Point Pleasant Hospital and admit him to a private facility in Pennsylvania.

Seely was a pudgy man in his midfifties with a notably round face, a deep tan, a thick Rolex watch and dark gray hair slicked back hard as in a 1950s Brylcreem advertisement. Upon his arrival, he spoke privately to Sal Coccaro in the hallway.

"We're going to take Rob out of here tonight. I

think he'll be much better off in Philadelphia," Seely said.

Half an hour later, Rob was whisked away through the emergency room exit and rushed to the temporary refuge of a neighboring state while Sal Coccaro drove his three sons back to the house in which, until three weeks earlier, they had lived as members of what had seemed to be a happy family.

That night, he sat up late with them. "Well, guys," he said, "I guess I'm all you got left for a while, except for each other. So it's time to stop calling me Mr. Coccaro. I'm Uncle Sal to you guys from now on."

The three of them nodded, tears in their eyes. The house was quiet and, except for the living room in which they sat, it was dark.

"It's time to level with each other, fellows," Sal said. "There's a very big question that I haven't heard asked yet in this house. Outside, it's different." He motioned toward the street. "Out there, all over town, it's the only question I hear. You guys aren't stupid. You know what it is."

The three of them nodded. But no one else spoke. "I don't know what your own feelings are and I don't care. You might not even know yourselves yet. And no matter what happens I'm never going to push you guys in any direction. I'm just here for you any way you need me, anytime.

"But I've got to tell you something, boys. You're going to have to help each other through this. There's things you can do for each other that nobody else can do for you, not even your dad. Maybe especially not your dad.

"Frankly, fellows, I'm concerned. There's a lot of things I'm hearing that I don't like. Your father is probably the best friend I have in this town, but a lot of things he's telling me don't add up.

"I'll come right out and say it, and then you can throw me the hell out of here if you want to: I'm worried that your father might have had something to do with killing your mother."

Sal stopped speaking. The silence grew. Nobody made a move to throw him out. Finally, Sal spoke again.

"Anybody else feel that way?" he asked softly.

John, the youngest, spoke first. He spoke immediately. He said, "No."

Roby said, "Once in a while. But I put it out of my head. It just can't be."

Chris said, "Yes."

No one else said anything. After a minute, Sal stood to leave. "There's only one thing I'd ask you, boys, and it'll be the biggest favor you can ever do yourselves. Whatever your own feelings are, and no matter how strongly you hold them, don't ever stop respecting the other guys'." He leaned forward and put one hand on Roby's shoulder and one hand on Chris's. "And no matter how angry you get at anyone else," he said, "don't let yourselves get angry at each other."

Then, with tears in his own eyes, he hugged all three of them hard and said good night.

10

THE suicide attempt prompted a new wave of outrage against Rob in Toms River. Had he succeeded in taking his life, he would have deprived the town of the spectacle of a trial. And already the trial had become a delectable topic of speculation. Would Felice testify? What would she say? What would she *wear?*

To Carl Seely, the strength and unanimity of the anti-Rob feeling in Toms River had come as a shock. He'd needed to spend only a day and a half in the town to learn that his client was viewed in approximately the same light as the Ayatollah Khomeini. He found this surprising, because Rob had assured him that he was a highly respected civic leader. "Beyond reproach" was the phrase Rob had used.

Now, as he looked ahead to the day when a jury might have to be chosen in the Ocean County Courthouse in the center of town to decide the question of Rob's guilt or innocence, Seely felt more than a passing twinge of dread.

Extensive negative publicity, however, if it rendered selection of an impartial jury impossible, was sometimes grounds for change of venue. Seely began to make himself available to the press.

First, he dealt with the apparent suicide attempt. In a series of interviews with wire services and area newspapers, Seely said that while he had not been able to listen to the tapes his client had made because the police had apparently confiscated them, it was his understanding that Rob, while professing his innocence, had wondered aloud whether anyone would ever believe him.

Rob had been under a lot of stress due to publicity surrounding the murder, Seely said, and from innuendo suggesting that he had been involved. Seely also said that any insinuations that there was "some kind of a causal relationship" between Rob's apparent overdose of sleeping pills and the arrest of Andrew Myers were way off base. "That, I don't believe and the doctors don't either," Seely said. "The primary reason seems to relate to his children. He feels this whole situation is putting his family in an unbearable situation. I guess he somehow felt it would put everything at peace. It was not like all of a sudden he heard about the investigation in Louisiana and said, 'I'm going to kill myself.' "

In regard to Myers, Seely said it was "no secret" that the Louisiana man and Rob had been involved in business dealings. He said that Rob, who had been getting into estate-planning work as well as life insurance sales, had prepared an investment portfolio for the hardware store clerk. He would not, however, disclose how the two men had met or how long they'd known each other. "I don't want to get into all the details of what our defense might be if we ever get to that point," Seely said. He added, "I can tell you categorically that we do not intend at any time to use an insanity defense."

While the county prosecutor's office continued to refuse all requests for comment or even to acknowl-

edge that Marshall was under suspicion, Seely kept
talking. In an October 3 interview with the Asbury
Park *Press,* which was printed under an eight-column
headline across the top of page one, the lawyer acknowledged for the first time publicly that Rob had
insured Maria's life for approximately $1.5 million and
that "it's pretty much a matter of record" that he'd
been having an affair.

He was quick to assert, however, that those factors
provided no motivation for murder. "If every man
who had an extramarital affair and had a life insurance
policy on his wife was automatically suspected of her
homicide, then we'd better start building a lot of pris-
ons real fast," he said.

Three days later, again under an eight-column, page-
one headline, Seely told the *Press* he expected his
client to be indicted for murder. He based this belief,
he said, upon his knowledge that authorities had
searched Marshall's offices and had taken, among other
things, records of long-distance telephone calls.

Seely explained that Rob was indeed acquainted
with the Bossier City, Louisiana, hardware store clerk,
Andrew Myers. Rob had met Myers in the spring of
1983 when Myers had been in New Jersey visiting
relatives.

In addition to advising Myers on investments, Seely
said, Rob had asked the clerk to put him in touch with
a private detective from Louisiana. Rob had suspected
that Maria was having an affair of her own, Seely said,
and he wanted someone to follow her. His reason for
hiring an investigator from as far away as Louisiana,
Seely explained, was confidentiality. "In Toms River,"
Seely said, "everybody sooner or later pretty much
knows everybody else's business."

The investigator, Seely disclosed, was a former deputy sheriff from Caddo Parish, Louisiana, named Ferlin

L'Heureux, who, in his dealings with Rob, had used the alias Ernie Grandshaw.

It was Seely's contention that the Ocean County prosecutor's office had made the erroneous assumption that Rob had hired L'Heureux, whose name he thought was Grandshaw, to kill Maria instead of to follow her. Such a notion, he said, was preposterous. "A reasonably intelligent person devising a well-thought-out, methodical plan such as the one the prosecution is suggesting would not make traceable phone calls and meet alleged accomplices in public places," he said.

Seely told the newspaper that he realized he was being unusually candid in discussing the case against his client in so much detail even before his client had been labeled a suspect. "What I'm trying to do," he said, "is to correct some of the misinformation which, in my opinion, is being designed to poison the minds of the public against my client. There's certainly been lots of publicity, innuendo and rumor."

Meanwhile, Rob was residing comfortably in a private psychiatric facility in Philadelphia. Having never ingested any of the Restoril mixture, he'd suffered no physical ill effects and, as far as Roby, who visited him daily, could tell, he seemed mentally and emotionally the same as ever.

It was Roby, actually, who was beginning to feel as if he were losing his grip. Every day he went to class at Ocean County College. Every evening he worked at Feet First. Then, every night, he had to drive seventy miles to Philadelphia to see his father in order to deliver the day's mail.

Rob, while hospitalized, insisted on keeping up with his work. He told Roby that it was a necessity that he stay absolutely current with his correspondence. What Roby privately believed was that his father was hoping

that Felice would write a letter saying she would take
him back again, but it didn't matter what the motive
was: the effect was that Roby had to drive 150 miles
round trip every night to deliver the mail.

With Chris back at Lehigh, his father hospitalized
and John temporarily sent to live with Gene Leahy's
family in Delaware, Roby would return home to a
silent, empty house every night. Sal Coccaro—Uncle
Sal, as Roby had actually begun to call him—was
nearby, but he had his own wife and three daughters
to take care of. Most of Roby's friends were away at
college, as he would have been had he not been sus-
pended. He had lost romantic interest in Susan Salzman.
And his mother, whom he'd always leaned upon first
at times just like this, was nothing but a few cupfuls of
ashes.

Roby himself began to think about suicide. The
death part was fine. That would be nothingness. Just
the absence of pain. It was the dying part that gave
him trouble. He didn't have a gun and if he did he'd
be afraid to use it. He could probably get sleeping pills
somewhere but he knew he'd be afraid to swallow
them. He could lock the car in the garage and turn on
the engine except they didn't have a garage. He'd
always been most afraid of the feeling of not being
able to breathe, so that ruled out hanging himself.
What he found himself longing for was some sort of
simple self-destruct button he could push.

I am, he told himself, *the definition of genuine chick-
enshit: I don't even have the guts to do a cowardly thing
like kill myself.* Still, he found himself pushing the
accelerator pedal of the Mustang to the floor on his
late-night trips back from Philadelphia. He'd go 100,
105, on flat, narrow, two-lane Route 70, not caring if a
tire blew, almost praying for a deer to jump into the

road, forcing him to swerve into the pine groves on the shoulder and the obliteration that waited there.

The feelings of anguish and despair continued to intensify throughout the first half of October, not helped by Roby's reading of the newspapers every day. What the hell was Seely talking about, his *mother* having an affair?

Roby had gone straight to Philadelphia when he'd read that and had confronted his father immediately. Not true, Rob had told him. He'd hired the detective from Louisiana because of the missing casino money. He had never suspected Maria of having an affair.

"Then how the hell can he say that to the papers?" Roby demanded. "That's a slander against the memory of Mom!"

"It's strategy, Roby. Lawyer's strategy. You can't let the victim get all the sympathy. You've got to make people realize that she might have some flaws, too."

"Screw that. That oily snake is talking about *Mom!*"

"Roby, we're playing hardball here and so is the prosecutor's office. Carl Seely knows exactly what he's doing and I don't want to hear you calling him names."

"Well, he'd better not call Mom names, either."

That was the way it had gone for ten days. Rob left the psychiatric institution and went to stay temporarily with an old friend of his mother's named Tessie McBride, who lived in Bucks County, Pennsylvania. Aware of how closely Ocean County detectives had been following him, and apparently fearing arrest, he was not eager to recross the New Jersey state line.

Then, on October 12, Ferlin L'Heureux was arrested in Louisiana on a charge of conspiracy to commit murder. He was taken to the Caddo Parish jail in Shreveport, where Andrew Myers was still being held on the same charge on $1.5 million bail.

"Neither arrest, of Myers or L'Heureux, will in any

way, shape or form change my client's position that he will continue to vigorously conduct an independent investigation and vindicate any innuendos and charges," Carl Seely told the newspapers.

Seely said that Rob's own condition was improving and that he was receiving care on an outpatient basis while staying with friends in the Philadelphia area.

The next day, Saturday, October 13, a self-employed steelworker name Ernie Grandshaw was arrested in Shreveport. It seemed there really was an Ernie Grandshaw. He, too, was charged with conspiracy to commit murder.

Seely told the newspapers he expected that Rob would be next. "Based on the prosecutor's theory, if the theory is what I believe it to be, then logic would dictate that at some point in time they're going to return or unseal an indictment against my client," Seely said.

By Monday night, October 15, it was all too much for Roby. Toward midnight, he left the silent, empty house and got into his car. He took a deep breath and drew back his right fist as far as he could. Then, screaming as loud as he could, he slammed his fist forward, punching a hole through the windshield. Then he threw the car into gear and drove as fast as he could in the direction of the bridge that stretched over the bay.

Later, Roby didn't remember much about his ride. Just fragments, like the fragments of windshield glass that lodged in his curly blond hair as they blew in from the edges of the hole his fist had made.

His eyes were closed. He remembered that much. He was driving at a hundred miles an hour over the bridge to Seaside with his eyes closed and the glass flying and the wind blowing, not caring if he lived or died, feeling only pain and rage and hopelessness.

He also remembered that he'd screamed the whole way.

And that he'd felt so alone it was as if he were the only person on earth who hadn't already died.

The eastbound bridge is the newer half, three lanes of smooth pavement with chest-high concrete barriers along both sides. It is not a bridge off which one can drive an automobile, not even at a hundred miles an hour with one's eyes closed. Not even when one's mother has been murdered and one's father is about to be accused of having arranged it.

Roby made it to Seaside, even though that hadn't really been his goal. He didn't remember slowing down, he didn't remember stopping, he didn't remember opening his eyes.

But there he was. Alive. Alone. Out of breath. With a hole in his windshield and his radio on.

Then he heard the high, haunting notes of a harmonica. It was the opening bars of what had been, for several years, his favorite song. This was too trite to be believed, but there it was—"Take the Long Way Home" from Supertramp's *Breakfast in America* album.

> *So you think you're a Romeo*
> *playing a part in a picture-show*
> *Take the long way home.*
> *Take the long way home.*
> *Cos you're the joke of the neighborhood.*
> *Why should you care if you're feeling good?*
> *Take the long way home.*
> *Take the long way home.*

The image that burst into his mind was of the first time his mother had heard the song. They'd been out together doing errands—in fact, buying supplies for a

surprise birthday party for his father—and the song
had come on the station wagon radio.

> *But there are times that you feel you're part of the*
> *scenery,*
> *all the greenery is coming down, boy*
> *And then your wife seems to think you're part of the*
> *furniture, oh it's peculiar, she used to be so nice. . . .*
> *You never see what you want to see*
> *Forever playing to the gallery*
> *You take the long way home*
> *Take the long way home*

The nice part had been that they were almost home
when the song came on and if his mother had driven
straight to the house they would have been there before it was over, so instead she took a circuitous route—
"the long way home," she'd called it—so that the two
of them could listen to the whole song together.

> *But then your wife seems to think you're losing your*
> *sanity,*
> *Oh, calamity, is there no way out?*
> *Does it feel that your life's become a catastrophe?*
> *Oh, it has to be, for you to grow, boy. . . .*

Roby sat very still as the song ended. Then he
brushed some of the glass out of his hair and out of his
lap and drove back across the bridge, slowly and with
his eyes open, to Sal Coccaro's house.

It was well after midnight when he knocked on the
door.

"Uncle Sal," he said, "do you know any psychia-
trists? I need help."

11

ROBY was admitted that night to the psychiatric ward of the Monmouth County Medical Center. Sal Coccaro contacted Rob in Pennsylvania to let him know. Rob, however, was obsessed by another problem: Felice, having rejected him, was not responding to any of his pleas for reconciliation. He'd called, he'd written, he'd sent flowers—*for Christ's sake he'd even tried to kill himself*— but she had shown no signs of interest.

Now, he went back to his ace in the hole: he sent a tape. This one began with not one but two love songs, string-filled, syrupy compositions.

Then he began to speak, in a voice presumably intended to be a romantic whisper. "Hello, babe," he said. "I can't help but feel that the message these songs convey will tell you what I'm feeling. I'm sure you're aware, too, of what's been happening as far as I'm concerned. It's all so crazy." There were long pauses between his phrases, as if the words were so weighty he could not utter too many at a time. "I wrote a letter to you that I was going to send but I'll read part of it to you and add my comments as I go.

"I'm terribly saddened by your concern about what other people—about what anybody is thinking or saying

about me. You must know that that doesn't matter.
People will think what they want to. People that I
thought were very close friends have turned against
me and others that I didn't know were friends have
been very, very supportive.

"None of that really matters. What does is you. You
and me. What you feel, what you felt, what I thought
we had. And from all the things we said to each other
over the past fourteen months it seemed to me that
nothing was really important except what we felt for
each other. The love that I was convinced existed."

From his voice now it was hard to tell whether he
was still reading, or commenting, or simply speaking.
"For some reason," he said, "something got in the
way. I can't believe that it was my deception of the
financial situation, or even the circumstances of
the case—of my situation. When I see you, if I ever see
you, I'll explain to you, but you must know that I was
in a corner, I really had no choice. You must know
that I've been truthful and honest with you with one
exception and that's the total extent of my financial
obligations.

"That really can't be that important in consideration
of what we felt, and hopefully still feel, for each other.
I guess I felt that there wasn't anything that could get
in the way of you and me, which is why I wanted to
tell you, started to tell you the rest of the story, the
rest of the problems that plagued me for the past year
or so—totally committed to resolve them, confident
that we could have."

To this point, his tone had been one of apparent
sincerity. Now there crept in an edge of bitterness.
"The other thing that I have to say, though, is that
you should have stood by me, babe, in spite of everything. In spite of the fact that Ocean County and the
rest of the world is dumping a load of manure on my

head. It shouldn't matter to you. If you love me, stand by me.

"You'd gain so much respect for standing by the man you love in spite of everything. You'd have been The Lady. The lady that, regardless of what everybody thought, stood by the man she loved."

His voice had sunk to a whisper so hoarse the tape almost did not pick it up. "You'd have been a hero," he said. "A goddamned hero." There was a long sigh, then a pause, then he resumed in a more conversational tone.

"I guess I wanted that so much. I didn't get it. And I couldn't understand it. I'm finding it difficult to discard the relationship that we had so recently. We had so much. There are so many reminders, especially the songs. Almost every other song, or every third or fourth song, is one of ours." He paused again, then put a harder edge on his voice.

"And I hope it's just as tough for you," he said. "Really. Because I'm finding it very difficult to just throw it all away. I can't do it. My friend Tessie McBride said something to me that seems to make sense now. She said, 'If your relationship was built entirely on sex, then that's not enough to hold it together in a situation like this.'

"I tried to convince myself and convince her that we really had more than that. She said, 'You didn't go out. You didn't do anything.' I said, 'A couple of times. We were afraid to get caught.' She said, 'Shame on you. No wonder it's falling apart now. Shame on you.'

"I thought about that and in a way she's right. We should have built some memories, maybe once in a while going to dinner somewhere, away from the threat of being discovered. I can think back to the few times we did have dinner together, the most recent being at

Garcia's, how much fun we had just being together, laughing and drinking together and eating and sharing our food. How wonderful that was.

"Certainly, sex wasn't something we needed to have every time. It was something we both craved, I realize, but it might have been more valuable to build a relationship on some memories, sharing things like dinner or doing something. After all, you had twenty-two years, we only had a year, and in our year all we did was make love.

"We talked an awful lot, and I—I felt that that was communication, that what we had, using our tapes, was more valuable than the things we might have done. Maybe it wasn't, given the fact that we've fallen apart over a relatively minor issue—considering the scope of our relationship, it really was."

Again, he paused, and when he went on it was in a tone of resignation. "The bottom line, babe, is there's a big hole in my life where you were, and I'm hoping—I don't want to fill it with anyone else. And I'd like to start over, with dinner and dancing, just you and me. My choice as to where, your choice as to when. A lot of talking. Let's try again.

"Part of the problem is that I don't know whether you've received my other tape or correspondence or the last rose I sent, or anything. I don't know what you're thinking and it's driving me crazy. I need to know that you either don't want any more contact, absolutely, positively, or that you might, or that you do. I just don't know, and that's the hard part."

Through almost the whole tape he'd sounded like a high school kid who'd been jilted by a girlfriend, as if there were no larger context in which he existed—as if he were not a forty-five-year-old suspect in a murder case, expecting imminent indictment and arrest. Now, he made brief reference to the circumstances that were keeping him out of New Jersey.

"Just to fill you in on some of the details of what's happened to me," he said, "first of all, let me say to you, don't believe all that you read in the paper. The rumors and stuff that have been flying around are just incredible. We're convinced that they're trying to play a pressure game, a psychological game, get somebody to break, but it isn't going to happen. Because no-body's going to admit to something that they didn't do. And so it's going to be a matter of circumstantial—stuff.

"Umm, I'm fairly convinced that we're going to end up in court. When I say 'we,' I mean me and my attorney. And that you will probably be a witness. I'm also convinced that eventually it will be resolved fa-vorably, in spite of all the circumstantial evidence that exists." There was a long pause here, the longest on the tape. Then Rob said, "It's gonna be a bitch, though."

He concluded in a more upbeat tone. "I can make it through, regardless. But I'd like to know that the light at the end of the tunnel is shining on both of us, not just me. And more than that I'd like to know how you feel. One way or the other, I've got to know. There's a return address on the back of this envelope that you can use to send a tape or letter. If it's your last one, let it be.

"And if it's the beginning, I welcome the beginning of the rest of our life. You've got to know that there's hope for us, babe, in spite of all my failings—and in spite of yours, too. There's a future if you want it. I don't know what you want. Please tell me. And just remember one thing—in spite of everything, regard-less of what happens, I love you and I always will. But you know that."

Felice did not respond. A few days later, Rob returned to Toms River.

Roby signed himself out of the hospital three days after he'd signed himself in. It was Sal Coccaro who drove to Monmouth County to bring him home.

And it was Sal, two weeks later, who swung by the Marshall house late one Saturday night to say hello to Chris, who he knew was home from Lehigh for the weekend.

He found Chris alone, studying at the kitchen table.

"Where's your old man?" Sal asked. "I heard he was back in town."

"At the Holiday Inn."

"What?"

"He went out a couple of hours ago, he said he was depressed about Mom, he needed to be alone for a while."

"He needed to be alone so he went to the Holiday Inn on a Saturday night?"

"Yeah, he said he'd be down in the lounge having a drink." Chris closed his textbook and looked at Sal. "Do you know what it's like?" he said. "It's like both of our parents got killed, not just our mother."

"I know what you mean," Sal said.

"We don't have a father anymore," Chris said. "First, he was with Felice all the time. Then when she dumped him he disappeared to Pennsylvania. Now that he's back, it's like he's not back. He's never at home. He's got some new girlfriend that the investigator who works for his lawyer introduced him to down in Cherry Hill, and he's got two or three others right in town. Roby and John say he brings a different one around here every night. His 'physical needs' is the way he explains it. Then he winks.

"Listen, Uncle Sal, we've got needs, too. Emotional

needs. Here I go sounding like a crybaby again, but I'm getting worried. Except for you, nobody seems to give a damn about us. Roby and I can get by, I guess, we're old enough. But what's going to happen to poor John?"

"I wish I could tell you, kid. I can't even tell you what's going to happen to your father."

"Do you really think he did it, Uncle Sal? Do you really think my father hired them?"

"Chris, it's like I keep telling myself. This is America. Innocent until proven guilty. Let's not convict the poor slob before he's even been accused."

"You know what I wish I had the guts to do?" Chris said.

"What's that?"

"To ask him. To walk right up to him and just say, 'All right, Dad, no more bullshit. Tell me the truth. Did you or didn't you?' Just like that."

"But you can't?"

Chris shook his head. "I'm his son and he's my father, and no matter what kind of doubts I might have privately, I owe it to him to give him support."

Sal stood up to leave. "You're a good kid," he said. "If I ever get in trouble, I hope my kids are one-tenth as loyal. But, Chris, I got to tell you. Faith in your father is one thing. But blind faith—where you won't face the facts—that's something else.

"Sometimes the hardest thing in the world can be to open your eyes and look at things the way they really are. But whatever you see, Chris, no matter how painful—it's better than not seeing at all."

"Maybe for now," Chris said, "I'd rather stay blind."

"Maybe for now," Sal said. "But not forever. You and Roby both—you're too smart and too strong for that."

"But suppose he is innocent," Chris said. "Which

he certainly might be. I mean, not even the police
have said he's guilty yet. How do you think it would
make him feel to find out that his own son had doubted
him? I don't think he'd ever forgive me. And I know
I'd never forgive myself."

"So what do we do, kid?" Sal asked, smiling.

"I don't know, Uncle Sal. You're the adult."

"I guess we just keep talking to each other," Sal
said. "And keep remembering your mother in our
prayers."

A week later, Rob took his new girlfriend, Terri, to
Florida for a long weekend. He told his sons he needed
to get away from all the pressure. He stayed in the
home of some old friends from Toms River named
Stevens. During the weekend, however, it became
clear to him that it was Molly Stevens, not Terri from
Cherry Hill, to whom he was primarily attracted.

He told Terri that their relationship would have to
end, but that he'd give her money to help her buy a
car. Molly Stevens moved out of the house she'd been
sharing with her husband and began to make plans for
a future with Rob.

"You'll love her, boys," he said once by long-distance
telephone. "She's just like Mom. We'll buy a house-
boat and we can all live together down here."

With no parents left, and no way to get a grip on the
future, Roby, Chris and John drifted their separate
ways through the remainder of the fall.

When they were together, the boys didn't talk about
their father's guilt or innocence—they talked about
anything but. Since the one subject they did not discuss, however, was virtually the only one they thought
about, it made for stilted conversation among them,
with many long, awkward silences between the words.

They themselves were all they had left, but they

didn't know how to deal with one another. They tried so hard to follow Sal Coccaro's advice to respect each other's feelings about their father that each of them found himself unable to *be* himself in the presence of the others. So, it was easier—or at least it seemed so—to stay apart as much as possible through the latter part of the fall.

Chris stayed at Lehigh, where he had fewer awkward questions to answer and fewer also to put to himself. He studied and he swam and he tried to avoid conversations with his brothers about his father. When he did speak to Roby on the telephone it made them both uncomfortable because they were, for the time being, standing—if not on opposite sides—at least on separate shores of a gulf, with the great unanswered question of their father's guilt or innocence looming between them.

To Roby, who had made a decision to have absolute faith in his father no matter what, any sign of ambivalence seemed disloyal. So Roby found it easier just not to talk to Chris. He found himself, in fact, uncomfortable in the presence of anyone who had not made the same decision he had. This included not only Chris, but most of Toms River. Even, in time, Uncle Sal, who made it clear that he would always be there for Roby, but not for Rob. That split was not one that Roby, blindly faithful, was able to tolerate.

As for John, at thirteen, what he had mostly was pain that no one seemed able to lessen.

The fact was, as far as Toms River was concerned, the boys had become something of an embarrassment. Here was their father, who had murdered their mother (for the town's mind was long since made up), still free to do what he pleased. That in itself was an affront to decency, no matter how many rumors had it that arrest was imminent.

And here were these three heartsick boys, stub-
bornly refusing to acknowledge his guilt (for even
Chris kept his uncertainty to himself).

In the minds and hearts of country club members,
that made it awfully difficult to feel all that sorry for the
boys. Sure, it was terrible what had happened to
them, but that still didn't give them the right to shut
their eyes to what was so obvious to everyone else.

And so a feeling—however hard to believe this may
seem—of something approaching *resentment* began to
build toward the boys. If they were going to stand by
their father, why, then, they'd just have to suffer the
consequences.

The biggest consequence was that they found themselves avoided, ignored, almost *shunned* by the very
friends and neighbors who had always seemed closest
to their parents.

It was as if they'd become a messy loose end to the
story and no one wanted to go near them to pick it up.

For weeks, following the arrests of Myers, Grandshaw
and L'Heureux, their lawyers had been trying to block
the extradition of the three to New Jersey. By late
November, however, the legal maneuvers were all used
up and the three men were flown north.

Suddenly, there they were, the three of them, "right
here in River City," as Toms River old-timers liked to
say, being publicly arraigned before Ocean County
Superior Court Judge William Huber on December 4.
All were charged with conspiracy to commit murder,
an offense that, under the new state death-penalty
law, could result in execution by lethal injection.

L'Heureux, forty-six, the former Caddo Parish deputy sheriff, was baby-faced, pale and grossly over-
weight. Standing six feet tall, he appeared to weigh at
least 250.

Next to him stood Grandshaw, swarthy and gaunt, a man with the hard, haunted eyes of an old hillbilly singer down on his luck.

And there, at the end of the line, stood little Andrew Myers. He looked like just what he was: a hardware clerk drawing a small Air Force pension. Short, nervous, bespectacled, with something vaguely lizardlike in his appearance. While the others seemed impassive, Myers looked openly terrified—as if he'd gotten trapped in somebody else's bad dream.

After pleading not guilty to the charges, and seeing bail set at $1.5 million each, the three of them, handcuffed and shackled, were led from the courtroom—looking, incongruously, like three bewildered dwarfs in search of Snow White.

But Snow White had been dead since September and the net around Rob Marshall was tightening fast.

Part Two

THE
LAW

12

BOB Gladstone, lieutenant in charge of homicide at the Ocean County prosecutor's office, was asleep at his home in Point Pleasant at 2:15 A.M. when he got a call telling him that a woman had been shot to death at the Oyster Creek picnic area on the Garden State Parkway.

By the time he reached the chilly scene, forty-five minutes later, Rob Marshall, bleeding from a cut on his head, had already been taken to Community Memorial Hospital. Maria was still lying facedown on the front seat of the ivory Cadillac in a pool of blood.

The first thing that struck Gladstone was how dark the site was, how thoroughly screened from the road. To reach it, a car entering from the northbound parkway would have to make a left at the end of the short entrance ramp, then, thirty feet further in, another left down a single lane of blacktop pavement lined with picnic tables and trash cans.

The Marshall car had traveled about fifty feet down this blacktop strip. The lane ended about one hundred feet further on, at an unlit cinderblock rest room structure. It was so dark that even with the lights of the several patrol cars that had now convened at the scene, Gladstone twice banged his knee against the grilles of cars he did not see as he walked about.

The evergreen growth on both sides of the lane was so thick (the picnic area, like that stretch of the parkway itself, had simply been hacked out of the Pine Barrens) that it was impossible to see and difficult even to hear traffic passing either north- or southbound on the parkway. It was no wonder, Gladstone thought, that there was a big sign posted at the entrance, warning, AREA CLOSED AFTER DARK, PARKING PROHIBITED.

Approaching the ivory Eldorado, Gladstone saw immediately that the car's right rear tire was completely flat. "What's the story?" he asked the state police officer in charge at the scene.

The officer read from a notebook by flashlight. The night was cold enough so that his breath made clouds in the darkness. "Robert O. Marshall, 884 Crest Ridge Drive, Toms River. Deceased is his wife, Maria P. Marshall. Mr. Marshall states that he and his wife had been to dinner at Harrah's Marina in Atlantic City, leaving there approximately midnight. After passing through the Barnegat Toll Plaza, he felt a vibration in the car. Says he knew the picnic area was nearby as he used the parkway frequently. Pulled in here to check the tire. Says he exited his vehicle and discovered that the right rear tire was flat.

"At that point, he observed a vehicle—dark sedan, possibly a Chrysler, pull into the area from the north-bound parkway and stop perpendicular to his car, approximately thirty feet away. Says he ignored the vehicle and did not see or hear anyone exit from it.

"Says he walked to his wife's door, she opened it, and he advised her to—what's this word?—to 'pop' the trunk. There was a button in the glove compartment, apparently, that opens the trunk.

"Then he says as he began to turn from his wife he was struck on the head and knocked unconscious. Did not see his assailant, had not seen or heard anyone approach.

Does not know how long he was unconscious. When he regained consciousness he noted that his wife had been shot. He was unable to awaken her and he ran out into the roadway to flag down help."

"Anything else?" Gladstone asked.

"Yeah. He says he's missing two thousand in cash, money he won at the casino. Says it was taken from his right front pants pocket."

"Is that it?"

"For now," the trooper said. "Except I asked him one other thing. I asked him if he'd noticed anyone following him, you know, along the parkway. Or paying special attention to him or his wife down at Harrah's. You know, in the casino."

"What did he say?"

"He said—I think I remember this exactly. He said, 'People always watch Maria because she is such a strikingly beautiful woman.' Then he started weeping. He was shivering and everything. We had to put a blanket around him, sit him down inside one of the patrol cars."

Gladstone looked around again at the dark, desolate and isolated location. "What is it," he asked, "three miles down to the toll booths?"

"Just about," the trooper said.

"And what, another three up to the Roy Rogers?"

"Maybe three point eight, maybe four."

Gladstone shook his head, then peered once more into the darkness, looking again at the nearly impenetrable barrier of forest that surrounded them. The high-speed, hectic New Jersey parkway world seemed not only miles but years away.

"The guy says he pulled in *here* to change a flat?"

"Yes, sir," the trooper said.

"And now he's gone?"

"At the hospital. He got whacked in the head, but it don't look too bad. Might take a few stitches is all. Oh, it's not in my notebook, but I can tell you one other thing."

"Go ahead."

"When he's leaving, you know, to go up to the ER, he walks back to his car and he climbs in the passenger side and he reaches over and he, like, pats his wife on the ass. You know, just put his hand there, on the buttock. Like he's saying goodbye."

Gladstone walked over to the ivory Eldorado and looked again at the body of Maria Marshall. From outside the car, it appeared as if she simply were sleeping, her body facedown across the two bucket seats, her shoes off, her head resting on her hands. She'd been shot in the back. There wasn't much blood. She was still wearing several pieces of gold jewelry—a necklace, a bracelet, two or three rings. On the floor, just beneath where her two stockinged feet hung over the edge of the seat, was a single, long-stemmed red rose.

"It's goodbye, all right," Gladstone said. "The long goodbye."

Gladstone then walked to the right rear of the car, got down on one knee, switched on a flashlight, and examined the tire. Right away, he saw a clean, straight cut, about an inch and a half long on the sidewall, just above where it rested on the ground.

Gladstone moved his light around the tire. The edges were smooth and undamaged, showing no signs of the tire having been driven on when flat or low on air.

He stood up. Gladstone was a jovial, soft-spoken, heavy-set man in his late thirties who wore a neatly trimmed gray beard, read a lot of books, and looked more like a college professor than a homicide detective. He was, in fact, an exceptionally talented homicide detective. But one did not have to be Inspector Maigret to get the sense here that something was wrong.

He called to the trooper. "Have somebody radio the

hospital," he said. "I don't want that guy going anywhere. I've got a few questions for him."

When Danny O'Brien, the county homicide sergeant dispatched to the emergency room by Gladstone, arrived at
4:15 A.M., Rob was just on his way out, accompanied by
Father Mulcahy, the priest from St. Joseph's, whom he
wanted to have by his side when he told Roby and John
about their mother.

Rob was wearing a blue blazer and tan slacks and had
a fresh white bandage high on his forehead, near the
edge of his deeply receding hairline, covering a cut that
had been closed with five stitches. He did not appear to
have been seriously injured and, to O'Brien, he did not
seem traumatized either.

"He didn't look like a man whose wife had just been
murdered," O'Brien said later. "He looked like a man on
his way to his yacht."

Because the murder had occurred on a state parkway,
O'Brien could not take an official statement from Rob
without a state trooper present. He did, however, ask
Rob where he was going.

"Home," Rob said. "To break the tragic news to my
sons."

O'Brien, with his mustache and his baleful eyes and his
unreconstructed nineteenth-century Irish face, gave Rob
a look in which the cynicism was palpable.

"Sit tight once you get there," he said. "We'll be
dropping by to say hello."

By 5 A.M., when O'Brien arrived at Crest Ridge Drive
in the company of two state police officers, Rob had
already been upstairs to see the boys. He was still dressed
in blazer and slacks and now seemed, to O'Brien, ready
to host a cocktail party. In fact, as the three men stepped
into the front hall, the first thing Rob said to them was,
"Gentlemen? Would you care for a drink?"

"No thanks," O'Brien said. "Let's take a ride."

Half an hour later, at the Bass River barracks, while waiting for the formal interview to begin, Rob lay down on a couch in a squad room and fell asleep. When the questioning did begin—and at this point, O'Brien said later, the atmosphere was of the neutral sort appropriate to a circumstance in which it had not yet been determined whether the individual being questioned was more likely victim or suspect—Rob repeated the story he'd given at the scene, adding, according to a state police report, that "the car did not seem right almost immediately and became progressively worse (seemed to have a sway) the farther north he went."

This made it seem all the more peculiar that he would have driven past numerous toll plazas and all-night service areas before pulling into such a secluded spot as Oyster Creek. Most peculiar of all, of course, was the one-and-a-half-inch slash in the tire which would have caused it to go immediately and totally flat, but at this point O'Brien chose not to mention that.

"How long you been married?" O'Brien asked.

"Twenty years," Rob said.

"A long time," O'Brien said. "I just got divorced myself. You have any problems with the marriage?"

"Well," Rob said, "we were having some financial problems. My wife, quite frankly, was living beyond our means. We briefly tried some marriage counseling as a result of that. Also, to be perfectly candid, I should say that my wife suspected me of cheating on her."

"Were you? O'Brien asked.

"No. No, of course not," Rob replied.

O'Brien just sat there, staring at him. O'Brien didn't like him. O'Brien didn't like that whole, phony, country club set, and Rob Marshall seemed as obnoxious an example of it as O'Brien had ever encountered.

"Did you kill her?" O'Brien asked.

"No. No, of course I didn't kill her," Rob said, his voice displaying sudden indignation. "What sort of question is that?"

"You have any reason to want her dead?" O'Brien asked.

"Listen, Sergeant. You'd better get one thing straight right from the start. I loved my wife."

"That wasn't my question," O'Brien said. "My question was, you have any reason to want her dead?"

This time, Rob didn't answer right away. He looked at O'Brien, for the first time, with something other than disdain. "Am I a suspect?" he asked.

"As much as anybody else who rode up or down the parkway last night," O'Brien said. "Now, how about I give you a ride home?"

As soon as he got in the car, Rob closed his eyes and fell asleep.

Bob Gladstone was downtown in the county prosecutor's office at nine o'clock in the morning, telling the county prosecutor what he knew—which was mostly that Rob Marshall's story about the flat tire didn't make sense—when the phone rang.

The caller was a private detective named Fred Grasso who had formerly been a state policeman. Gladstone knew Grasso. In Toms River, everybody knows everybody, especially if they work in law, law enforcement or real estate.

"There's a client of mine," Grasso said, "in whom I think you've recently developed an interest."

"How recently?" Gladstone asked.

"Oh, maybe one, two o'clock this morning."

"Marshall, Maria P.?"

"That's the lady. And, Bobby, she was one hell of a lady. Nicest woman you'd ever want to meet."

"Somebody didn't think so."

"Yeah, and I can tell you who."

"Well, don't be shy."

"She was the nicest lady, Bobby, I swear to God. Not a mean bone in her body."

"Who disagreed?"

"Her husband."

"That would be Robert O. Marshall, eight eight four Crest Ridge Drive, Toms River?"

"Rob-O himself. And what a horse's ass he is. Bobby, this woman calls me last December, just before Christmas. She'd been talking to Tom Kenyon, the attorney. Said she suspected her husband was having an affair, wanted to talk to him about her options. Turns out Kenyon knows the broad involved in the affair, so he don't want any part of it. But he has her call me, do some surveillance, get the goods, so whatever lawyer she winds up with will be holding a few face cards when the game starts."

"Hey, Fred? Why don't you come on in, do this in person. And bring me whatever you've got."

"I'll be right over," Grasso said. "Listen, Bobby, this one is a nasty piece of business. There's all kinds of wrinkles in this. But Mrs. Marshall, she was such a fine lady, Bobby. The kind of lady you wish you'd had her for a mother when you were a kid."

Fred Grasso had a clear and vivid recollection of his first meeting with Maria. Kenyon had called him and had explained the circumstances and had told him to expect her call. It came within the hour. Maria said her husband was having an affair with Felice Rosenberg, wife of David, daughter of Fred Frankel, and vice principal of Seaview Regional High School. Maria said she wanted to see Grasso right away but she said she couldn't just go to his office, she might be seen.

So he had told her the way to arrange it. He described his car to her and told her he'd be parked in it at the far

end of the parking lot by the Super Foodtown on Route
37. It was one of the biggest parking lots in Toms River,
not counting the mall, and a meeting there would not
attract attention. She was to pull her station wagon up
next to his car. He'd be facing north, so she should face
south, so the driver's side windows would be next to one
another. They would stay in their own cars to escape
detection.

As he explained this to her carefully, Grasso thought
she seemed almost too nervous to comprehend it. She
seemed terrified at the thought that she might be observed.

"I understand," Maria told him. "I'll be there. I'll
drive up to you slowly, but if I don't stop I don't want
you to follow me." This must be a big step for her, he
figured, and up to the last moment she wanted to be
able to change her mind.

She did stop, however, and Grasso was impressed
by his first sight of her. Not only attractive but very
well spoken, with her nervousness now firmly under
control. She had, as he'd told Gladstone, a strong
smile, a lively expression on her face. Fred Grasso
liked her right away. *Her husband has got to be some
kind of shmuck,* Grasso thought, *to give this lady a
hard time.*

They did not linger in the twilight of the mid-
December afternoon. Maria handed Grasso a photograph. It was a picture taken at one of the country
club's many costume parties. The photo showed Rob
and Maria and David and Felice, with Felice dressed
as some sort of belly dancer who'd been taken captive
by the pirates. Her hand was reaching out toward,
almost touching, Rob's crotch. He was grinning and
holding a sword to her throat.

"What's this for?" Grasso asked.

"You said to bring a picture of her."

He shook his head. *Jesus, Jesus, sometimes he wished*

he'd never left the state police. "Yeah, Mrs. Marshall, I said bring a picture, but that was for identification purposes, so when I see her I can be sure that it's her." He held up the photograph. "This would be great if they ever sell her into white slavery, but I don't think they let her into Seaview Regional dressed like that."

Maria looked crushed. Her first investigative assignment and she had botched it. "Never mind, never mind," Grasso said. "It'll be fine. I've seen her around town, I'll recognize her. And if she's not the one, I'll also be able to tell you that."

She still looked so sad and hurt that Grasso felt sorry for her. Two weeks before Christmas, twenty years of marriage, three kids back at the house, this couldn't be any fun for her.

"Listen, Mrs. Marshall," he said. "Don't worry. I'll get right on this. Maybe I can't solve your problems for you, but I promise I'll get you the information you need."

"Thank you," she said.

"And, listen, I've seen this kind of thing a lot of times. It happens more than you'd ever guess. And usually it all works out fine."

She smiled at him. "Thank you," she said again. Then she reached into her purse and handed him a hundred-dollar bill. "Is this enough to start with?"

"That's fine, Mrs. Marshall. You don't even need to give me this. I can just bill you as we go."

"No," she said. "That won't do. The way our money's disappearing, I'd better pay you in advance."

"That's fine," Grasso said. "I'll get right on this. Do you want me to call you directly or do you want me to call Tom Kenyon when I've got something?"

"Don't call," she said hurriedly. "Don't call anyone. I really don't want anyone to know. I'll call you. I'll wait a few days and then I'll call you."

"Okay, Mrs. Marshall, we'll leave it like that. And hey—try to have a merry Christmas anyway."

She smiled once more, then raised her window and drove off.

And now she was dead. Shot to death in the front seat of Rob-O's Cadillac. With Rob-O standing outside, holding a hanky to his head, according to what Grasso had heard on the radio. Well, he had his whole file with him and Bob Gladstone was welcome to it, pictures and all.

In midmorning, Gladstone got a second call, this one from a lawyer named Michael DeWitt, whose practice was in Bricktown, a raggedy collection of blue-collar tract homes and mini-malls that had sprung into existence just north of Toms River.

DeWitt said he had been Maria Marshall's lawyer. He had begun to represent her the previous December, after she'd been referred to him by Tom Kenyon, the Toms River lawyer whom she had first consulted.

Her problems, DeWitt said, had been twofold. First, her husband was having an affair. The woman involved in the affair was sufficiently well acquainted with Kenyon so that, when he'd heard her identity, he'd decided it could pose a conflict of interest for him to represent Maria and thus he had referred her to DeWitt.

Mrs. Marshall's second problem had been financial. She had discovered that her husband had plunged the family horrendously into debt and had attempted to disguise the problem by taking out a $100,000 home equity loan. In order that she would not know that he had done this, he'd signed her name on the loan application.

DeWitt had prepared both a bankruptcy petition and a divorce filing for Mrs. Marshall, he said, but whenever she'd reached the point that action was required, she'd pulled back. Her goal, she had told him repeatedly, was to save her marriage, not destroy it.

Over the summer, however, she had grown increasingly concerned that her husband might be involved in activities that were criminal in nature. She feared he might be using, or even selling, cocaine, or that he'd fallen in with people engaged in such illicit trafficking. She was also deeply concerned, even fearful, about the depths of his involvement with the Atlantic City casino-gambling world. And she feared, too, that his desperate financial plight might have made him dependent upon people connected to organized crime. She had taken to listening in on his phone calls and to searching through the contents of his desk, but she'd been afraid to confront him with what she had learned or suspected.

DeWitt said he had worked actively in her behalf in December and January. There had then followed several months when she had hoped, apparently, that she would be able to resolve her difficulties without any legal assistance. In July, however, she'd suddenly gotten back in touch with DeWitt and, by the end of the month, he'd prepared all the paperwork necessary for a public divorce filing, including the naming of Felice Rosenberg as corespondent, and a notice of Lis Pendens, which would place a lien on the Marshall house, so that Robert Marshall could not employ it as an asset in any way.

The papers were ready on July 26, DeWitt said. But she'd told him to hold off on filing, that the family was leaving on vacation the next day, and that she still hoped to resolve matters privately. Except for one day in mid-August, when she'd stopped by the office to pay her bill, DeWitt said, he'd never heard from Mrs. Marshall again.

By noon, Gladstone had the results of the autopsy. Maria Marshall had been shot twice in the back at very close range with a .45-caliber pistol. The entrance wounds were so close together that a fifty-cent piece would have covered them both. The trajectory of the bullets made it apparent that she'd been lying face-down on the front seat of the car when she'd been shot. It was obvious that whoever had shot her had done so with the definite intention of killing her. This had not been a panicky overreaction during a robbery attempt gone awry. To Bob Gladstone, it had the mark of a professional execution.

By one o'clock he'd already assigned a detective the task of determining how much insurance had been carried on Maria Marshall's life.

By three o'clock he'd given the order that Felice Rosenberg should be brought in for questioning.

No question about it, they did it up right. They waited until she left Seaview Regional at 3:30 that afternoon, waited until she got that black Buick Skyhawk cranked up to about eighty, eighty-five on the parkway, and then, lights flashing, unmarked car in addition to patrol car, pulled her over to the side of the road.

No, they told her, they didn't want her license and registration. Speeding wasn't what was on their minds. It was more along the lines of, "Follow us, ma'am. We're bringing you in for questioning." About what? About the murder of Maria Marshall.

When they brought her in, they booked her, they fingerprinted her, they took a mug shot. This was real. This wasn't a fortieth-birthday surprise. Gladstone had assigned Detective Al McGuire to the interview. Al

was really a very sweet guy, but from a distance of
more than, say, forty feet, he was hard to distinguish,
in size and shape, from a grizzly bear.

Alongside him sat Detective Tony Mancuso of the
state police, who without even trying gave off the air
of a man who wasn't the least bit bothered by anything
you said because he didn't believe a word of it anyway.

Felice took one look at those two and she wanted a
lawyer. In fact, she wanted two of them, Lou Minsky
and his partner, Jay Jarvis. They were social friends,
as well as lawyers—all part of that big, extended family up in Brookside.

Minsky and Jarvis wasted no time getting down to
the prosecutor's office. (Though Minsky had the unen-
viable task of first calling David Rosenberg at the car
dealership and giving him a double dose of bad news:
[a] your wife's been having an affair; [b] she's about to
be questioned in connection with a homicide.)

The two lawyers consulted with Felice privately and
then informed Detectives McGuire and Mancuso that
she would be willing to submit to questioning.

She was advised of her rights several times, given a
consent-to-question form to sign, advised again after
she'd signed it that she had the right to terminate the
interview at any time, that she was not under arrest
and that the procedure they were going through was
entirely voluntary on her part. Then they took her into
the polygraph room and started to talk—without hook-
ing her up to the machine.

The story she told them was that yes, there had
been an affair, commencing in the summer of 1983.
Maria had grown suspicious in the fall, especially after
finding records of Rob's dozens of phone calls to her
at Seaview. Felice herself had mentioned the affair to
only one or two very close friends, and Rob, she was
certain, had never confided in anyone about it.

Rob, she said, had been unhappy in his marriage. He'd complained that Maria was overly possessive and spent too much money. She herself was unfulfilled in her relationship with her husband and she and Rob had planned to leave their respective spouses and live together.

Plans for such a move had been in the works for some months, she said, and in fact, had just about come to fruition. Within a week, she and Rob had planned to make their respective announcements and take up residence in a beach house they'd just rented in Manahawkin. They'd already obtained a safe deposit box together, into which Rob had placed "a couple thousand dollars' worth" of silver ingots, and they'd already signed papers for a joint checking account. Also, she said, for months they'd been sharing a downtown post office box, which they used for the exchange of tapes—little love messages they sent one another when they could not be together.

She outlined in detail her activities of the previous day, acknowledging that she had met Rob at 4 P.M. in the parking lot of a shopping center not far from Seaview Regional. She had left her car there, she said, and had ridden with him to one of their favorite parking spots. It was an area of scrub pine, beyond a sign that said FOR OFFICIAL USE ONLY, behind the site of a new housing development. He had mixed Cuba Libres (rum, Coke and lime) for them as he usually did, and they had talked for what she guessed was an hour, an hour and a half. She said she remembered him complaining that he didn't want to go to Atlantic City that night, but that he had to because his wife had "insisted."

They'd parted at about five thirty and she'd proceeded to a Toms River exercise salon to lead an exercise class. Then she'd gone home, changed clothes, and had taken a small party of friends to a birthday dinner she was giving for her father at the Wall Street restaurant in Bricktown. She'd ordered a Caesar salad as a main course. She'd been waited on by a blond woman named Nancy. On the way home, they stopped at Carvel's for ice cream.

McGuire asked her how she'd heard the news of Maria's death. She said Rob had called her at school that morning. "Are you sitting down?" he'd said. When she'd said yes, he'd said, "Maria's dead." Then, she said, he'd started to cry. He'd also said, "It's terrible. I didn't want it to be like this." Then he'd described how it had happened. He'd pulled into the picnic area, got out of the car, heard a car pull in behind him but paid it no attention, asked Maria to "pop the trunk," and then was hit on the head. When he'd regained consciousness he'd found her dead, shot in the back.

McGuire stood up. He said, "We're going to leave you here alone for a while, Mrs. Rosenberg. Just give you a little bit of time with your attorneys here, Mr. Minsky and Mr. Jarvis. What I want you to do is keep thinking. See if there might be anything else you can think of that might be helpful." Then he and Mancuso left the room.

When they returned ten minutes later, Felice had thought of something. She said, apropos of the financial difficulties that she knew Rob had been experiencing, she'd remembered that he had taken out a $100,000 second mortgage on his house.

McGuire nodded. "That's fine," he said. "That's the sort of thing I mean. In a situation like this, you just never know what might be helpful. Now why don't you stay there a few minutes longer with Mr. Minsky and Mr. Jarvis and think some more. We'll be back soon."

This time, when they came back, she said she had thought of one other thing. Both McGuire and Mancuso found it to be of sufficient importance that they included it in their written reports of the interview.

McGuire wrote: "During a conversation with Robert Marshall before Christmas of 1983, Marshall had stated to her, while discussing his financial difficulties, that 'the insurance on Maria would take care of his debt.' [He'd said,] 'I wish she wasn't around. Do you know of anyone who could take care of it?' Felice Rosenberg stated to Rob Marshall at that time that she only knew of a subject by the name of Patsy Racine as the only person that she knew who had ever gotten in trouble with the law. She (Felice) stated she never wanted to be involved with [Marshall] if he could do anything like that to his wife."

Mancuso wrote: "Mrs. Rosenberg described one conversation when Rob asked her if she knew of anyone who could help him get rid of his problem (speaking of his wife). Mrs. Rosenberg advised that she was shocked and told Rob that if he was serious, she did not want to have anything more to do with him, but she added that the only person she knew who might be able to help him was Patsy Racine, but again added that she never wanted to hear him talk of it again."

McGuire figured that was enough for one day. But he told Felice before she left—in the company of attorneys Minsky and Jarvis—that they might be asking her back to take a polygraph examination.

13

WHILE Felice was being interviewed in the polygraph room, Bob Gladstone was in his office down the hall, talking on the telephone with a local insurance agent named Philip Girard, who had called as soon as he'd heard news of the murder broadcast on the radio.

Girard said he thought he should mention to someone that on Monday he'd been contacted by Rob Marshall, who said he needed an insurance policy taken out on the life of his wife, Maria, in the amount of $100,000.

Marshall had stressed that he was in "a very big hurry" to get the policy into effect. He insisted that all paperwork be handcarried to speed the process and that a medical examination be completed within forty-eight hours. He said he and his wife would be leaving on a long vacation by the end of the week and it was essential that the policy be in force before then.

Girard said a medical examination had been conducted in the Marshall home at ten o'clock on the morning of September 6, and that he had arrived there shortly after noon to sign the papers, just as Marshall, his wife and a tall, handsome young man who appeared to be their son were leaving, apparently on their way to lunch.

"Holy shit," Bob Gladstone said to himself.

Before he could say more, to himself or to anyone else, he was interrupted by the sound of raised voices in the hallway outside his office. He opened his door and looked out to see Felice's father, Fred Frankel, demanding to see someone in authority.

"I'm the lieutenant in charge of homicide," Gladstone said quietly. "If this has anything to do with the Maria Marshall murder, I'll be happy to talk to you about it."

"What the hell's your name?" Fred Frankel demanded.

"Gladstone. I'm Lieutenant Gladstone."

"You listen to me, Gladstone. I understand you've got my daughter down here and I demand to see her immediately. I want to know just what the hell is going on. What right do you think you have to drag my daughter in here off the streets like some common criminal? Do you know who she is? Do you know who I am? Listen, Gladstone, I'm a close friend of Ray DiOrio's. And goddamnit, I'm going to call him about this. What the hell do you think this is, Russia?"

"Mr. Frankel," Gladstone said calmly, "your daughter is in the presence of two attorneys of her own choosing, she's been fully advised of her rights, she has signed a consent-to-question form, she is speaking voluntarily and, as she and her attorneys know, she is free to terminate the interview at any time."

"Goddamnit, I want to see her. What the hell is this all about?"

"I'm sorry, Mr. Frankel, but I'm not going to interrupt the interview," Gladstone said.

"Didn't you hear me the first time? I said I'm a close friend of Ray DiOrio's. I'm going to tell him about this and I guarantee you, Gladstone, there is going to be hell to pay!"

"That's fine, Mr. Frankel. You call anybody you

want to. And as soon as the interview is completed, I'll let your daughter know that you're eager to speak to her."

"You son of a bitch, you might not believe me, but the minute I walk out this door I'm calling DiOrio."

"That's fine, Mr. Frankel. If you'll excuse me now, I've got a few calls to make myself."

In early evening, McGuire and Mancuso came into Gladstone's office to report on their session with Felice. Their impression, they said, was that she knew more than she was telling. Gladstone was not surprised to hear this.

Marshall, when asked, had denied he was having an affair. That, apparently, had been a lie. And now it turned out that it was not only an affair, but one that soon would have resulted in both parties' leaving their spouses. And it turned out that Marshall had been so heavily in debt that, months earlier, his wife had seriously explored the possibility of filing for bankruptcy. And it also turned out that he'd embarked upon a frantic quest for life insurance on his wife the very week she was murdered. He ran through these circumstances with McGuire and Mancuso. Then one other thought occurred to him.

"Felice works at Seaview, right?"

The two other detectives nodded.

"That means she drives past the murder site twice a day. That would give her a chance to know it pretty well. To know just how dark and secluded it was."

"But she wasn't there," McGuire said. "She was up in Bricktown having dinner with her father and a bunch of other people, and boy, does she remember every single drop of salad dressing."

"She wouldn't have to have been there when it happened to know it was a good place to get the job done," Gladstone said. "It's just a thought, just a thought. Incidentally, her old man was just in here. I'm surprised you didn't hear him. He sounded like a wounded water buffalo. By now he's on the phone to Ray DiOrio, complaining that his daughter's not getting enough respect."

"We were respectful," McGuire said. "We were very respectful. We fingerprinted her with the utmost of respect."

"We said 'please,' 'thank you,' the whole bit," Mancuso said.

"She wants respect," Gladstone said, "maybe she ought to hire Ray DiOrio as her lawyer."

The three of them laughed about that.

But then, after the others had left, Gladstone began to ponder the implications of Felice's mention of the name of Patsy Racine.

His real name was Patsy Ragazzo and, among other things, he ran a restaurant called Patsy Racine's Rainbow Room in Toms River. He was also, Gladstone knew, at least a minor-league figure on the fringes of organized crime. The question in Gladstone's mind was, how come he was a friend of Felice's? Or at least a good enough acquaintance so that when Robert O. Marshall asked her for the name of someone who might assist him in disposing of his wife—just kidding, of course—Patsy Racine/Ragazzo was the name she came up with?

Well, it wasn't so strange that she would have had some name to give him. If he'd tried, Marshall could undoubtedly have come up with a name on his own. The Mafia was not exactly a low-profile presence in Toms River.

It had started, like everything else, with the real estate boom in the midsixties, when Ocean County suddenly became a land of opportunity for illegal as well as legal enterprise. That was when Vinny Gigliotti

had been sent down from north Jersey by "Big Top"
Tornicelli of the Lucchese crime family, to organize a
gambling and loansharking operation.

Like everyone else in Toms River, Gigliotti got
caught up in the real estate boom and, in addition to
his bookmaking and loansharking, he started a con-
tracting business. In fact, he built a number of the
town's more expensive homes, including many in
Brookside that came to be occupied by members of his
extended family.

Gigliotti himself had lived only a few blocks away
from Robert Marshall. He had, that is, until his un-
timely demise back in June, when three men in ski
masks had shown up at his construction company office on Route 9. Ski masks in June were strange enough,
but what even more quickly caught the eyes of witnesses
(who very soon thereafter made themselves scarce)
was that the three men in ski masks were carrying golf
clubs. The men had begun to swing the golf clubs at
Vinny Gigliotti. They kept swinging until he was dead.
Then they walked out the front door, climbed into a
gray Lincoln Continental, and drove away. No one
happened to catch the license number. And no one
had ever happened to get arrested for the crime.

Gigliotti had been one of three first cousins in Toms
River. A second, Vito Quadrozzi, was a lawyer who
had been, for a time, a municipal judge. His days on
the bench had come to an end in 1980 when the
proprietor of a pornography shop and homosexual sex
club in Bricktown had been shot to death through the
living room window of his home, and the three
.38-caliber revolvers used in the shooting were found in
a shoebox in Judge Quadrozzi's basement. He explained that he had simply been asked to hold a pack-
age for a friend.

Quadrozzi's son, Gino, was also a resident of

Brookside. In 1979, he and *his* cousin, Michael Gigliotti, son of Vinny Gigliotti, had opened a beachfront night-club called the Key West Lounge.

As it happened, the Key West Lounge became the chief distribution center for a cocaine-trafficking ring headed by Gino Quadrozzi that sold more than seven million dollars' worth of the drug annually in Ocean County.

The ring included such Toms River notables as John Maloney, former operator of Sultan's Delight Pleasure Spa in Bricktown, and Richard Bianchi, owner of River City Automotive, another Route 37 car dealership.

Also included were a former assistant football coach at Toms River East High School and a recent graduate of Toms River East named Joseph Maselli, who, when once stopped in a school hallway and found to be carrying more than five thousand dollars in cash, explained that it was "lunch money."

Maselli turned out to be the brother of Gino Quadrozzi's wife. In all, five other members of the Quadrozzi and Maselli families were charged with being part of the ring, including Joseph Maselli's mother. Gladstone remembered the joke that Maselli was one teenager who didn't have to worry about his mother going through his pockets and finding drugs: she was probably the one who put them there.

The other joke was that, at River City Automotive, when they told you a car came fully equipped they really meant it. Bags of cocaine, available for quick sale, were kept stashed above removable panels of the main showroom ceiling. Of the fifty-seven people charged with being part of the ring, twenty-one were River City employees.

The other of Vinny Gigliotti's cousins was the quiet one: John Riccio. He owned a restaurant on the board-walk but his primary business was sanitation. He had

affiliations with most of the private garbage haulers
between Asbury Park and Atlantic City. He, too, lived
in the Brookside neighborhood, Gladstone recalled.
In fact, Riccio lived only three blocks away from Robert Marshall.

Gladstone's phone rang. It was Fred Frankel, speaking in a much softer voice. He said he wanted to
apologize for his behavior that afternoon and told
Gladstone he had spoken to his daughter and had
learned of the affair. He also stressed that he could
personally account for her whereabouts during the
hours immediately preceding the crime and he assured
Gladstone that both he and his daughter would do
anything they could to assist the prosecutor's office in
its inquiries. The name of Raymond DiOrio was not
mentioned.

Also, that evening, Detective Mancuso got a phone
call from Felice. In fact, he got two. In the first, she
said she wanted to change a statement she'd made
during her interview. Now, she said, she remembered
that Rob had, in fact, told three or four people about
the affair, including lawyers Patrick Reilly, Jay Jarvis
(who, along with Minsky, had been representing her
that afternoon) and Tom Kenyon (in whom Maria had
also confided). She added that Rob had even asked
her to call Jarvis and inform him of Maria's death that
morning, after he had called to tell her.

Then she said, "Don't you see? It would be stupid
to suspect Rob of killing his wife, with Rob knowing
that all those people knew he was having this affair."

After he'd hung up it occurred to Mancuso to wonder if she had, in fact, "forgotten" those facts that
afternoon, or whether it wasn't more likely that in a
subsequent conversation with Marshall he'd instructed
her to call back with the new information, as well as

with the theory that it somehow should relieve him of suspicion.

Ten minutes later, Mancuso received his second call. This time, Felice told him that she'd forgotten yet another name—that of a divorce lawyer, Martin Manning, whom Rob had consulted several months earlier and whom he had informed of the affair.

On Monday morning, September 10, Michael DeWitt, the lawyer from Bricktown, brought the Maria Marshall file to Gladstone's office. He seemed a calm and deliberate man whose disposition, Gladstone sensed, had probably been well suited for a nervous, troubled woman just starting the plunge into the brief dark side of her life.

DeWitt called Gladstone's attention to a note that Maria had sent him on July 23.

It said, "Dear Mike—More 'stuff' for the file. Holding my own, pray for me." Attached were three telephone numbers, each in the 318 area code.

"Three one eight," Gladstone said. "Where's that?"

"Louisiana," Michael DeWitt said. "Western Louisiana. Not New Orleans. Shreveport."

"Why did she give you these numbers?"

"They worried her. You might even say they frightened her. But then she went on vacation and only came back to pay her bill."

" 'Holding my own, pray for me,' " Gladstone read aloud. "She sounds frightened."

"She was a lovely woman," DeWitt said. "One of the nicest people you could ever hope to meet."

"But a frightened woman in late July," Gladstone said. "Frightened by phone numbers from Louisiana."

"Or maybe," DeWitt said, "by the people at the other end."

Gladstone placed the file in a desk drawer. "It all

depends," he said, "on who they are. Don't worry. We'll find out."

As soon as DeWitt left, Gladstone had McGuire contact New Jersey Bell headquarters and arrange to obtain a complete printout of all toll calls to and from Rob Marshall's home and office for the past six months.

By late afternoon, McGuire was back, document in hand and a big grin on his bearded face. "You're not going to believe this," he said. "Where are those numbers? Those three numbers you got from DeWitt?"

Gladstone took them out of his desk drawer.

"Look at this," McGuire said, standing over Gladstone's desk. "This first one. There's got to be twenty calls back and forth between Marshall's house and this number, starting in June. And look at this—this last one, September fifth. That's the day before she was killed.

"This other number shows up at least ten or twelve times. And the third is there a couple of times, too."

"So what's it mean, Al?"

"It means Marshall was doing a lot of business in Louisiana all summer long. Business that worried his wife. And business that ended the day before she got killed."

"Hardware business," Gladstone said.

"What?" McGuire looked puzzled.

"That first number," Gladstone said, "5314. That's the number—we learned this afternoon—of the Caddo Hardware Store in Shreveport, Louisiana."

"A *hardware store?*" McGuire said.

"Yup. And this second one that shows up so much? That's the home number of a Shreveport resident named Andrew Myers. And, McGuire, being that you're such a hot-shit detective, I'll bet you can figure out where Mr. Myers is employed."

"Caddo Hardware?" McGuire said.

"You got it. Now if I can just get somebody in the Shreveport police department to answer the phone, maybe I can persuade them to send somebody over there to find out from Mr. Myers just what kind of hardware Rob-O was so interested in."

"Maybe a forty-five?" McGuire said.

"Could be. They sell them. Hell, I think I could've bought one over the phone this afternoon."

"Yeah, but if you had," McGuire said, "you wouldn't have had to have another twenty-three conversations about it. What about the third number?"

"Pay phone at an Exxon station ten miles west of Shreveport. That one I haven't figured out yet."

Gladstone stayed up late that night, trying to figure them all out. For hours, he studied the printout of Marshall's calls, but the significance, if any, was hidden in a code he did not yet know how to decipher. In addition to the abundance of Louisiana calls, however, three others in particular caught his eye—all from the morning of September 6, the last day of Maria Marshall's life.

At 9:46 A.M. Marshall had called Felice's number at Seaview Regional.

At 9:48 A.M. she'd called him back from a different phone. That conversation had lasted ten minutes.

In her interview on Friday, she had not mentioned either of those conversations. And she hadn't called Mancuso that night, either, to say that she'd suddenly remembered them.

The third call in which Gladstone was especially interested had come to Marshall at 9:59 A.M., almost the moment he'd hung up from talking to Felice. In fact, given that Marshall had more than one line in his office and a secretary to answer the phone, he might have still been talking to Felice when the new call came in. Conceivably, it might even have been the

new call that prompted him to end his conversation
with Felice, in order that he might receive it.

This call had been placed from a coin box in Atlantic City. A further check with the phone company
disclosed that the pay phone in question was located at
a motel called the Airport Motor Inn.

Early Tuesday morning, Gladstone called O'Brien into
his office.

"Hey, Danny," he said, "take a ride down to Atlantic City. Go to the Airport Motor Inn. Check their
registrations for the first week in September. In particular, see if just by chance there might have been
somebody from in or near Shreveport, Louisiana,
staying there on the nights of September fifth or sixth."

O'Brien called in just before noon.

"Guess what, Bobby."

"There was."

"That your guess?"

"That's my first guess. If you say no, then my second guess is that there wasn't."

"No second guess needed, pal. We've got an Ernest
Grandshaw, Jockey Club Lane, Shreveport, Louisiana, operating a 1980 Cadillac with Texas plates. He
checked in at seven oh five on the morning of Thursday, September sixth, and checked out the next day. I
should say 'they.' Grandshaw paid the rate for double
occupancy."

By Tuesday afternoon, much of the insurance information had come in.

In addition to two separate $100,000 policies on the
life of Maria Marshall issued by the Provident Mutual
Insurance Company of Philadelphia—Rob's company—
some years earlier, there was enough to cause small

beads of perspiration to break out on Bob Gladstone's brow.

—A $500,000 policy on the life of Maria Marshall issued by the Banner Life Insurance Company of Rockville, Maryland, in September 1983.

—A $500,000 policy on the life of Maria Marshall issued by the Manhattan Life Insurance Company of New York City in February 1984.

—A $100,000 policy on the life of Maria Marshall issued by the Fireman's Fund Company of San Rafael, California, in February 1984.

—A $100,000 policy on the life of Maria Marshall issued by the Minnesota Mutual Life Insurance Company of St. Paul, Minnesota, in April 1984.

That put the total at $1.4 million, not even counting the $100,000 worth of coverage that Rob had rushed into effect on September 6. And $1.2 million of it, Gladstone noted, had been obtained after the affair with Felice had begun.

"Jesus Christ," Gladstone said to himself. "No wonder the poor woman was frightened."

Bob Gladstone was a loving and considerate husband under most any circumstances, but that night when he got home, he went directly to his pretty wife, Amy, an elementary school teacher, and gave her an especially tight hug.

"What's that for?"

"Don't ask," Gladstone said. "You don't want to know."

She smiled at him. "I get it. You're making some progress with the Marshall case."

"Amy," he said. "I sure am happy you're my wife. And you know what? Just to celebrate, let's cancel all the life insurance we've got."

*　　*　　*

On Wednesday, September 12, Gladstone learned from phone company records that eight minutes after Rob Marshall had received the call from the Airport Motor Inn, someone had made a call to that pay phone from a pay phone at a 7-Eleven store located only five minutes from Marshall's office.

"Do you get the feeling," he asked Dan O'Brien, "that we ought to be thinking about heading for Shreveport?"

"I get the feeling," O'Brien said, "that Rob-O ought be to thinking about heading for the Falkland Islands."

"Are you kidding?" Gladstone said. "You've met the man. He's a pillar of the community. Pillars don't run, Dan. They crumble."

On Thursday, Gladstone received a report from the credit department at Harrah's Marina that showed Marshall had made twenty-five visits to the casino between the first of the year and September 6. He could have made others, of course, and he could have frequented other casinos—Gladstone had men in Atlantic City checking that out—but in order to qualify for the "comps" that meant so much to him, Marshall had apparently made a point of letting Harrah's know when he was there and betting actively.

The records showed that he'd played blackjack for ninety-three hours and seven minutes during the course of his twenty-five recorded visits, and that his average bet had been $131. He had a credit limit of $10,000, but owed the casino only $3,000 at the time of Maria's death.

Gladstone tried to figure how much money a person could lose betting $131 a hand through ninety-three hours of blackjack.

Then he studied reports from the credit check his office had made on Rob. A $100,000 home equity loan raised to its $130,000 limit in the spring. A $20,000 loan from the First National Bank of Toms River in April, and, in May, another $15,000 loan from the same bank. A $30,000 loan from the Navy Federal Credit Union. A $12,000 loan from Citibank.

"Jesus Christ," Gladstone said, "he's borrowing more money in a week than I'm earning in a year."

Rob had seemingly hit the limit in midsummer, though, when his application to raise the credit limit on his Visa and MasterCard accounts from $2,500 to $10,000 each had been denied.

Unless, of course, he'd turned to other sources. The sort of sources who don't turn up in credit checks. The Vinny Gigliotti sort of sources, who can get you in more trouble faster than you would have ever believed possible, no matter how much trouble you'd been in before.

Gladstone spent all day Thursday looking at those numbers. And then he thought of how much extra it might cost if you walked out on your wife and kids and set up house with someone else. Especially with someone whose tastes ran to silver and Acapulco, like Felice. And especially if you were playing ten or twelve hours of blackjack a month at $131 a pop.

And then he thought again the thought he'd been thinking most of all—of how much money $1.5 million was, and of how it could dig a man out of the deepest of holes almost overnight.

Unless he obtained it through murder.

By Friday, Gladstone and his men had been through every registration card for every hotel and motel in Atlantic City back through the first week of June, when Marshall's phone calls to Louisiana had started.

They found that the September visit of Mr. Ernest Grandshaw of Jockey Club Lane, Shreveport, Louisiana, had not been his first to the area. Mr. Grandshaw had also been in Atlantic City on June 18, staying on that occasion at the far more luxurious Harrah's Marina, the casino hotel most frequented by Robert Marshall.

"June the eighteenth," McGuire said. "There's something funny about June the eighteenth."

Gladstone looked at him, puzzled.

"Wait a minute," McGuire said. "It's the insurance. We just got word back on two more insurance policies on Maria. There was one for about thirty-three thousand—some exact amount, not a round number—to cover remaining college tuition costs. That was taken through some outfit in Boston sometime in July.

"But the other one—it was a twenty-thousand-dollar term policy on Maria from Bankers Life in Chicago. And the date he applied for it was June the eighteenth."

"The same day Mr. Grandshaw is in Atlantic City," Gladstone said. "So what?"

"I don't know," McGuire said. "Probably nothing. Just a coincidence, I guess."

"File it away, but don't forget it," Gladstone said. "I've got a feeling that before this is over we're going to have to build a new wing on the building just to store the coincidences."

Finally, on Monday, September 17, Gladstone heard from a Shreveport detective named Tucker.

"Stopped by there at the Caddo Hardware, like you wanted," Tucker said. "Me and Shooter. Shooter, he's my partner. Short little fellow but he sure knows how to throw a dart. That's why he's called Shooter, you see. Has nothing to do with firearms. Lot of folks have that misunderstandin'. It's darts, not firearms, why he's called Shooter."

"How about Myers?" Gladstone asked, as patiently as possible.

"Well, I did like you told me. He's just a little squirt, too, this Myers. Hell, he ain't much bigger than Shooter. A real little piss ant. And shakin' like hell, the minute we showed him our badges. I said right off, I said to Shooter, 'This boy's got one a them guilty consciences.' "

Gladstone debated with himself whether screaming would do more harm than good and decided that it probably would. So he practiced slow, deep, rhythmic breaths, of the sort that he'd read in a book were supposed to relax a person, bringing a sense of peace and inner tranquility.

"Pretty nice store they got there. Now Myers, he don't own it. The owner is a fella by the name of, let's see, I got it here—Train. That's T-r-a-i-n. Arthur Train. He wasn't in at the time, he was next door at the barbershop. He owns that, too. This is Arthur Train I'm talkin' about, not Myers. Shit, Myers, I think all he owns is a couple a bowlin' trophies. The man was scared to death. I'm tellin' you—and I said this to Shooter right there in the store—I said, 'I think this boy's fixin' to wet his trousers, Shooter, what do you think?' And Shooter said, 'Hell, yeah. Either that or crap in 'em.' "

"Tucker?"

"Yes, sir?"

Gladstone spoke very softly and slowly. "Did you ask him if he knew either Robert or Maria Marshall?"

"Hell, yes, we asked him that. What do you think we went over there for? He said he met the two of them up there in New Jersey in May. Met 'em at a party. Told me what a lovely woman Mrs. Marshall was. Said he even danced with her at the party a couple of times. Fast dances, not slow ones. Said her husband was right there the whole time, he danced with her, too. So then Shooter, he comes right to the point: he says, 'Myers, were you puttin' it to that lady? You have anythin' goin' with her?' And Lord God, I want to tell you, he just turned red as a sugar beet. Said, 'No, no, no. She wasn't that type at all. She was a *lady*.'

"So I said, 'Well, Myers, she's a dead lady now.' And, you know, here I got to tell you somethin' funny. That boy, he had a very strange reaction. It was like he was surprised but he wasn't surprised, know what I mean?"

"I think so."

"It was like we just broke bad news to him and he was shocked, but it was bad news that he was afraid he was going to hear. So it wasn't really news in a way. Even though it was news. You follow me?"

"I follow you."

"Anyway, once he heard she was dead—murdered, we told him. Shot right in the back with a forty-five, right there in that picnic spot like you told me. Right there on that Garden Gate highway."

"Garden State," Gladstone said.

"What's that?"

"It doesn't matter. Never mind."

"Yeah, well, if he was nervous before, once we told him that lady was murdered, he started shakin' so hard I thought his teeth was gonna crack. Shooter noticed it, too. Spotted it right away. We were remarkin' about it later on. Shooter says, 'Damn, that boy nearly swallowed his tongue.' "

"Did you ask him," Gladstone said wearily, "what he and Marshall talked about?"

"Hell, yes, we sure did. That was why we went over there in the first place. He said IRAs."

"He said what?"

"IRAs. Retirement accounts. He said Marshall was in the financial business and they got talkin' about

IRAs, and Marshall said he had a plan he thought
might be just the right thing for Myers and so they
chatted about it a while and then a couple of days
later, he said, Marshall sent him down some brochures. He had 'em right there in the store, too. He
has a desk behind the front counter there and he
reached right down to the bottom drawer and pulled
'em out. Didn't hesitate but a second. It was like he
was expectin' to be asked, knew right where they were
right away. He had a bunch of 'em. Said Marshall just
kept 'em comin', even though he hadn't bought one
yet. The latest was from a bank up north there, Mas-
sachusetts, I think. Shooter, he recognized it. He said,
'Hell, yeah, that's a damn good one. That's the plan
we have in the police.' Myers, though, by that time,
he was shakin' too hard to care much one way or the
other about IRAs."

"Okay," Gladstone said. "Thanks a lot. This has
been a big help. Just one more thing. Did he happen
to mention whose party this was, where he met Mr.
and Mrs. Marshall?"

"Hell, yeah, you don't think we would have forgot
to ask him that, do you? He said it was a birthday
party. It was in a restaurant in some town, I got it
here, town of Point Pleasant. You know, you folks up
there have some mighty pretty names for your geography. Point Pleasant. Garden Gate."

"Whose party?" Gladstone said. "Did he say whose
birthday party?"

"He sure did. The people were givin' the party for
their son, who was just turnin' twenty-one, and the
father's name, I got it here, was John Riccio. That's
R-i—"

"Never mind," Gladstone said. "I know how to
spell it."

John Riccio lived three blocks from Rob Marshall.

John Riccio was big in sanitation. John Riccio was a cousin of the Quadrozzis and Gigliottis. John Riccio knew Patsy Racine/Ragazzo. Patsy Racine/Ragazzo knew Felice.

On Friday, September 7, as Felice was being questioned and booked as a potential suspect in the murder of Maria Marshall, her good friend Raymond DiOrio, one of the most influential political figures in New Jersey, was attending the U.S. Open Tennis Championships at Flushing Meadows, New York.

At 7:30 A.M. Saturday, September 8, he was back in Toms River, huddled over a Formica breakfast table at a diner on Route 37, agreeing to represent Felice's lover—and his social friend from the country club—Rob Marshall, in the matter of the murder of Marshall's wife.

But even before that meeting, as his $4,750 bill to Marshall for legal services reflects, Ray DiOrio was busily working on the case.

For Friday, September 7, the bill shows "extensive telephone conferences (long distance) concerning the death of Maria Marshall." It does not specify with whom, or about what, DiOrio conferred.

For the same date, the bill also shows "various miscellaneous telephone conversations." Again, neither the subject matter nor the other parties to the conversations are specified, but these talks all occurred before DiOrio's first meeting with Marshall about the case.

For Saturday, September 8, the bill does reflect that in-person discussion.

It also shows that between September 8 and September 16, DiOrio performed a number of other services as Rob Marshall's legal representative. The influential political figure met at least twice with one of his closest aides "regarding factual circumstances" of the murder; he had numerous telephone conferences and at least one office meeting with Marshall; he made a personal visit to the crime scene; he engaged in an unspecified number of "miscellaneous telephone conferences and discussions" with unnamed parties; and, on at least one occasion, according to the bill, he had a telephone conference with the Ocean County prosecutor.

On one level, Ray DiOrio's relationship with the prosecutor was very simple. DiOrio had arranged for his appointment. Now, he was planning to see to it that the prosecutor became a Superior Court judge, which was something that the prosecutor wanted to be.

Ray DiOrio had a number of friends in Toms River, including Felice Rosenberg, who was, in fact, rather a close friend. He also had a number of political enemies. If his enemies became aware that one of his friends was suspected of conspiracy in the most sordid and sensational murder in Ocean County history, it would not redound to his benefit. And if Rob Marshall had, in fact, asked Felice for the name of someone who could help him murder his wife, and if she had given him such a name—as she'd already told the prosecutor's office she did—and if he had then acted upon her suggestion in any way that, however indirectly, had ultimately resulted in the murder of Maria Marshall, Felice could certainly face the possibility of a criminal charge.

If, however, the prosecutor were to determine or decide that Rob's original conversation with Felice was in no way connected with Maria's death, then, of course, there would be no need to charge her—thereby sparing her, and her family, and her friends, much embarrassment.

Within the ten-day period, from September 7 to September 16, that Ray DiOrio was active as Rob Marshall's attorney, Felice retained new counsel for herself. The new lawyer's name was Anthony Trammel and he, like many other people in New Jersey, was well acquainted with Ray DiOrio.

And during the same period that DiOrio was in contact with the prosecutor's office regarding the case, so was Anthony Trammel, notifying detectives that he was now representing Mrs. Rosenberg and that if she were needed for any further questioning, arrangements should be made through him.

And at or about the same time, the prosecutor apparently made the determination that there would be no need to question Patsy Racine/Ragazzo. At least, no one from the Ocean County prosecutor's office ever did.

And shortly after September 16, Ray DiOrio made the determination that it might be in Rob Marshall's best interests to find himself another attorney. Criminal defense work, after all, was not really the influential political figure's specialty.

14

"GENTLEMEN," Gladstone said to O'Brien and Mancuso on Tuesday, September 18, "we're going to Shreveport."

There were no direct flights, so they flew from Newark to Dallas at 5:25 that afternoon and then drove from Dallas to Shreveport. It had looked close on the map but it was 238 miles and they did not check in to their rooms at the Holiday Inn until two o'clock Wednesday morning.

They spent much of the day at Shreveport police headquarters, explaining the nature of their business. Then, in late afternoon, the three of them drove to Caddo Hardware on North Market Street. Andrew Myers, small and gray and, yes, with something vaguely lizardlike about him, was right there at the front counter, looking eager to please.

They showed him their badges immediately.

"We'd like to talk to you," Gladstone said pleasantly.

"Fine, fine," Myers said. "How about in the back there?"

"How about downtown," O'Brien said. It did not sound like a question.

"Downtown?"

"Downtown," O'Brien said. "Police headquarters.

We're not here to talk about Phillips screwdrivers, Myers, we're here to talk about a murder."

They went downtown. They went into a long, narrow, featureless detective's conference room and took seats around a well-worn table. O'Brien reached inside a manila envelope and removed a photograph and slid it across the table to Andrew Myers.

"You know these people?" he said.

"Sure," Myers said. "That's Mr. and Mrs. Marshall."

"You see Mrs. Marshall?" O'Brien asked, pointing.

"Yes, I sure do, that's her right there. A lovely lady."

"You know she's dead?"

"Well, now, yes, as a matter of fact I did just happen to hear about that."

"From who?" O'Brien said.

"Well, those detectives mentioned it to me last week. Those two gentlemen from the Shreveport police here. But, in fact, I'd already known about it. It was Mrs. Riccio who told me. Carol Riccio, up there in Toms River. As I told the gentlemen from the Shreveport police, it was at her birthday party for her son that I first made the acquaintance of Mr. Marshall and Mrs. Marshall. And just last week I happened to call her and she informed me at that time of the very sad news."

"You called her last week?" O'Brien asked.

"That's right."

"What for?"

"Why, to wish her a happy birthday."

"When's her birthday?" O'Brien asked.

"Well, see, now that's the funny thing. I really do think I happened to call a few days early, or else it might have been a day or two late. Her birthday, you see—well, I know it's sometime right around this time of the month. We're old friends, Mrs. Riccio and I.

We used to sell vegetables together back in Perth Amboy when we were children. Her family, the Capodilupas, they had a fresh-produce stand, and my own folks—"

"Myers!" O'Brien said.

"Yes, sir?"

"You call to wish her a happy birthday every year?"

"Well, sir, it's one of those things that's always on my mind to do, but I can't swear to you right now that every single year I get around to where I actually do it. Sometimes you get so caught up in your own business you overlook these little niceties."

"Myers?" O'Brien said.

"Yes sir?"

"You know a guy named Ernie Grandshaw?"

"No, sir. No, I don't."

"How about this address—Jockey Club Lane. You know where that is?"

"No, sir, I sure don't. Would that be in Shreveport?"

"Myers, what did you and Marshall talk about that night you met him?"

"As I said to the gentlemen from Shreveport, it was mostly IRA accounts."

"Anything else?"

Myers appeared to take a minute to try to recall. "No, I think that was it. IRAs."

"Listen, Mr. Myers," Gladstone said. "If you don't mind, we're just going to take your picture and then you can be on your way. We appreciate your coming down here with us on such short notice as this."

"Oh, I'm happy to oblige, officer. Happy to oblige."

"You haven't heard from Mr. Marshall recently, have you? Like since his wife died?" Gladstone asked.

"No, no, sir. Not a word."

"Listen, Myers," O'Brien said. "You being such a

thoughtful guy and everything—maybe you'd want to send him a sympathy card."

"Why, yes," Myers said. "That's a very nice idea. I think I might do that."

"Yeah," O'Brien said. "Try not to forget. I'm sure it would mean a lot to him. I understand he's pretty broken up."

Bob Gladstone felt like a man who was trying to do a jigsaw puzzle blindfolded. The pieces were there, he could feel them, could feel their shape. He could run his fingers along the edges and could turn them over slowly in his hands. But he still didn't have the slightest idea of how to fit them together. Or of what picture would emerge when he did.

"You know," O'Brien said, "Myers—he must be pretty tight with the Riccios. We've just found out what a bitch it is to travel between New Jersey and Shreveport, and that guy flies up there just to hit a birthday party for their son."

"Well, you can tell just by looking at him," Mancuso said, "what a real party animal he is."

"Dancing up a storm with Mrs. Marshall," Gladstone said.

"Only fast dances," Mancuso said.

"Yeah, the slow ones she danced with her loving husband," O'Brien said.

"When he wasn't too busy selling Myers IRAs," Gladstone said.

"That guy must really be a super-salesman," Mancuso said. "Pitches an IRA account to a hardware clerk from Louisiana at a party and then follows it up with half a dozen brochures and thirty-one phone calls just to get the guy's annual contribution of what, two thousand, twenty-five hundred, what's the limit?"

"Two thousand," Gladstone said.

"So his commission," Mancuso said, "is what? Fifty bucks?"

"Shit, he spent more than that on the phone calls," O'Brien said.

"Hey, I got an idea," Gladstone said.

The other two detectives looked at him.

"Let's go bowling."

So they did, across the river in Bossier City, but they didn't run into Andrew Myers.

On their way, however, they stopped by the home of Ernest Grandshaw of Jockey Club Lane, who made it clear from the outset that he was not pleased to see them. He was a tall, thin, darkhaired man who had a loud voice that he was not reluctant to raise. It seemed apparent to Gladstone that the New Jersey contingent was not the first group of law enforcement officers he'd ever encountered.

They showed him the picture of Rob and Maria and he told them he'd never seen either one of those people in his life.

Then they told him they wanted to talk to him about the murder of Maria and about his two brief visits to Atlantic City that summer, one of which coincided with the night she was killed, at a site only twenty-five miles from the motel at which he'd stayed.

He told them he didn't know a goddamned thing about any murder and he'd never been in Atlantic City or anywhere else in the goddamned state of New Jersey in his life and he wasn't going to say one more goddamned word to them without first talking to a lawyer. Then he told them they could get the hell off his front steps and they could move their goddamned car out of his driveway.

The next day, Thursday, September 20, Bob Gladstone went to the barbershop next door to Caddo

Hardware and got a haircut. "Just trying to soak up local atmosphere," he explained.

Then he went before a Caddo Parish judge and obtained a search warrant that would permit the three detectives to return to the home of Ernest Grandshaw of Jockey Club Lane and pay him a more serious visit.

"Tell me again," O'Brien said, "what are we looking for? I mean, besides his Dale Carnegie videotapes."

"More pieces, Dan," Gladstone said. "Just to make blindfolded jigsaw more challenging. It could be anything. It could be the forty-five used to shoot Maria. He was in Atlantic City the night she got killed, and except for Rob-O himself, there's nobody else we've turned up who we can say that about. And somebody using the pay phone at the motel he stayed at called Marshall early that morning. And eight minutes later got a call back from the 7-Eleven just down the street from Marshall's office. And yesterday he tells us that he's never been to New Jersey in his life. I think that justifies a little authorized snooping around."

As it happened, Gladstone was proven correct. Later that day, in a desk drawer in Grandshaw's house, Mancuso found a receipt for a Western Union money order sent to Grandshaw from Toms River on June 25 by a James McAlister of Philadelphia.

In another drawer, Gladstone found a piece of paper torn from a Caddo Hardware memo pad. On it was written the name James McAlister, with a Philadelphia address, and the notation that McAlister would be sending a three-thousand-dollar money order to Ernie Grandshaw.

"You know anything about these?" Gladstone asked.

"Not a damn thing," Grandshaw said.

"That your handwriting?"

"It sure ain't. And I ain't gonna answer no more questions without a lawyer."

Grandshaw's wife had been standing by, watching all this, and growing ever more agitated. Now, she erupted.

"Goddamn, you, Ernie Grandshaw, what in the hell are you into now?"

"Be quiet," he told her.

"The hell I'll be quiet, while you go dragging our name down into the gutter where all those friends of yours belong!" Then she turned to Gladstone. "You step outside here with me," she said. "I want to talk to you alone."

"Goddamnit, woman, don't you go talkin' to that cop!" Grandshaw shouted.

"If I left it to you you'd have both of us arrested before midnight. This is a *murder* these men are down here about, Ernie, and there are a few things I think they'd better know. Before they take you home with 'em in handcuffs."

Grandshaw's wife took Gladstone into the kitchen and, speaking in a much softer voice, explained that her husband had been in trouble with the law on prior occasions, but had never been involved with murder. If it was murder they were investigating, she felt they would do better to focus on a friend of her husband's named Ferlin L'Heureux. L'Heureux, she said, was a former policeman and "the kind of person who would do a murder."

She also said that following their visit the night before, her husband had left the house to meet with L'Heureux but upon his return had refused to say what they'd talked about, though she was sure what it had amounted to was L'Heureux threatening to hurt him or kill him if he said anything to the police.

The three detectives left the Grandshaw house. They went back to downtown Shreveport and obtained a subpoena for all Western Union records pertaining to money orders sent from Toms River, New Jersey, to Ernest Grandshaw of Shreveport.

They also asked local detectives what was known about a Ferlin L'Heureux. And that turned out to be a question with many answers.

The L'Heureuxs were a family well known in Shreveport. Ferlin's father had "been in real estate," which is one of the expressions people in Shreveport used to describe a wide range of activities, most of which were probably even legal.

Ferlin himself had been involved in a wide range of activities, some of which unquestionably were legal. For twelve years—to take just one example—he'd been a deputy sheriff in Caddo Parish. His law enforcement career had come to an end in 1978, after he'd been sent out to investigate a traffic accident involving an overturned tractor trailer that had been carrying a full load of plywood.

In northern Louisiana, it was explained to Gladstone, a load of plywood—like a brand-new Cadillac—is one of those things a man would do just about anything to have. Never mind that he didn't need it— plywood had cachet. The possessor of a full load of brand-new plywood was, de facto, a man of substance and accomplishment, a man with whom to be reckoned.

It was in such terms that Ferlin had thought of himself anyway—the plywood would simply confirm it. Therefore, in the course of investigating the accident, Ferlin acquired the plywood. Eventually, this led to his rather abrupt resignation from the department and the end of his formal career in law enforcement.

Ferlin, twice married and the father of six, went "into real estate," as his father had done. He also went into car sales. He would buy a car in Texas and sell it in Alabama. And vice versa. Or he would buy a car in the morning and sell it in the afternoon. Or sometimes sell it in the morning and not get around to buying it until the afternoon. All of this was very informal—especially as regards the original ownership of the vehicles involved—but at no time did it lead to Ferlin's arrest.

He also dabbled for a time in the field of private investigation. The story they loved to tell in Shreveport was of the time he was hired by the wife of an airline executive who suspected (correctly) that her husband was having an affair with his secretary. The executive suspected (also correctly) that the wife was using an investigator to try to compile evidence that would be useful in a divorce suit, so what he did was, he drove his customized van with the dark-tinted windows into the middle of a big open field and stayed inside with the secretary. He had the tape deck, the champagne bucket, the waterbed mattress, everything he needed, in the back of the van.

Except a toilet. The secretary had to leave the van in order to pee. It was Ferlin's notion to photograph her in the act, making sure to get the van in the same frame. The problem was that the field in which the man parked was so big and so empty that you would have to take the picture from the edge of the highway, and Ferlin did not own a telephoto lens powerful enough to produce a useful picture from that distance.

His solution, which they loved to tell about in Shreveport, was to drag a cardboard washing-machine box into the middle of the field and climb inside and hunker down, cutting a small hole in the side for the camera lens. When the executive parked his van, Ferlin figured, he could just waddle forward until he was close enough to take the picture when the secretary got out of the van to pee.

Seeing that Ferlin was six one and 250 pounds, it was no easy waddle. Especially when the thought occurred to Ferlin (as it did) that the executive might decide to start blasting away at the box with the .357 Magnum that Ferlin knew he kept inside the van. Which he would do, Ferlin was convinced, if he had the slightest suspicion that it was anything other than a gentle Louisiana zephyr that had caused the washing-machine box to wind up fifty yards closer to the van than it had been when the executive had first parked it.

"Target practice," was all the man would have to say if anyone ever asked. What could be more innocent, especially in northwestern Louisiana, than an airline executive engaging in a bit of target practice to impress the secretary he'd brought with him to share a picnic lunch on a lovely spring day? No reason in the world for him to have suspected that a former Caddo Parish deputy sheriff had been squatting inside trying to focus a 35-millimeter camera.

Not that anyone would ever ask. Ferlin, all 250 sweaty pounds of him (it would be less if you figured in the blood loss) could lie inside that box for weeks—riddled with bullets—and nobody but the carrion birds would even know it.

Eventually, his overwrought imagination became too much for Ferlin and he burst forth from the carton, threw his camera in the air, and, with his empty hands raised above his head, sprinted for the highway at top speed, shouting, "Don't shoot! Don't shoot! I resign!"

At least that's the way they liked to tell the story down in Shreveport. But they told plenty of others about Ferlin, too, and not all were in quite such a humorous vein.

Ferlin liked to race stock cars. For a time, he'd even owned his own little racetrack in east Texas, but he'd

drive anywhere in the South there was a race: Mont-
gomery, Biloxi, Nashville, anywhere.

Often, there would be a bank or two in the towns in
which Ferlin drove. And often, friends of his would
have an interest in the banks. Not a proprietary interest, as in, say, the case of a stockholder, and not a
managerial interest, either. This was more an interest
in what was inside the banks—i.e., money—and an
interest in seeing it removed.

Ferlin, it was explained to Gladstone, was involved
with a gang of bank robbers who had made successful
scores all across the South. He wasn't a hard-core
member of the gang. He was more out on the fringe,
sometimes included, sometimes not, and never en-
trusted with any task more central to the enterprise
than the driving of the getaway car.

This was where his informal career in law enforcement entered the picture. For, Gladstone was led to
believe, Ferlin had a little something going on the
side. A little something with the federal authorities,
whereby he kept them advised, from time to time, as
to the gang's plans for the future. Not to mention its
membership.

Some might describe this as trying to have your cake
and eat it, too. Others might see it as suggestive of a
death wish. In either case, it meant that Ferlin
L'Heureux led a complicated life, and that, in the
opinion of the Shreveport police, it was entirely possible (though they couldn't quite imagine how) that he
could have gotten ensnarled in a plot to murder a New
Jersey woman for insurance money. Especially if the
payoff was big enough.

"A million five?" Gladstone said.

"Big enough," said the Shreveport detective to whom
he was speaking. But then he added a cautionary note.

"Ferlin's a no-good bastard," the detective said, "but he probably wouldn't have the heart to kill a woman."

On Friday, September 21, McGuire called Gladstone in Shreveport with the results of his Western Union inquiry. Ernie Grandshaw had received not one but two money orders from Toms River in June. The second, for three thousand dollars, had been the one for which they'd already found the receipt in Grandshaw's house. The name listed as sender on that one was James McAlister, as the memo written on the Caddo Hardware pad had indicated.

But there had also been a twenty-five-hundred-dollar money order, transmitted June 13, from Toms River to Ernie Grandshaw of Shreveport. The sender's name on that first money order was Robert O. Marshall.

The handwriting on the two money orders, McGuire said, appeared to be identical. It appeared to be the handwriting of Robert O. Marshall.

"You know, Al," Gladstone said, "here's what I think you'd better do. I think you'd better swing by eight eight four Crest Ridge Drive this afternoon and put a couple of questions to Mr. Marshall. We know he knows Myers, that's not the point. But Myers isn't the guy he sent money to. He sent money to Grandshaw. And five days after he sends the first installment, Grandshaw turns up at Harrah's Marina. The next time Grandshaw turns up, Maria Marshall turns up dead.

"So ask Rob-O if the name Ernie Grandshaw means anything to him. And watch his face closely when he answers. Then try out one other name. Ask him if he knows anyone named Ferlin L'Heureux."

"And you know what else, Al? Long as you're in the neighborhood, stop by the Riccios' house. Have a little talk with them, if you can. Ask them what's the story with Andrew Myers. I'd like to know a little more about that friendship."

When he hung up, he turned to O'Brien and Mancuso. "Gentlemen, what's your pleasure? A haircut, perhaps? Or would you rather we had another go at tenpins?"

"I saw a poster back at the hardware store," O'Brien said. "Advertising a crocodile barbecue. I think it's tonight at the Legion hall."

"That sounds good, Dan," Gladstone said. "I know Mancuso here hasn't had a good piece of crocodile since we left Newark."

"That's not all I haven't had," Mancuso said.

"You want to go back to Caddo Hardware and check the details?" O'Brien said.

"No," Gladstone said. "I don't think so. I'd rather arrange for our own crocodile barbecue. Dan, why don't you call the store and see if you can't persuade Mr. Myers to come downtown here this evening and be the crocodile. I think a few of the pieces are starting to fit."

O'Brien made the call at 5 P.M. "Yeah, he said he'd be down," O'Brien reported. "He just wanted to call his wife and say he'd be a little late for supper."

"Like maybe thirty years late," Mancuso said.

"Thirty years?" Gladstone asked.

"Yeah. That's the minimum sentence before parole eligibility following a conviction for conspiracy to murder in a case involving the use of firearms."

"But all Myers did was dance with the broad," O'Brien said.

"Yeah," Mancuso said, "but what did he do with her husband?"

15

THIS time, they read Myers his rights.

Through the money orders and Atlantic City motel registrations they had linked Myers to Marshall. The link in itself was not necessarily suggestive of criminal activity, but at least they had established a connection.

Through the meeting at the Riccio party and the dozens of phone calls that followed, they had linked Myers to Marshall. Again, there was no evidence of wrongdoing, but the three detectives did not believe for a minute that Marshall's repeated calls to Myers at both work and home had been intended solely or primarily (or at all) to sell him a plan for his Individual Retirement Account.

The problem now was to link Myers with Grandshaw somehow. And then, once the links were in place, to see where they led. All three detectives strongly suspected that they would lead to the Oyster Creek picnic area on the Garden State Parkway and to the body of Maria Marshall, facedown on the front seat of her husband's ivory Cadillac with two closely spaced bullet holes in her back.

"Andy," Gladstone was saying, "I'd like you to tell us a little more about this telephone conversation you had with Mrs. Riccio. The one where she told you that Mrs. Marshall had been killed."

"Right. Well, like I said, I called her and when she answered, I said, 'Happy Birthday. I know it's early.' You see, the more I think, I think her birthday is actually the eighteenth. But I knew I was calling either early or late. Anyway, I talked to John, too, and I said, 'What's going on?' And Carol, Mrs. Riccio, she told me that her son, the one from the birthday party, was engaged to get married. And I asked when the wedding was going to be and she said June of next year, June '85, and I said, 'Are you going to send us an invitation?' And she said, 'Sure, we will.' And I said, 'Thank you.' And then she said John's cousin passed away, and I said, 'John's cousin?' And she gave me a name, and I said, 'I don't think I know him.' And she said, 'No, I only think you met him once.' "

"Golf clubs," O'Brien said. "He passed away due to golf clubs."

"Excuse me?" Myers said.

"Never mind," O'Brien said. "Keep talking."

"All right. And then she says, I believe she just said, 'Maria got killed.' And I said, 'Who?' 'Maria Marshall, the one you danced with.' And I says, 'What happened? What are you talking about?' And she said that she was—they were coming back from Atlantic City and he got hit over the head and she was shot. And I said, 'Oh, my God.' And then we talked generally about everything else. And that was it."

"You known her a long time, Andy?" Gladstone asked. "Mrs. Riccio?"

"I knew her when we were twelve, thirteen, fourteen years old up in Perth Amboy and she was a Capodilupa at the time."

"And you stayed in pretty close touch over the years?"

"Yeah, we just continued—my ex-girlfriend, more or less, at one time. And we just continued the friendship. My wife and I, and my daughter, we went up there a few years ago, visited them at their house. And I met them in New Orleans about a year ago. They were down there for some kind of convention, and I had a bowling tournament and we happened to hook up for a while."

"So how'd you happen to go up to the party?" Gladstone asked.

"You see," Myers said, "my daughter was in some advanced classes and from January on my wife and her were staying up to the wee hours of the morning and she was helping her. And, more or less, I felt left out in the cold, neglected, depressed. I tried to communicate and I wasn't getting anywhere because she was looking at it from my daughter's point of view instead of looking at it from my point of view. So instead of having a big family fight, when the invitation came in the mail, I just told her I was going somewhere and I went the other way.

"You see, since I was going up there by myself, my wife would say, 'Why are you going? Why don't you just stay home?' And I would have tried to explain to her my feelings of what was going on. And my wife is a very sentimental person. She cries very easily. And I can't stand it for her to cry.

"So I told a little white lie. I told her my knee was bothering me. I told her I was going to have it looked at. In a hospital. In San Antonio."

"How far's San Antonio, Andy?" Gladstone asked.

"Three hundred, maybe three hundred fifty miles."

"There's no hospitals in Shreveport?"

"Yes, there is."

"Your knee," O'Brien said. "Up until that time had

you complained to your wife about any problems with
your knee?"

"Now and then," Myers said, "but not every day."

"But that wouldn't cause a fight? If you told her you
were going to a hospital in San Antonio?"

"No."

"But it would cause a fight if you told her you were
going to New Jersey?"

"Yes, if I told her why I was going up there, to go
to the party. So I just told her I was going to San
Antonio and then I went the other way."

"How long were you up there?" Gladstone asked.

"Three days."

"Where'd you stay?" O'Brien asked.

"My stepbrother, Bill Henderson, he has a place in
Perth Amboy. I stayed with him."

"What'd you do?" Gladstone asked.

"Oh, this and that. Took Bill's daughter—she goes
to a Catholic or private school—we would take her to
school, we would stay around the house, b.s. a little
bit. In the evening, his wife's relatives came over and
we played nickel-dime poker."

Yes, Mancuso thought to himself, *a real party animal.*

"About the party, Andy," O'Brien said. "How'd
you get there?"

"Rent-a-car."

"What time did you arrive?" Gladstone said.

"Approximately six o'clock. I was early, so I sat at
the bar. I had, I guess, two drinks, and then the guests
started showing up."

"You didn't join them?" O'Brien asked. "All these
Riccios and Capodilupas and all these old friends from
Perth Amboy who you'd just flown fifteen hundred
miles up to see?"

"Well, no, see, it got sort of crowded all at once
there, and then Mr. and Mrs. Marshall showed up and

all the tables had been taken and they was just standing there at the bar and he was having difficulty getting attention, and since the bar lady knew what I was
drinking I waved at her and she came over, and I said,
'These people would like to have an order.'

"And then we just started general conversation,
because he was thankful that I got him a drink."

"What'd you talk about?" Gladstone asked.

"We talked about everything. We talked about me
being in the service, how I knew the Riccios, what
kind of business I was in. I told him I was a retired Air
Force and he told me that he was in the Navy. We
discussed IRAs. I told him I was interested in IRAs,
and I told him my reason which was, we—my wife and
I—we had CDs, see, and the money is there and I
pull it out too quick and I have to pay a penalty on it.
And since I did have relatives, family, in New Jersey,
I thought that if I can get something out of the state of
Louisiana it would be harder for me to get the money
back because I would have to write."

"Go on." Gladstone nodded as if he were interested.

"See," Myers said, "I think we had two five-thousand-
dollar CDs, if I'm not mistaken, in Commercial National Bank in Shreveport, and I told him that every
time we put money away, either in the savings account
or into a CD, I draw them out early and we pay a
penalty. And I wanted something that was not within
state. That if I needed the money I would have to send
a letter. And by the time I did all that and the letter
come back I wouldn't need the money."

"But every once in a while," O'Brien said, "you'd
take a break from these financial discussions in order
to dance, is that right?"

"I just danced with her one time," Myers said.
"Fast dance. Every slow dance they would dance together. And when they were sitting, she would rest

her elbow on his leg. I thought they were very much in love."

It was at this point that Bob Gladstone opened the folder that contained the memo about the Western Union money order. The memo on Caddo Hardware stationery.

"Ever seen this before?" Gladstone asked.

Myers's Adam's apple seemed to bob quickly up and down. Then he nodded. "Yes. I wrote that. That was a message I took for Ferlin."

Now it was Gladstone's pulse that quickened.

"Who's Ferlin?" Gladstone asked.

"Oh, he's just a fella stops by the store sometimes. Kind of a wheeler-dealer, that type of guy."

"I don't understand, Andy. This note that you wrote says that James McAlister of Philadelphia is going to send a three-thousand-dollar Western Union money order to Ernest Grandshaw here in Shreveport. If I remember correctly, you told us on Wednesday that you don't know anyone named Ernest Grandshaw."

"That's correct. Ernest Grandshaw is just a name that Ferlin was using."

"Ferlin who?" Gladstone said.

"I don't know his last name. He's a big fella, like I say, a wheeler-dealer type, but Ferlin is all I've ever known him by."

"How about McAlister?" O'Brien said. "You know him?"

"Well, now, you see, that's another thing. McAlister isn't real, either. That was the name Mr. Marshall told me he had used."

"Mr. Marshall?" Gladstone said.

They could all see that Myers was beginning to perspire. "Listen, I haven't done anything wrong," he said.

"Nobody's talking about wrong, Andy," Gladstone

said. "Just help us clear up this confusion. Then you can go home to your wife and a nice hot supper."

Myers was beginning to tremble as well as perspire.

"You see, nobody really asked me this before, but, you know, Mr. Marshall called me a couple of times after the party, to see if I'd received the information he'd sent me about the IRAs. And I said, 'Yes, sir, but I haven't looked at it.' And, ah, one of those times—you know, he might even have mentioned this at the party, now that I think about it—he wanted to know if I knew any investigators."

"Investigators?" Gladstone said quietly.

"Yes."

"He say what kind of investigator?" Gladstone asked.

"No, no. Not at all. He just wondered if maybe there was somebody I could recommend, but I told him no, I didn't know anybody in that line of work."

"Did he say he wanted an investigator?" Gladstone asked.

"No, he didn't. But that same day I think it was, just after Mr. Marshall had called me, this fellow Ferlin drove up and he drove up in a pretty nice-looking car. I'd seen him as a customer before because he was buying supplies, and I said, 'What type of work do you do?' And he says, 'Well, I'm more or less a wheeler-dealer.' And I said, 'What is a wheeler-dealer?' And he said, 'I just bought this vehicle. I'm going to sell it and make a couple grand, and then I'm going to buy another. And if somebody wants to buy a piece of property, I act as the intermediary. And I get a commission.'

"So then I asked him, 'Do you know anybody who does investigations?' And he asked me what type. I said, 'I don't know. There is a gentleman up north who wants an investigator.' And he says, 'Well, I do investigations.' So I said, 'Okay.' And I called Mr.

Marshall and said, 'I think I found an investigator for
you and he'll be here at five thirty this afternoon if
you want to call and talk to him.' "

"Did he call?" Gladstone asked.

"Yes, it was about quarter to six, and he apologized
for calling so late. He wanted to know if the gentleman was still there. And I said, 'Yes, just a minute.'
And I said, 'Ferlin,' and he said, 'I'll take it on the
phone in the back.' "

"How long did they talk?" Gladstone asked.

"Twenty, maybe twenty-five minutes," Myers said.

"You hear any of the conversation?"

"No, no, I wouldn't listen. The only thing I couldn't
help hearing was that Ferlin gave Mr. Marshall his
name as 'Ernie Grandshaw, from Mississippi.' And
that made me curious, so after he hung up and we
started to walk out, I asked him, 'What's Ernie Grandshaw—or who's Ernie Grandshaw in Mississippi?' And
he says, 'I never give my real name to a client until I
know who I'm dealing with. I don't know who this
person is. And since I don't know him, I gave him that
name.' And that was it. I walked out with him, locked
up the store and went home."

"Listen, Myers," O'Brien said. "We've got the phone
company records. We know you and Marshall talked
on the telephone thirty-one times between June fourth
and the night Maria Marshall was murdered."

"I didn't have anything to do with it," Myers said
loudly. "I didn't even know about it until after it
happened." Under the table, his legs were shaking up
and down so hard that all three detectives could feel
the vibrations.

"You're telling me," O'Brien said, leaning in fast,
"that every time Marshall called you or you called him
all you talked about were IRAs?"

"No," Myers said. "I never said that."

"The hell you didn't," O'Brien said. "What did you tell those two Shreveport detectives last week?"

"I answered their questions," Myers said. "There were just certain questions they didn't ask."

"Like what?" Gladstone said quietly.

"Listen, I swear to God, I didn't know anything was supposed to happen to that woman. She was a beautiful lady. You'd have to be crazy to want to hurt somebody like her."

"Or greedy," O'Brien said.

"Or desperate," Gladstone said.

Myers looked as if he were about to start to cry. "If anybody had asked me I would have told them. I don't have anything to hide. Mr. Marshall and Ferlin used me to pass messages back and forth. Ferlin didn't want Mr. Marshall to have his real phone number, or even to know who he was, so every time Mr. Marshall wanted to get in touch with him, he had to do it through me. But it was only for an investigation. That's all that was going on, I swear it. At least, that's all I knew about."

"Just sit tight, Andy. You want a cup of coffee?" Gladstone said. "I'm going out to get a few pictures."

"I don't want to see her dead!" Myers called. "I didn't have anything to do with it and I don't want to see that lady dead!"

"Relax, Andy," Gladstone said. "These are just some ID photos to see if you can help us pick out your buddy Ferlin. You take anything in your coffee or you want it black?"

But Myers now had his head in his hands and was starting to sob.

He picked out Ferlin. Among eight photographs he was shown of white males in the Shreveport area, he pointed instantly and unerringly to the picture of Ferlin L'Heureux.

"So what were you, Andy, a messenger boy?" Gladstone said softly.

Myers nodded. "If Ferlin said he was going up to New Jersey, I'd call Mr. Marshall and tell him when. Or if Mr. Marshall called down here trying to reach Ferlin—which happened a lot more often—I'd pass the message along. It got so, in July, that Mr. Marshall was really bugging me. Finally, I told Ferlin he had to give me a phone number where Mr. Marshall could reach him directly. And he did, he did. He wouldn't give me his home number, but he gave me a number he said he'd be at at specified times. It was a pay phone at some gas station near his house."

"Andy, did you call up there on September fifth?" Gladstone asked.

"I don't know, I don't know. I might have."

"What did you say, Andy, that time?"

"I don't know, I don't know!" Myers cried.

"Did you say Ferlin was coming back up?"

"Ernie Grandshaw." Myers sobbed. "Ernie Grandshaw. That's the only name Ferlin ever wanted me to use."

"And he did come back up!" O'Brien shouted suddenly. "And the next night that lady was murdered!"

"I swear, I swear, I didn't know anything about it," Myers said. "All I was ever told was that it was an investigation. I didn't even know what the investigation was about."

"Hey, Andy," Gladstone said. "It's ten o'clock. Maybe you want to call home. Tell your wife you're going to be a little later."

When he reentered the room ten minutes later, Myers suffered a sudden panic attack. He fell to the floor and started to shake. Gladstone dumped out the coffee from Myers's cup and called down the hall for a shot of something—brandy, vodka, anything—to replace it. Vodka was what the Shreveport police supplied. Gladstone measured a careful ounce into the cup and handed it to Myers, who was still on the floor but sitting up now, and crying, literally crying, that he wanted to go home.

"You can go home, Andy," Gladstone said. "All you have to do is tell us the truth."

"I have told you the truth," Myers moaned.

"The whole truth, Andy. The whole truth and nothing but the truth."

"I want a lawyer," Myers said. "Why didn't you give me a chance to get a lawyer?"

"Andy, we read you your rights," Gladstone said. "We read them slowly and carefully and we informed you that you could consult an attorney of your choice at any time."

"Yeah," Myers said, "but the only lawyer's card I've got in my pocket is the one that Ferlin gave me this morning. And he's Ferlin's lawyer, not mine."

When they propped him up again, Myers told them about the earlier portion of his day.

At 8:30 that morning, he had been standing behind the counter at Caddo Hardware, coffee in hand, just opening up for the day, when he heard a horn honking out front. He went to the door to see what was happening. Ferlin was what was happening. Honking, and now waving for Myers to come to the car.

"It was sprinkling," Myers said. "I ran out to the car—he was driving a Jeep was what it was. I had the cup of coffee in my hand, and he waved to me and told me to get in. And I said, 'What's the problem?' Normally we talk—if you want to say something to me—we talk right there.

"He said, 'Please. The police may be listening.' And I said, 'What are you talking about?' We went riding around and he says, 'The police went over to Ernie

Grandshaw's house and they got the money order receipts.' And I said to him, *'There is an Ernie Grandshaw?'* And he said, 'Yeah.' And I said, 'God, what have I got involved in? The police here are questioning me and I don't know what's going on and I have a lot to lose and I don't know nothing.'

"And then Ferlin says, 'They're tryin' to make a mountain out of a mole hill.' He says, 'Be cool. Don't say nothin'. You know you got a lot to lose. Just don't say nothin'. Don't talk.' And I said, 'Please, take me back to the office,' which he did. He took me back to the office. And I was shaking.

"Then he called me from his lawyer's office. He told me he was down there talking to his attorney and his attorney says for me not to say anything, to get a lawyer and just keep quiet. And I didn't have a lawyer, and he says, 'Well, write this man's name down, and he gave me the name and number of his lawyer. But I didn't even want to be on the phone with Ferlin anymore. I just wanted him to leave me alone. I told him I had to get back to work. 'Just leave me alone and let me get back to work,' I said, and I was still shaking."

"Not as much as you're shaking now," O'Brien said. "What I want to know is, when was the first time you saw Ferlin *after* Maria Marshall was murdered?"

"Oh, Lord," Myers said, "Oh, Lord. Don't make me remember that." But they did.

He'd been in the store late on the afternoon of Monday, September 10, when Ferlin L'Heureux—all smiles —had driven up in his big white Cadillac, this time with his wife along.

"Hi, Andy," he'd said, grinning, "how are you-all doing this fine day?" Then he'd introduced Myers to his wife.

"I'm kind of thirsty, Andy," he'd said, walking toward a case where soft drinks were kept. "I find myself kind of thirsty today. Maybe I'll just take two of these Co'-Colas here, one for me and one for my wife."

"That's fine, Ferlin. You just help yourself."

"Yup, I'm feelin' good, Andy, my man. Your friend up there in New Jersey, Mr. Marshall, he ought to be feelin' good, too." He grinned broadly. "Andy," he said, "I have completed my investigation."

"Well, that's fine, Ferlin. That's just fine. I'm sure that'll be a great relief to Mr. Marshall. He did seem to be getting kind of harried toward the end there."

"Yes, sir. Well, it's all taken care of for him now. Say, Andy, I was wonderin' if you could do me a favor. I'd sure like to get a newspaper from up north."

"Newspaper? What do you want a newspaper for?"

"Well, I'll tell you. Drivin' back down from New Jersey I heard on the radio there that there was some sort of robbery and a shootin' on one of their parkways. Some man got hit over the head. Some lady got killed. And they broadcast it like it was somebody very important was involved. You got some kind of relative up there, don't you?"

"Yes, sir, I sure do. My stepbrother Bill Henderson up in Perth Amboy."

"Well, would you do that favor for me, Andy? Would you give him a call, say tonight or tomorrow, and ask if he could send you down a paper? I'd sure like to read more about this thing."

"Sure thing, Ferlin. I'll give him a call."

"Did you call him?" O'Brien asked.

"I did. The next day. We talked about family, about how everybody was doing, and I asked him could he send me a *Daily News,* because I knew he got the *Daily News.*"

"Why'd he get the *Daily News?*" O'Brien asked. "He do the Jumble words?"

"He is a sportsman," Myers said. "And he also plays the horses. And I said, 'If you can get me one for Saturday or Sunday I would appreciate it. And he said he would see what he could do. But he never did locate the paper. And when Ferlin came back in a few days later, and I told him I had some good friends in Toms River, he said maybe I should call them, and I did. And Ferlin was standing by me the whole time, wanting to know what they'd say."

"Happy Birthday," O'Brien said.

"That's what *I* said," Myers said.

"Right," Gladstone said. "A few days early. Or late. Or whenever. Listen, Andy, I'm getting tired of your bullshit. I want the truth. You knew all summer long, you knew right from the start, that what they were planning was the murder of Maria Marshall."

"I did not," Myers said. "That's not so."

"Andy," Gladstone said. "You didn't pull the trigger. You weren't even there. If you tell us the truth, the whole truth, right now, we might be able to do something for you down the line. I'm not saying no time, and I'm not making any promises at all, but I am telling you that this might be the last best chance you'll ever have."

But Myers stiffened. "No, sir," he said. "I didn't know anything about anything. All I knew was an investigation was going on."

"It's midnight, Andy," O'Brien said. "You're still here. You'd better call home again."

This time, they gave him a phone in the conference room.

"Vivian," he said to his wife, "I'm still here. They

want me to say something I can't say." There was a
pause, during which all three detectives could hear the
shrill sound of Vivian Myers's voice at the other end
of the phone.

Myers took the receiver from his ear and covered
the mouthpiece with his hand. "She says the pizza on
the stove is getting burnt. She wants to know how
much longer I'll be."

"Thirty years," said Mancuso, who had been sitting
quietly at the end of the table, taking notes.

"That all she said, Andy?" O'Brien asked. "The
pizza?"

"She also said that Ferlin called. He wanted to
know where I was."

"You tell her," O'Brien said, "next time he calls,
tell him to come down here and we'll help him find
you."

There were tears in Andrew Myers's eyes. "Vivian," he said. "I think maybe I should have got a
lawyer." Then he hung up.

He turned to the three detectives. "What now?" he
said.

"Now," said Gladstone, "we're going to place you
under arrest."

It took an hour for the paperwork to clear, but at
1:30 A.M. on Saturday, September 22, Andrew Myers
earned the dubious distinction of being the first person
arrested for involvement in the killing of Maria Marshall. The charge was conspiracy to commit murder.

Gladstone called McGuire in Toms River on Saturday
morning and learned that the Riccios had said little,
though they did acknowledge that Myers was an old
friend and that he had attended the birthday party in
May. Marshall, however, had been a different story.
When he'd heard the names of Grandshaw and L'Heu-

reux, O'Brien said, Rob had almost spilled his drink
and then had refused to answer any further questions,
invoking Raymond DiOrio's name.

Next, Gladstone went to Andy Myers's house to tell
Vivian that her husband had been arrested. Bail, he
said, had been set at $1.5 million. She didn't think she
heard him right and he had to repeat the figure. She
turned pale.

"What's the charge?" she said.

"The charge," Gladstone said, "is conspiracy to commit murder."

She was sitting on a couch and he was sitting on a
chair across from her. They were separated by a coffee
table so crowded with bowling trophies that Gladstone
could barely see her through the glitter of gold and
silver plate.

She said she'd never heard the name Robert Marshall in her life. She said she had no idea that her
husband had gone to New Jersey to see the Riccios
after telling her he was going to Texas. She said she
thought Andy should probably have a lawyer. Gladstone agreed.

Then she said that Ferlin had called again to see if
Andy were home yet. She was afraid, she said, that
someone would try to hurt her or her daughter as a
means of discouraging Andy from cooperating with
the police.

What surprised Gladstone most about all these apparently typical semisuburban ranch houses he was
visiting was the obvious attention paid to security.
There had been a high brick wall around Grandshaw's
house. Here, there were wrought-iron bars on all the
windows. Not the sort placed there for decorative
purposes—the kind that were put up to keep intruders
out.

The security, Gladstone thought, and the cars. At

Grandshaw's house, there had been a customized van
that was worth at least twenty-five thousand dollars, as
well as a Cadillac. And Grandshaw was supposedly a
self-employed, part-time steelworker. Here, in the driveway of a hardware store clerk who earned maybe two
hundred dollars a week at his job, there were a Chrysler
Le Baron and a Lincoln Town Car. And Ferlin
L'Heureux, who didn't seem to have a full-time job,
was said to drive the flashiest cars of all.

On Sunday afternoon, Gladstone got a call from a
Shreveport detective who'd just been to see Myers at
the Caddo Parish jail. "He wants to talk," the detective said. "He's got more to tell you."

He began talking as soon as the detectives arrived,
shortly after 6 P.M. He said he now remembered that
L'Heureux had made three trips to Atlantic City, in
June, July and September, and when he'd come back
from his July trip he'd told Myers an elaborate story
about hitchhikers and a stolen car and an auto accident, and having to leave town in a hurry. He had said
that if Marshall called, Myers should repeat that story
and explain that that was why "Ernie Grandshaw" had
not been able to complete the investigation.

He also said he now remembered that Marshall had
called him on Tuesday, September 4, the day after
Labor Day, asking, "Where's your friend? He's not up
here yet." Marshall had seemed surprised, Myers said,
because in an earlier call he had told Myers to give
"Grandshaw" the message that "there's an extra fifteen in it for him if he completes the investigation by
Labor Day."

Myers was not in good shape. He was crying inter-
mittently, and twisting about in his chair, and already
they'd taken away his belt and shoelaces because of
his seemingly overwrought emotional state.

At 6:45, a man named Bascombe Reade arrived at the jail and said he was there to represent the interests of Mr. Myers on behalf of the law firm that had been retained by Mrs. Myers. He requested permission to sit in on the remainder of the interview. Gladstone agreed.

With each new question, Myers grew noticeably more upset, until he was approaching incoherence. At one point, Reade (who, as it turned out, was not himself an attorney but a paralegal employed by the firm) said to Myers, "Hey, either tell these fellows the truth or keep your mouth shut. I've picked up three inconsistencies already."

Gladstone said, "Andy, all we want is the truth. You tell us the truth now, we'll take that into account. It'll help you further down the line."

"Yeah, Andy," O'Brien said. "You're going up north with us. There's a grand jury up there ready to indict. You're going on trial up there, Andy. A murder trial."

"The truth is all we want, Andy," Gladstone said. "Just tell us what happened, what you know. At this point, telling us the truth can only help you."

Myers then began to cry again. Through his tears he started blurting out phrases. " . . . Ferlin said it was gonna be a robbery . . . He told me there was gonna be a robbery on the parkway . . . in a dark place . . . she was gonna be shot . . . he was gonna get hit in the head . . ."

At this point, Reade insisted that the questioning go no further until he'd had a chance to speak to Myers privately. The two conferred for more than an hour, at the conclusion of which Reade told Gladstone that he would have to insist that the interview be terminated because his client "knew more than what he was telling," and because, Gladstone later reported, "he feared Myers would get in further trouble."

Before leaving the jail, however, Reade told a couple of Shreveport police officers to whom he spoke that Myers had told him that the murder was "an insurance job."

On Tuesday, September 25, Gladstone received a call from a lawyer named Lawton Garner, who said he represented Ferlin L'Heureux. He said he had become aware that New Jersey law enforcement agents were in the Shreveport area, expressing interest in Mr. L'Heureux's possible involvement in the murder of a New Jersey woman. He wanted to inform Lieutenant Gladstone that Mr. L'Heureux had assured him that he had no involvement in the murder whatsoever. It was Mr. L'Heureux's view that he could shed no light on the matters that appeared to be of concern to the New Jersey authorities and that therefore he would not be making himself available for any sort of questioning or interview.

Ernie Grandshaw, however, having become aware of the fate of Andrew Myers, had agreed to talk. Accompanied by his attorney, he met Gladstone, O'Brien and Mancuso at Shreveport police headquarters on Tuesday evening.

"I've known L'Heureux for about fifteen years," he began, "ever since he used to be a deputy sheriff. See, I do construction work and ever' now and then somebody wants him to do a job and he knows *nothin'* about construction work so he comes to me for information as to how to do it and what it costs.

"Now, in June I was workin' a job just across the river in Bossier City, and Ferlin comes by the job site and he asks me to pick up some money he said he had comin' in for some investigation services he'd been doin'. He said when he had 'em send it he didn't know whether he'd be in town or not so he just had 'em send it in my name.

"Tell you the truth, this happened twice. One time I went with him right then and the other time he brought me some kind of paper with the information on it and I picked it up for him later that day."

Gladstone showed Grandshaw the note Myers had written on the Caddo Hardware memo pad.

"That was it. That's what Ferlin gave me. See, both of 'em were from some northern address and I believe one was for twenty-five hundred and the other one for three thousand. I wouldn't guarantee that, but I believe that's right."

"Did he give you any money for doing this?" Gladstone asked.

"He never has paid me for what I done for him," Grandshaw said. "It's always a favoritism deal."

"Did you think you were going to get money for doing this?"

"No, sir. Not knowing Ferlin, I sure didn't."

"Now, you recall when we came to your house last week?"

"I surely do, sir. Both occasions. So does my wife."

"Did you get in touch with Ferlin to let him know we'd been there?"

"Yes I did, I made it a point to because I knew he was the onliest man who would pull somethin' like this on me, get me mixed up in somethin' this bad."

"What did you tell him, or what did you ask him?" Gladstone said.

"I asked him what in the hell was goin' on. I asked him what he done pulled and what he had me mixed up in."

"And what did he say?"

"He wouldn't comment on much of nothin'. All he done was look like his momma had slapped him. Turned kind of pale. Yes, he looked like he was pretty well shaken."

"Do you know Andrew Myers?" Gladstone asked.

"No, sir. I'm not even familiar with the name."

Grandshaw repeated that he'd never been to New Jersey in his life, that he'd never met, spoken to, or even been aware of the existence of either Robert or Maria Marshall, and that Ferlin had never discussed with him any aspect of the "investigation" for which the money from New Jersey was being sent.

They let him go that night but the next day they gave him a polygraph test. The results indicated to Gladstone that Grandshaw had not told them the whole truth: that, in fact, he knew who had fired the shots that had killed Maria Marshall and that he was aware of the involvement of other people in the conspiracy that had led to her death.

Gladstone informed Grandshaw's lawyer of the results of the polygraph test and the lawyer said that under those circumstances he would have to advise that his client have no further contact with the New Jersey authorities. That was fine, Gladstone said, but he should inform Mr. Grandshaw that unless he told everything he knew, he would soon be arrested on the same charges that Myers faced.

Wednesday, September 26, was also the day when Gladstone got the warrant that enabled the three detectives to search Ferlin L'Heureux's house. They found nothing of interest and Ferlin himself was nowhere in sight. He was, however, represented at the search by both Lawton Garner and his son Moss, who was also an attorney, and by his own sister, Bonnie, who worked as a paralegal in the Garner office, and by a blond man wearing a gaudy cowboy shirt and expensive new leather cowboy boots, who was introduced to them as Gary Hamilton, "a member of the firm."

What Gladstone noticed most about Hamilton, other than his clothes, was that he remained utterly silent throughout the search, not even engaging in the small talk or pleasantries that seemed to come so naturally to the others. Only much later would it occur to Gladstone that the likely reason for Hamilton's reticence was his desire not to reveal that he lacked a Louisiana accent.

On Thursday, September 27, Gladstone finally got access to the Louisiana telephone records that would disclose toll calls made to and from the home of Ferlin L'Heureux.

Between June 17 and June 19, the records showed, nine calls had been made from L'Heureux's home to various numbers in Atlantic City, including three to the main number at Harrah's Marina and two to different pay phones within the hotel. Before June 17 there were none and between June 19 and the night Maria Marshall was murdered there were none.

The lack of calls prior to June 17 was consistent, Gladstone thought, with Myers's story that L'Heureux and Marshall had not spoken for the first time until the second week of June, and with the fact that the first money order had not been sent until June 13.

The absence of any calls after June 19 suggested to Gladstone that from that point forward L'Heureux may have recognized that he was engaged in a criminal enterprise and did not want there to be any traces of contact between Marshall and himself. Thus, the use of Myers to relay messages.

With Ferlin L'Heureux, Gladstone realized, they were not dealing with a stupid man.

That night, Gladstone, O'Brien and Mancuso, who by now had been in Shreveport for nine days, went out to a club called Chevy's that had been highly recommended by several Shreveport detectives. Gladstone had the feeling that he was slowly working free from his blindfold and getting a first, hazy sense of the picture the pieces might someday form.

They could assume, he told O'Brien and Mancuso, that it had been L'Heureux, signing in as Grandshaw, who had been at Harrah's in June and at the Airport Motor Inn in September. And that, according to Myers, L'Heureux apparently had also made a trip to Atlantic City to meet Marshall in July. That it had been L'Heureux who had called Marshall's office on the morning of September 6, and that it had been Marshall, leaving the office for the presumably greater security of a pay phone, who had called him back eight minutes later.

Felice had told them that Marshall had said that he'd love to "dispose of" his wife, but of course he had only been kidding. She had mentioned a name to him. A few months later, at a party given by a friend from the neighborhood, who happened to be John Riccio, who was big in the sanitation business and was closely related to the Quadrozzis and Gigliottis, Marshall happened to meet Andrew Myers, who happened to be sitting alone at the bar after having flown fifteen hundred miles north to be at the party, while his wife thought he was in a hospital in San Antonio.

Ten days later, Myers put Marshall in touch with an "investigator" whose last name he didn't even know and who just happened to drop by the hardware store the same day that Marshall had called to ask for assistance.

On at least two occasions, Marshall had sent money to this "investigator," who made sure to use an alias in all of his dealings with Marshall. On the second of these occasions, Marshall, too, had sent the money under a false name.

The more they talked, the more the detectives could see a picture dimly emerging. But it was all so circumstantial: dots on a page that seemed to form a picture, but with no one to connect the dots.

"There's no question," Gladstone said, "Ferlin is our man. He's the one we'll have to try to put the heat on."

At that moment, Mancuso interrupted. There was dancing at Chevy's, although the three New Jersey detectives were not there to dance, they were there to talk about their case. But Mancuso, staring through the gloom and smoke and dim lighting, observed a large, bulky figure bounding energetically across the dance floor. He'd seen the same pictures that had been shown to Myers and he thought he recognized the man.

"Bob! Dan! You see out there on the dance floor? You guys aren't going to believe this but I think I just saw L'Heureux!"

Gladstone stood up to get a better look, but the first recognizable person he saw was not L'Heureux, but Gary Hamilton, the blond, silent, cowboy-booted member of L'Heureux's law firm.

Hamilton peering back through the gloom, spotted Gladstone, and with him the other two detectives. As Gladstone watched, he ran onto the dance floor in search of . . . yes . . . yes, it was . . . unmistakably . . . Ferlin L'Heureux. In the flesh. All 250 pounds of it.

After a moment's whispered conversation, the two men walked quickly off the dance floor and headed toward a rear exit.

"Son of a bitch," Gladstone said, "I bet they thought we came here to arrest him."

"Wish we could oblige," O'Brien said.

"We're not ready," Gladstone said.

"Yeah, but we can bust his chops a little bit," O'Brien said. "Follow him around for a while. That's one hell of a law firm he's got, by the way. Did you see that clown he had with him?"

"Hamilton," Gladstone said. "The guy who never opened his mouth. Even for down here, he doesn't look much like a lawyer to me."

The three detectives paid for their drinks and ran out to the parking lot, hoping to spot L'Heureux and Hamilton as they left.

"There he goes," Mancuso shouted. "I see them both. They're pulling away in that Cadillac."

"Okay," Gladstone said, "let's play tag for a while."

The three of them ran to their rented car.

"Holy shit!" O'Brien shouted. "I don't believe this."

The right rear tire of their car was flat.

"He must have just done it," Gladstone said.

O'Brien bent down and picked up a ballpoint pen. "Yup," he said. "Just hold this against the end of the valve for thirty seconds, there goes your air."

"How did he know it was our car?" Mancuso asked.

"Hamilton, that rhinestone cowboy, must have seen it yesterday when we drove over to do the search," O'Brien said.

"Son of a bitch," Gladstone said. "He picked the right rear tire, too."

"Well, of course," O'Brien said. "That's the area where he's had the most experience."

The next morning, Gladstone got a phone call from Toms River. He was told, first, that Felice had given a further statement to detectives, and, second, that Marshall had staged an apparently fake suicide attempt at the Best Western Motel in Lakewood, leaving behind an envelope that appeared to contain a tape cassette. The envelope was currently being held in the prosecutor's office, pending issuance of a warrant that would permit it to be opened and the tape to be played.

"Gentlemen," Gladstone said, "I think it's time to go home."

16

ON the morning of Thursday, September 27, New
Jersey and Philadelphia newspapers carried the news
of Myers's indictment by an Ocean County grand jury.
News of the arrest itself several days earlier had not
been reported. So September 27 was the first day on
which the public knew that genuine progress in the
investigation was being made.

It was on the same morning, after news of the
indictment had been printed and broadcast, that the
Ocean County prosecutor received a phone call from
attorney Anthony Trammel, who was representing Felice Rosenberg.

In the words of the report prepared by the prosecutor's office, Trammel "suggested" that detectives "respond to his law office" in Trenton for the purpose of
reinterviewing Mrs. Rosenberg, whom, he said, "may
possess certain information which would be helpful to
the investigation into the death of Maria Marshall."

Upon their arrival in Trenton, detectives were required to go through a preliminary screening with an
associate of Mr. Trammel's before being permitted in
Mrs. Rosenberg's presence. As McGuire wrote in his
report, he "assured [Trammel's associate] that Mrs. Rosenberg was not a primary target of this investigation."

This was a little different from having the Skyhawk flagged down on the parkway and being dragged into the prosecutor's office in Toms River and being finger-printed and booked.

Whether in return for the heightened degree of cour-tesy and respect extended to her, or simply because she felt that as a responsible citizen it was her duty to assist law enforcement personnel in the performance of their duties, Felice in Trenton on September 27 was far more forthcoming than she had been in Toms River three weeks earlier, before Raymond DiOrio's brief involvement in the case.

She began by saying that Rob had become "very nervous" the previous Friday night, after being asked by McGuire whether he knew L'Heureux or Grandshaw.

The next day, she said, she had gone with him to meet with his new lawyer, Carl Seely. Also present had been a private investigator named Gary Hamilton, whom Seely was employing for this case. The meeting had lasted several hours, she said, during which time she'd been required to remain in Seely's kitchen so she could not overhear what was being discussed.

On the way home, Marshall, who had been ex-tremely tense and subdued before the meeting, seemed almost exuberant. He told her that Hamilton, the in-vestigator, would soon be leaving for Shreveport to "come up with alternative reasons," for any contact he'd had with "Ernie Grandshaw." He told her he could not elaborate further because Seely had insisted that he not share "Shreveport information" with her.

The next day, she said, Rob had received the mes-sage from Roby on her answering machine about the urgent call from "Grandshaw" in Louisiana. She said he "became visibly shaken and turned pale." He told her he "didn't know what to do," but thought he should speak to Seely before returning the call. She said she had become "concerned" over his "obvious distress" and had asked him why he was so upset.

The story he told her was the story of the bet on the NBA games. He'd met a man named Myers at the Riccios' party, had wagered on the outcome of a basketball game they were watching at the bar, and had lost the bet. He'd had to pay in two installments, the first of twenty-five hundred dollars and the second of three thousand. When wiring the money the second time, he said, he'd used a fictitious name. He also said he had wired the money to a party named Ernie Grandshaw rather than to Myers himself for reasons that were simply too complicated to get into, but involved other business dealings he was engaged in down there.

She also reported that Rob and Carl Seely each made phone calls to Shreveport on Sunday in response to the message received on her answering machine and that at least one of the calls had been to a Shreveport lawyer representing someone connected to the case, and that another had been to that lawyer's father, who was also, apparently, a lawyer.

She said Rob was so "desperate" for money that he had already begun to sell Maria's jewelry. She even gave the name of the Toms River jeweler with whom he'd placed it on consignment. She also said that he'd brought all of Maria's furs to her house and had asked her to sell them in New York, along with some of her own, in order to raise additional cash.

It had been her earlier impression, she said, that Rob had been only $100,000 in debt. Since then, she'd come to learn that his indebtedness was actually $200,000. According to McGuire's report, "she assumed this is from gambling and losing at the Golden Nugget and Harrah's Casino in Atlantic City." In addition, she said, he had used at least $50,000 of the money obtained through the second mortgage on his home to buy stock which had subsequently lost more than half its value.

She also said that Rob had confessed to her that he had signed Maria's name not only on the home equity loan application but also on at least one of the insurance policies he'd taken out on her life.

At 7 P.M. Tuesday, she said, Rob had called her to say that he had "good news" from Shreveport. But by this time, she said, she had become "increasingly nervous" about Rob. Thus, when he came to her beach condo later that night and started to apologize for fabricating the story about the NBA bet, and offered to tell her the truth, she asked him to leave.

He came back a second time and again she asked him to leave.

The next day, Wednesday, just one day before she decided to make this statement, she said she'd come home from work to find a cassette and letter waiting for her at her door. On the tape, Rob again apologized for lying about Shreveport. Since then, she'd had no contact with him.

Then, again, she described the conversation months earlier into which she'd interjected the name of Patsy Racine. She said it had occurred "during November or December" of 1983, when Rob was feeling pressured by Maria's suspicions regarding the affair. "I swear," he had told her, "if I thought there was a way of getting rid of her, I would. Do you know somebody who would do it?"

In this recounting, there was nothing jocular about the remark. In fact, as McGuire wrote in his report, "according to Mrs. Rosenberg, there is no doubt in her mind that Marshall meant to murder his wife."

One area, however, about which Felice apparently did not volunteer information and about which she was not questioned, was the morning of September 6, when, as Gladstone had already discerned from his examination of the phone company records, she had received a phone call from Marshall at 9:46 A.M.

She had called him back at 9:48 A.M. from a different phone at Seaview Regional and they'd talked for ten minutes—or until the call from L'Heureux at the Airport Motor Inn had come in at 9:59.

What had been the purpose of Marshall's call?

Why had Felice chosen to leave the phone she took the call on and, uncharacteristically, go to a different phone to return it?

What had they talked about during those ten minutes, at a time when Rob already knew, from Myers, that "Ernie Grandshaw" had come back north to finish his "investigation"?

These were questions that apparently did not interest the Ocean County prosecutor, a man who had been put in his job by Felice's close friend Raymond DiOrio and who was now hoping that DiOrio would arrange for him to be a judge. Whether this lack of interest was in any way connected to Raymond DiOrio's brief involvement in the case could not, of course, be determined from official reports.

Back in his office on Monday, October 1, Bob Gladstone heard and read the full report of Felice's second interview.

"So that's who he was," he said to McGuire. "Hamilton. A private dick down there to cook up a story with L'Heureux that would get them both off the hook. I knew that son of a bitch was no lawyer, not even a Louisiana lawyer."

"I knew he wasn't a cowboy, either," O'Brien said.

"Wonder what the 'good news' from Shreveport was Tuesday night," Gladstone said.

"He must've heard that Hamilton and L'Heureux had started cooking."

"Cooking what? Jambalaya? Crawfish pie?"

"Nah," O'Brien said, "that's the bayou. That shit town we were in, that's really more like part of Texas. The bad part of Texas. Chicken-fried steak and a six-pack, that's about it."

"So Tuesday night he gets good news from Shreveport," Gladstone said.

"And Thursday he checks into his favorite motel."

"And tries to check out."

"Or pretends to."

"So he has an excuse for creating a farewell tape."

"Which he's actually dying to get into our hands."

"Because?" Gladstone said.

"Because you know what's gonna be on that tape when we finally get the fucking warrant and we can play it?" O'Brien said. "There's gonna be his 'alternative reasons' for jacking around with Ferlin L'Heureux all summer long."

Not long after Rob had checked into room 16 of the Best Western on the afternoon of September 27, the motel's desk clerk, who recognized him from his many prior visits, and who was aware of the published speculation that he was considered a suspect in the murder of his wife, notified the Ocean County prosecutor's office that he was there.

That he would check into a motel room—his special motel room—alone seemed sufficiently peculiar so that a team of detectives was dispatched to the Best Western to keep him under surveillance. Arrangements were made at the front desk to permit three of them to occupy room 17, immediately adjacent to his.

Thus, when Rob left his room at 10:45 to walk down the hall to buy a Coke, a detective observed him.

And at 11:30, when he walked to the front desk in the lobby, carrying an envelope with him, a detective followed. The detective observed Rob put the envelope into a tray that rested on the front desk.

The detective, whose name was James Vandermeer, remained in the lobby after Rob left to return to his room. He walked over to the open tray, into which outgoing motel mail was placed for later pickup by a U.S. mail carrier, and noted that on the back of the sealed envelope Rob had written, "To Be Opened in the Event of My Death."

Turning it over, he saw that it was addressed to someone named Eugene Leahy in Wilmington, Delaware.

Vandermeer took the envelope from the tray and returned to room 17. The envelope was not opened by the detectives, but the message on the back caused them to consider the possibility that Rob might be planning to take his own life. They called the Lakewood police department emergency squad and asked that an ambulance be dispatched to the Best Western to stand by in the parking lot. Then, at regular intervals, they began calling Rob's room, hanging up when he would answer.

At 12:55 A.M. they got no answer and, using a passkey given them by the desk clerk, entered his room. There, they found him asleep on the bed. Next to him, on a night table, was a glass filled with a foamy mixture of Coca-Cola and the contents of fifty Restoril sleeping capsules, each of which had been opened by hand so the contents could be poured into the glass.

Rob woke up almost immediately and told detectives that he'd stirred the mixture with his finger, licked his finger, and fallen asleep. He said he'd been planning to kill himself at exactly the same moment that his wife had died on the parkway but apparently he'd overslept.

They found a tape recorder, three cassettes and a photograph of Maria and her three sons on the floor next to the bed. These they collected, along with the Restoril bottle and the glass containing the mixture.

They took Rob to Point Pleasant Hospital, where he was admitted for observation as a possible suicide attempt, even though he had ingested none of the liquid and physically there was nothing wrong with him.

The envelope containing the tape to Gene Leahy was taken to the prosecutor's office, along with the three other tapes, which turned out to be one each to Roby, Chris and John.

And on Tuesday, October 2, proper authorization having been obtained, Gladstone, O'Brien and Mancuso gathered around a tape recorder to hear what Rob Marshall had to say.

"Where should we start?" Gladstone said.

"Let's do the boys first, get those out of the way," O'Brien said. "Shit, he didn't even put them in an envelope. What the hell were they supposed to do, drive to the Best Western and pick them up?"

"Saving postage, Dan. The guy's in debt," Gladstone said. Then he put the cassette marked for Roby into the machine.

"As I lay here," Rob's voice began, "looking at your beautiful face, with your mother right next to it, and Chris and John, I can only think of how much I love you and the fact that I have loved you almost as long as Mom.

"Roby, I hope that someday you'll understand that I just could not go through this ordeal. You know that I wouldn't hurt Mom, but there's so much stuff that so many people try to make it seem as though I would, and I feel the inevitable will happen and I will be dragged through the courts and found guilty. And I can't bear that—not for me or you—so I'm taking the shortcut, buddy, to be with Mom, I hope. I know where she is and I will pray to God this evening that He lets me be with her.

"I know this makes it awful tough on you because you're left to deal with everything, but I know how strong you are and I know you can do it. You're the oldest and the biggest and I want you to be strong for everybody—be a leader. Finish school. Go back to Villanova in January and kick ass, as Chris says. Do the best you possibly can do. Go to law school, get your own practice, whatever, and go for it, Roby. I know you said you want to be President someday, and God, I think you can. I believe you can.

"But whatever you do, do the best, do the best you can do. Give it everything. Never forget your family, and that's talking about me and Mom and Chris and John, and me and the Leahys, and all your cousins, and the nice people like Sal Coccaro, who's been so helpful.

"Roby, I'm so proud of you. You've grown up to be such an intelligent, bright young man. I just know that you're going to do so well for yourself. By the way, I told Uncle Gene to arrange to purchase the Mustang for you so you'll have a car. Roby, I'm so proud of you. Please be strong and never forget how much I love you. I love you so much."

The tape ended.

"Found guilty, huh?" Gladstone said. "Guess he doesn't have much confidence in Seely."

"I like the Mustang," O'Brien said. "Now it's all starting to make sense. You kill your wife so the insurance money can buy your kid a new car."

"You know how it is around the country club, Dan. You've got to keep up appearances."

He put the second cassette, the one for Chris, in the machine.

"I'm lying here," Rob began, "looking at your beautiful face, in the same frame with your mother and Roby and John. You look so handsome. You're getting so tall—so big.

"I'll never forget that time many summers ago when something happened to you and you started swimming like a dart. I looked at you and it was as though someone was pulling you with a rope. You had found the secret, it seemed, and you have gotten better, so much better, ever since.

"Mom was so proud of you. She loved to see you in the water. So proud of what you're doing at Lehigh. She was just so pumped for you—so pleased that you got in and that you're happy there—and so am I. I'm just tickled and I know that you're going to do well—not only in the pool but with your studies.

"You'll go on and get your degree in architecture and you'll be one of the best around, buddy. I know you will. Tell Jennifer how much I love her. If you two end up together, and I hope you do, but if you do, you're going to have beautiful kids. Just raise them with the kind of love that Mom and I have raised you with.

" 'Specially Mom. She was the one that poured everything she had into you guys. Every ounce of energy she had. She loved you so. We both believed that you will make the '88 Olympics. I want you to try for that, 'cause I know you can do it.

"Chris, I'm so sorry for breaking the promise I made to you, but everything seems to point to me, and although I never hurt your mother there's so much circumstantial evidence that I know I'm going to get dragged through the courts and I'm so afraid that they'll find me guilty. I couldn't bear that. Not for me—not for you boys, either. I want to maintain some dignity if I can. Please try to understand. Forgive me. I love you so much.

"I told Uncle Gene to make arrangements to purchase the car, the Jeep, so even though the lease is not finished, that will be taken care of for you. Be careful. Please stay close to your family. They need you as much as you need them. I hope and pray that all of this will work out for you guys.

"I've also told Uncle Gene to be sure that you have plenty of spending money in your account at Lehigh so that you can come home when you want to and maybe even go see Jennifer from time to time, because I know that you're going to need her now and I want you to do that. So I'll be sure to tell him to let you go. God, I love you, Chris. Please love me."

The second tape ended.

"Yeah," said O'Brien, "I'm really starting to see it. It was either Mom or the Jeep."

"It takes a big man to make the tough choices, Dan," Gladstone said, as he began to play the tape to John.

This was similar in style and content to the first two, except Rob told John that when he turned seventeen, Gene Leahy would buy him a Porsche. But "not a brand-new one," he warned. "Nothing too outrageous."

"Yeah, shit," O'Brien said, "you wouldn't want the kid to get his hopes up."

Then Gladstone played the tape that had been removed from the envelope addressed to Gene Leahy. If their theory were correct, the entire suicide attempt had been staged because Rob wanted to document a version of events that would coincide with the story L'Heureux would give when they eventually arrested him. A perfectly innocent explanation for everything that looked so suspicious. An explanation that, according to Felice, Gary Hamilton had gone to Louisiana to help L'Heureux concoct and that someone then—in all probability—had relayed to Rob before he went to the Best Western to make this tape.

"As I lie here," Rob began, "wondering where to start, I think back fourteen months ago, when I went out with a lady who—for years we just winked, across the pool or across the room—was nothing but a friend. A good friend, a friend that Maria didn't care for too much, but a friend of mine who was a lot like me. I began a relationship that developed into a torrid love affair that was going to tear my marriage apart, and—if it were not for Maria's death—that would have happened within a month.

"I guess my problem began long before that, though, really. Because, for some reason—and I'm to blame— whatever we wanted, to do or to buy, we just went ahead and did it. If it meant borrowing to do it, we did it anyway. And I always assured Maria that it was okay, that there was enough—even if there wasn't.

"I think she knew, but she knew that I wanted it and I know that she wanted it, whatever it was, and we did it, and that created a spiral—a spiral that accelerated to almost a two-hundred-thousand-dollar debt, not including the mortgage on the house. A debt that I was determined to try to pay off, but just couldn't seem to—climb out.

"We were starting to work on it together, and I had emphasized the importance of spending less. I knew, of course, that within a month I was going to be leaving, and I would make the necessary changes to eliminate the debt—by putting Maria on an allowance and taking whatever cash was left and applying it towards debt reduction. However, that never happened.

Never had the chance, because some bastards followed us home—from what I can gather—perhaps after tampering with one of the tires on my car, knowing that I would have to pull off somewhere, or pull over, and—were either going to rob us, or—do what had to be done to take the money we had on us."

"Smart bastards," O'Brien whispered, "to tamper with it so he'd have to pull off at Oyster Creek and not four miles further at Roy Rogers."

Rob's voice continued. "The circumstances that surround the entire evening are bizarre," he said.

He went on to explain that because casino money was mysteriously missing—"five or six thousand dollars had disappeared without explanation," from their joint checking account—he'd felt "compelled to hire somebody who I thought was—had a good reputation, was out of town, didn't mind coming the distance," to determine what had happened to the money.

Then he bemoaned the fact that none of the people who apparently knew that Maria had hired her own investigator had bothered to tell him. "And if they had, this entire thing would not have happened because we wouldn't have been in Atlantic City that night."

That, apparently, got him thinking about Maria. "She wanted to start over. It didn't matter. She loved me. She would forget anything. And when I think about that now, how incredible she was, how much she loved me, and how foolish I was to walk away from her . . . I miss her so. And as each day goes by, it gets worse and worse."

He then said to Gene Leahy, "You must communicate to everybody my love for Maria, in spite of our problems, and that I wouldn't hurt her, in spite of what seems apparent. You must also let the authorities know that Felice was not involved in any way."

He went on for a long time about financial details—outstanding loans, insurance policies, premiums due, and he stressed that Gene was to see to it that Roby, Chris and John each wound up with a fully paid-up car of his own.

Then he shifted back to a more personal mode. "As I lay here," he said, "I'm really tormented. In spite of my innocence, I feel I'll be found guilty because of all the circumstantial evidence that points in that direction, and I can't bear the thought of that. I'm convinced that the inevitable will happen and a jury of men and women who do not know me will be compelled to find me guilty and I'll be sentenced to death. Not only can I not bear going through that, but the embarrassment for the family would be far worse than anything else I could think of. I want a little dignity to remain, if possible.

"So I believe what I will do, at twelve forty-five tonight, which is approximately the time we pulled off the parkway three weeks ago to look at a flat tire, is I will join Maria. I hope that God forgives me, and I'll be praying right until the end that He does.

"I'm sorry for letting everyone down. I'm especially sorry for the boys. As I sit here, I'm looking at their beautiful faces with their wonderful smiles, and Maria, her beautiful . . . everything. The love shining through. Gene, you've got to help the boys. Somehow, the love has to continue."

And then, scarcely pausing for breath, he said, "When you get a chance, call Felice. She can be reached at school or at her apartment, and tell her that I loved her. That I'm sorry for disappointing her. Tell her that as I speak to you, I'm in room sixteen at the Best Western, where I was my happiest—and now where I'm the saddest.

"Tell her that I knew that she was going to go back

to David, and that I understand, in spite of the feeling that I think it all would have worked out for us if I had stuck around to see it through. With her gone, her not there, I'm alone, really . . . and . . . I can't go on alone. Tell her I love her. Tell her I wish her the best. Tell her to . . . stay straight. Tell her I said, 'Stop smoking.'

"And, this is silly, but I ordered some draperies recut from the drapes we took down in the family room that I was going to give to her for the apartment. They'll probably be delivered sometime next week. Give them to Felice, if she wants them. Ask her if she wants them.

"Give Sal Coccaro a call, too. He's been absolutely super. Tell him I love him, both him and Paula, and that I appreciate him standing behind me. Tell him I'm sorry for not having the courage to see this through. I think he might understand. And tell him that I said I was still thinking of business, even tonight—and remind him that Paula's premium is still overdue."

"Make a note, Dan," Gladstone said. "Tell Paula she's overdue."

There was a long pause on the tape, and then, finally, Rob got to what appeared to be the point. "I think," he said, "it's probably best that I fill you in with what I know up to this point. As I mentioned the other day—I said I had wired money to a fellow in Louisiana to pay off a bet. In fact, that money was, uh, being sent out to the investigator that I mentioned earlier in this tape.

"This was a guy who was recommended by this fellow Andrew Myers. Supposed to be a very good investigator. He made two trips, uh, to New Jersey. One in June after I wired him twenty-five hundred dollars. He said he was going to be busy for a little while, but if I wired him some additional money he would come back and check things out. The objective was to do this quietly, without anybody in the area knowing. People in the area are not reliable, from what I know of the people that work in Ocean County, and that was the logic behind getting somebody out of town.

"Uhhh, this guy would apparently work as cheap as somebody in the next state, uh . . . and he was supposed to have a good reputation. I saw him the second time at Harrah's the evening Maria was killed. I gave him an additional sum of money, approximately eight hundred dollars, which was all I had, which he took, and he said that he would, uh, stay around to do a little checking. I found out later that he left, and that his only purpose was to rip me off.

"So I sent him two installments, one for twenty-five hundred, one for three thousand. Waiting for him to come back, I called Andy Myers, several times, inquiring as to the whereabouts of the person that I knew as Ernie Grandshaw, and, uh, at the same time tried to do, uh, some business with Andy Myers on the telephone, some investment business.

"The police, as I understand it, have indicted both Myers and this fellow Ernie Grandshaw, whose name is Ferlin something, as, uh, conspirators, and I'm convinced that the third sealed indictment that's in Toms River is for me.

"Those are the details that I haven't told anybody, except my lawyer, Seely, and his investigator who is down there getting a confirmation statement from, uh, Andrew Myers. I did meet Myers, by the way, at the Riccios' son's birthday party, back in May.

"Uhh, I'd like you to sit down and explain to Roby and Chris as much of those details as you feel comfortable explaining to them. Try to make them understand the kind of pressure that I felt. I just feel that that, plus the life insurance, the debt and Felice, that, uh, it just looks so bleak. I can't stand the thought of what's going to happen—or what could happen.

"And so, my friend, my dear friend Gene, I hope you understand and I hope you won't stop loving me because I lacked the courage to face it all.

"I hate doing what I'm going to do because of the boys. I know how it's gonna hurt them. So please help them. They're good boys. They don't deserve this. Just like Maria didn't deserve what happened either. But, Gene, I want to be with her, and I pray God will allow me to be . . .'cause I can't go on like this. I love you all, especially Roby, Chris and John."

The tape ended.

"What do you think?" Gladstone asked.

"I think he should've swallowed the fucking potion," O'Brien said.

17

JOKING aside, Gladstone, O'Brien and Mancuso agreed that the making of the tape had been, on Rob's part, a mistake. If nothing else, it now gave them what they had not had before: a sufficient factual basis for returning to Louisiana to arrest Ferlin L'Heureux.

The chain had started with Myers identifying the "investigator" as L'Heureux. The next link had been provided by Grandshaw, who said L'Heureux had used his name as an alias and had in fact used him to pick up money wired by Marshall. Then there had been the documented series of phone calls from the L'Heureux home to Atlantic City between June 17 and 19.

Now, on tape, Marshall had acknowledged that "Grandshaw" was really a man named "Ferlin something" and that he'd met with Ferlin in Atlantic City in both June and September.

Samples of L'Heureux's handwriting obtained from Shreveport police department records matched the "Ernie Grandshaw" writing on the registration cards at both Harrah's Marina in June and the Airport Motor Inn in September.

And now, providing the most vital link of all, Marshall had admitted, on tape, to meeting L'Heureux, *and to paying him money*, at Harrah's Marina, only hours before the murder. On the same date, Gladstone emphasized, that "Ernie Grandshaw" had registered at the Airport Motor Inn and that someone using the Airport Motor Inn phone booth had called Marshall's office and, eight minutes later, had received a call back from a pay phone outside a 7-Eleven store just down the street from the office.

There still was no one remotely ready to admit that *investigation* had been a code word for *murder,* but the three detectives knew they had enough facts to return to Louisiana, armed this time with arrest warrants for both Grandshaw and L'Heureux.

They wanted Grandshaw for two reasons: because the polygraph examination had indicated he was withholding significant information, and because the testimony he would have to give at trial to clear himself would, of necessity, link L'Heureux directly to Marshall, who had sent the two Western Union payments.

They flew down on October 11 and arrested both L'Heureux and Grandshaw the next day without incident. With L'Heureux behind bars, Gladstone, an assiduous reader of the works of Herman Melville, felt a bit as he imagined Captain Ahab would have had he succeeded in conquering Moby-Dick.

But the truth was, Ferlin L'Heureux wasn't Moby-Dick, physical resemblances notwithstanding. In this case, Rob Marshall was the Great White Whale, and success would be earned only by seeing him convicted for the heartless, malicious, greed-soaked, lust-soaked, fear-soaked murder of his wife.

Bob Gladstone, truly, earned less money in a year from doing a difficult, distasteful and occasionally dangerous job well than Rob Marshall *borrowed* in a week while lying on sheets covered with rose petals (a kinky detail that Vandermeer had learned while on his

Best Western detail), his limbs intertwined with those of the wife of a man who lived down the street.

Yes, it was Rob Marshall who was Moby-Dick. Ferlin L'Heureux, however crucial to the case, was no more than an overfed pilot fish who could lead Gladstone to the main prey.

Six weeks passed as L'Heureux, Grandshaw and Myers resisted extradition to New Jersey. These were weeks during which Bob Gladstone continued to fret.

He liked to think in terms of links in a chain, but he knew that a good defense lawyer could make the prosecution's theory—that Marshall had imported a hit man from Louisiana to murder Maria for her insurance money so he could pay off his debts and continue his affair with Felice—seem a hodgepodge of supposition and coincidence, pasted together with a handful of phone bills.

More, he knew, would be needed to prove guilt beyond a reasonable doubt. But he didn't know how he could get more, when Myers and Grandshaw both insisted that "investigation" meant no more than that, and when Ferlin L'Heureux simply flat out refused to talk.

"We've got to get them up here," Gladstone kept saying. Once the suspects were brought to New Jersey, they could be kept isolated from one another and Gladstone could practice a bit of psychological warfare. If Ferlin didn't know what Andy might be saying, and Ernie didn't know what Ferlin might be saying, and Andy didn't know but what maybe even Marshall himself had started to talk—that sort of thing could put a lot of pressure on a man. Especially when the man was fifteen hundred miles from home and facing trial in a state that had recently reinstituted the death penalty.

"Once we get them up here," Gladstone kept saying, "one of them will flip."

                        *   *   *

They arrived in Toms River on December 3, their
fight against extradition having been lost. Each was
placed in solitary confinement, with no knowledge of
the whereabouts of the others. Through their attorneys, however, each of the three knew that the prosecutor's office was interested in talking about a deal:
drastically reduced charges in return for the right kind
of information.

The one to whom this proposition seemed most
tantalizing was L'Heureux. He was, after all, the one
most directly implicated in the murder itself. He was
the one against whom they had compiled the most
damning evidence. That made him the one most likely
to be convicted of murder, and therefore the most
likely to face death. Ferlin had been a cop himself for
more than ten years. He knew how the game was
played. And he knew who usually won.

Ferlin L'Heureux had two lawyers. Moss Garner,
the son of Lawton Garner, had flown up from Shreveport, and, in addition, L'Heureux had been given a
New Jersey state public defender.

Bob Gladstone talked to these lawyers. He and the
county prosecutor explained that the deal was still out
there, dangling, but time was short. The deal would
not dangle much longer.

It was, without question, a good deal. L'Heureux, as
long as he could demonstrate to their satisfaction that
he had not been the actual killer, would serve a very
brief sentence in a minimum-security state prison, after
which he and his family would be relocated through
the Federal Witness Protection Program (for which he
was eligible as a result of bank robbery information
he'd given the FBI in Shreveport).

No one disputed that this sounded much better than
death.

They showed L'Heureux's lawyers little bits and pieces of their evidence. The phone records. The motel registrations. And something new: a statement from a young woman who said she'd driven past the Oyster Creek picnic area at the time of the murder and had seen a white Cadillac with a dented right side (just like L'Heureux's) roaring down the southbound exit ramp at high speed. They talked about what Myers had said, and what Grandshaw had said. Then they mentioned that Rob Marshall had made a tape. A tape that, whatever its original purpose, served to implicate Ferlin deeply.

The lawyers went to the jail and conferred privately with Ferlin. They came back and said he was interested in the deal and had the right kind of information to offer, and that, no, he hadn't been the shooter, but first he wanted to hear the tape.

So they played him the tape. They let him hear Rob talk about his torrid love affair, his crushing debt, his plans to walk out on his wife and kids. He heard Rob talk about all the insurance he'd taken on Maria's life, and about how L'Heureux's only purpose had been "to rip me off." Then he heard about how he and Rob had met at Harrah's on the night of the murder and how Rob had paid him more money.

Ferlin L'Heureux began to frown as he listened to the tape. Then the frown deepened into a scowl. Then he began to clench his fists. When the tape ended, he jumped to his feet and shouted, "That squirrelly, no-good son of a bitch is tryin' to frame me!"

He sat back down and raised his hands in a gesture of helplessness.

"Goddamn it," he said. "The story I gave to Hamilton was all about how Marshall was a well-organized, well-settled individual who was happy with his lifestyle and family ties. And how since the time he'd got in touch with me, he and his wife was havin' a second honeymoon, and things had taken such a good turn that he didn't need an investigator anymore.

"Goddamn! That's what the loony bastard was supposed to put on the tape." He stood up again, his face now red.

"I never from the start should have trusted that crazy motherfucker." He clenched a fist and pounded the table on which the tape recorder sat. Then he turned and looked directly at Bob Gladstone.

"That man," he said, pointing to the tape recorder, "is so *stupid* that you ought to put him to death just for *that!*"

"Does this mean," Gladstone asked mildly, "that maybe you'd like to take the deal?"

"Shit, yes," Ferlin said. "Shit, yes, I'll take the deal. After hearin' that, I don't see that I got much of a choice."

"But, Ferlin," Gladstone said, "there's no deal if you're the one who pulled the trigger."

"I didn't pull the fuckin' trigger."

"And you do know who did?"

"I sure as hell do."

"And you are going to tell us. As part of the deal. And you're going to testify to it in court."

Here, Ferlin hesitated. "You know," he said, "I'd like to think some on that."

"No shooter, no deal, Ferlin. Simple as that."

Ferlin stared out the window of the prosecutor's office. It was the first window he'd had to look out of in ten days.

"Got to be some other way you can come up with the shooter besides me," he said.

"No shooter, no deal, Ferlin," Gladstone repeated. "Simple as that."

"And what are you givin' me? Tell me again?"

"You give us the whole story. And it better fucking check out as true or this deal is gone faster than anything you ever saw in your life," Gladstone said. "And you testify in court to everything you tell us. And after you've done that we let you plead to conspiracy to commit murder, which as your attorneys can tell you—"

"They've already told me."

"—is a lot different from a conviction for murder for hire. Then we recommend a sentence of no more than five years with a special request that you be paroled on the first day you become eligible."

"And time I'm servin' now counts toward that?"

"That's right."

"So if I sit on my ass here for another year or so, waitin' on this case to get to trial, I could be free after that?"

"Just about."

"And if I do go somewhere, it's somewhere easy?"

"If you do go somewhere for another few months or whatever, it'll be a prison out in the western part of the state that's mostly for women. It's called Clinton. Low security. There's a special wing there in which you'll be housed."

"But you've gotta have the shooter's name."

"We've gotta have the shooter's name and everything else."

Ferlin L'Heureux looked around the room. He took a deep breath which turned into a sigh.

"Okay, boys," he said. "We got a deal."

18

On the morning of December 14, Ferlin L'Heureux
started to talk. Except for a few hours for sleeping, he
didn't stop until the night of the fifteenth. By the time
he had finished, Bob Gladstone was a satisfied man.

The way Ferlin remembered the start of it was quite
different from the story Andrew Myers had told. For
one thing, Ferlin said that Myers knew very well who
he was—last name, as well as first—and knew also (or
thought he did) that Ferlin would be just the right man
for this job. There had been nothing casual or coincidental about the contact.

"See," Ferlin said, "I guess I was his idea of what
the Mafia looked like down there. One day I'd be in
old clothin' and the next day dressed to a T and drivin'
different cars—lookin' like a guy that was connected.

"So he started with me, but he was smart enough
not to—for me not to know that he was doin' what it
was that he was doin'. See, he never come right out
and told me that what Marshall wanted was his wife
murdered, but I'm sure Marshall told him, you know,
'Get this done for me and I'll take care of you.'

"Anyway, he called me at home. Told me he had a
friend of his who needed some help in New Jersey. He
called—talked to my wife, actually—asked me to stop

by the next mornin'. Said at ten or nine or somethin' like that, a friend of his was goin' to call and talk to me about doin' some kind of divorce work, or some kind of domestic case on his wife.

"So I stopped by. Myers told me the man was very well off, had plenty of money. Told me he had met Marshall at some Mafia friend of his's party. Somethin' to do with restaurants, garbage collectin' or somethin'. He'd been accused of bein' in the crime family and also his son or somebody had just been beaten to death with golf clubs.

"So Marshall called. I went to the back of the store and took the phone. Marshall told me who he was and that Myers had told him about me, that I was an investigator, and he wanted to hire someone from outside the New Jersey area who wouldn't be familiar with his wife, so it'd be less likely this business would get out, because he knew so many people.

"He said he was a man with a lot of status in his town. So he didn't want me to meet him there. He wanted me to come to Atlantic City. Told me that he was also well known in Atlantic City, so even there he had to be extremely careful. Well, I come to find out that he was weller known in Harrah's than anywhere else in the world and that's where he wanted me to meet him, and I thought that was kind of stupid. But that came later.

"Anyway, I said, 'That's going to be expensive.' Told him I'd need five thousand expenses up front. Wired to Shreveport, Louisiana. I told him to send it in the name of Ernie Grandshaw. Purpose of that was, I don't want to pay no more taxes than I have to.

"In a couple of days, Myers calls and tells me the money is in and to come by Caddo Hardware, he had the information written down on a piece of paper. I went by and he gives me a sheet of paper which says the money was sent in the name of Ernie Grandshaw, and had some other information written down there— that Marshall wanted me in Atlantic City on such and such a date, at the O'Hara's, or the Harrah's, whatever the hell it is, the Marina motel or hotel—the gamblin' casino.

"So I went and got Ernie off the job site where he was at and we went to the Western Union and he went in and picked up the money order. Then I drove him to the nearest bank and cashed the check. I took the money and took him right back to the job site. Told him it was for a gamblin' debt."

But what he'd found, he said, was that the money order had been for only twenty-five hundred dollars instead of the five thousand that had been agreed upon.

"I went back to Caddo Hardware and told Andy Myers that Marshall had not sent me all the money that I asked for. Told Myers I had a good mind to not even go. So he had another phone conversation with Marshall and then he told me, 'When you get there, he'll give you the other twenty-five hundred.' I said, 'Look, I ain't goin'. The guy didn't send the money that I asked for.' He said, 'He'll give you that other money as soon as you arrive.' I said, 'Okay, I'll think about it.' And Myers told me to go to Harrah's Marina, register in the name of Ernie Grandshaw, and that Marshall would call me there on the morning of June the eighteenth."

The way he saw it at that point, Ferlin said, was that he'd already received twenty-five hundred dollars for no more than a twenty-minute phone call. That would more than pay the plane fare and hotel bill for a two-day trip to Atlantic City, which Ferlin had never seen before, even if he never laid eyes on Robert Marshall. Besides, the way Myers had been talking, it sounded like there was a lot more money where the first twenty-five hundred had come from.

"The thing is," Ferlin said, "I like to take advantage of opportunities and this sure looked like an opportunity."

He'd gone home and told his wife to make the necessary reservations. Harrah's was booked, but after calling around a bit, she'd found him a room at the Islander Motel.

As Ferlin reached this point in his story, Gladstone flipped to the page of his notes where he had a list of the toll calls made from L'Heureux's house. June 17: to Harrah's Marina, to the Clipper Ship Motel, to the Islander. It checked.

He said he'd flown Delta to Philadelphia on the afternoon of June 17. From Philadelphia he'd taken a commuter flight to Atlantic City. From there, he'd taken a cab to the Islander.

Rather, he'd tried to take a cab to the Islander. The cab driver, a Korean fellow, couldn't find it. They drove around for more than an hour, L'Heureux said, to no avail. By now it was almost 10 P.M. Ferlin had received an extensive tour of Atlantic City and environs and had not been impressed.

"Just a slum, a cruddy place. I couldn't believe it. Finally, I told him, told the Chinaman, just take me to O'Hara's and that I would walk in and try to get a room. If not, I'd just mess around in the casino for the remainder of the night and advise the desk clerk in the mornin' that I was expectin' a call."

It turned out that a room was available at Harrah's and, using the name Ernie Grandshaw, L'Heureux had signed in. The next morning, he said, he'd eaten a big breakfast (that part of the story Gladstone found easy to believe) and had dressed up in what he considered his "investigator's clothes—slacks, sports shirt, leather-cashmere coat, dark sunglasses." He'd laid a briefcase and a notebook on the table and waited for the phone to ring.

Shortly after 9 A.M., it did. It was Rob Marshall. Saying he was running a little late. Saying he'd be down about eleven. But it was almost noon, Ferlin said, before he heard from Rob again, this time a call from the lobby to say he was on his way up.

Ferlin opened the curtains to let bright sunlight flood the room. He made sure to keep his dark glasses on. The man didn't know his name and Ferlin didn't want him to know his face, either. At least not until he learned for certain what this was really about. "You have to understand," he said, "there was an air of mystery about the whole thing."

His first impression, he said, was that Rob Marshall was a very nervous man. "The minute he showed up, he was jumpin'. He was scared. It was like somebody was pursuin' him. Like any day the bottom was going to fall out."

L'Heureux's "investigator's greeting" didn't do much to put Rob at ease. "I shook him down," Ferlin said. "Patted him down to make sure he didn't have any kind of recordin' device on him. He was kind of squirrelly-lookin' to me. I thought he might be part of some kind of federal strike force to entrap me, to coerce me into cooperatin' with some of those other matters they might have goin' on."

The next thing he did, Ferlin said, was remind Rob that they had some "unfinished business." There was no argument. Rob said he had already stopped at the casino cashier before coming up to the room and had drawn $2,500 on his credit account. He then handed L'Heureux twenty-five crisp, new one-hundred-dollar bills.

Then he started to talk. "At the outset," Ferlin said, "he told me that it was his impression that his wife was havin' an affair with someone, he didn't know who, and he wanted a domestic surveillance conducted on her."

Ferlin's first question was the obvious one: why hire a detective from Louisiana for that? But Rob explained that he was so well known, such a prominent citizen of Toms River, that no local or even nearby detective could be trusted to maintain confidentiality. The temptation to gossip about a man of Rob's social status would simply be overwhelming. "He said anybody he went to up here had a way of leakin' out his business," Ferlin recalled.

Rob had then given him various details concerning Maria's daily life, "what she drove, where she played tennis, clubs she went to, where she banked, her friends, things of that nature, so I could pick her up and follow her around."

But Ferlin noticed that Rob seemed strangely distracted, jittery, impatient. As if he were having trouble coming to the point.

"I could see there was somethin' that wasn't right. He lingered on in the room. Then he took two pictures out of his wallet. One of them was of his house and the other one was his wife. He gave them to me. And then he said, 'What I really want—' And then he stopped. Then he tried it again. He said, 'What I really want is my wife done away with.'

"So I asked him, 'Done away with?' He said, 'Yes.' I said, 'You mean divorced?' He said, 'No. I want to get rid of her.' And I asked him, 'What do you mean, get rid of her?' The strange thing was, he just wouldn't say 'killed' by himself. He would say 'disposed of.' He would say 'get rid of.' He would say 'done away with.' But he just couldn't make himself say 'murdered.'

"So I finally done it. I said, 'You're tellin' me that what you want done is your wife murdered?' And he

said, 'Yes.' I looked down at her picture and then I
looked up at him and I said, 'Why in God's name do
you want to murder her?'

"He went on to say he was in debt from gamblin',
he just overextended himself, he had a big house and
new cars and kids in school—three boys, he kept tellin' me—and he owned a condo in Florida, and just a
number of things. He had just more or less been livin'
out of his means."

Ferlin asked him if there were another woman
involved.

"He first told me no, but I knew just from how he
said it that that was a lie. So I said, 'Just what is the
problem?'' And he said, 'We're not compatible.' I
said, 'Well, why don't you just *divorce* her?' But he
said, 'No, that would ruin me. It would be devastatin'
to me. I couldn't handle that.' Then he said, yes, he
did have a girlfriend that he intended on marryin' one
day, and that he had his wife heavily insured and that
he wanted, he needed the money.''

"So what did you tell him, Ferlin?" Gladstone asked.

"I said, 'These things can be done.' And he wanted
to know how much it would cost. Of course, I was
thinkin' in my mind that no money at all could make
me commit any crime such as this, but through talkin'
with him I was faced with a man that I thought could
afford, ah, a reasonable sum, or what he would consider a reasonable amount of money. A man who was
desperate. So I told him a hundred thousand dollars.
He said, 'That's too much,' so we haggled back and
forth there and finally come up with a figure of
sixty-five."

Five thousand had already been paid. Rob agreed to
go right back downstairs and draw another ten thousand from his casino credit line. The remaining fifty,
Rob said, would be paid after he collected the insurance.

"But I was skeptical about that," Ferlin said. "I said, 'That could be, ah, that could take forever to collect.' No, he was an insurance man, he was on the board of the bank or board of the city, or whatever. He was an influential person and he didn't anticipate any problems in collectin' this insurance money. The amount he told me it was, was one hundred and thirty thousand, but he said it was double indemnity so he'd be collectin' twice that. Guess he didn't want me to know how much he really had comin' or he figured I'd be up here pesterin' him the rest of his life."

"That's the only thing he figured right all year," O'Brien said.

Rob left the room at that point, Ferlin said, to go downstairs and get the ten thousand. But when he came back he had only seven. "I told him, 'This is seven. We said ten.' And he said, 'I'll have the rest with me tonight.' I said, 'Tonight?' And he was gettin' all jittery and jumpy again. He said, 'Yes, tonight. That's when I want you to kill her.' "

"Wait a minute," Gladstone said. "Twenty minutes after he walks into your room, he's not only telling you that he wants you to murder his wife, but that he wants you to do it *that night?*"

"Listen, Gladstone," L'Heureux said. "I was kind of taken aback by that myself. I had considered that I could string him along a while, tell him some kind of something and then blow the deal off—just never do it, after taking him for as much as I could. I didn't like that 'tonight' shit, either."

"What did you say?" Gladstone asked.

"I said, 'No, no, you got to wait for the proper time, the proper atmosphere. It may take six months. Or a year.' But he said right away again, as if somethin' powerful was closin' in on him, 'I don't have six months. I want you to do it tonight.' "

Ferlin said that Rob had explained to him that he'd be taking Maria to dinner at a posh restaurant called the Ram's Head, in a town called Absecon, just across the bridge from Atlantic City. He already had it all figured out. He and Maria would come out to the parking lot after dinner and get into Rob's ivory Cadillac. Then Rob would tell her that he had to run back inside to use the men's room. "Then, he says, 'You can walk up to the Cadillac and kill her.' Simple as that, he thinks. While he's standin' inside there, wonderin' why the pee won't come out."

"So, what did you say?" Gladstone asked.

"I says, 'How do you want it done?' See, I'm still just stringin' him along. And he tells me how he *don't* want it done. He didn't want a shotgun used on her, he didn't want a knife used on her, he didn't want it done in his house where his kids might be present, he didn't want her carried off in a rape, he didn't want anything that could tear her up. He said, and these were his exact words— 'I don't want to mar the beauty of my wife, Maria.' "

"And what did you say?" Gladstone asked.

"I said, 'You know somethin'? You're *crazy.*' "

But Rob was also in a hurry. He kept looking at his watch. He said he had to get back up the parkway to meet his girlfriend. But before he left, he wanted to be sure it was settled: the murder would be committed that night, in the parking lot of the Ram's Head, in a manner that would not mar the beauty of Maria.

"So I said, 'I'll look at it. See if it can be done.' Hell, I already had twelve thousand dollars just for talkin'. I was in no hurry to shut down the well.' "

Ferlin said the two of them walked together to the parking garage across from Harrah's, where Rob pointed out the ivory Cadillac and made sure Ferlin copied down the license number. Wouldn't want the

wrong lady killed by mistake. Rob said they had an 8
P.M. reservation, which meant they should be out between ten and ten thirty. He said he would park at the
outer edge of the lot.

"I told him," Ferlin said, "I told him, 'You know,
it's gonna be hard. There's gonna be a lot of heat, a
lot of pressure. They're gonna rake you over the coals.
Your business, your girlfriend—they're gonna look at
everythin' you got.'

"But he told me not to worry about any of that.
That he was an outstandin' member of the community
and had a lot of influence and he could handle that. So
I told him, okay, I would check it out. And that if it
could be done, you know, well, it would be done."

Then Ferlin told the men from the prosecutor's office that he actually had ridden up to check it out. He
said he'd spent the afternoon playing blackjack and
wandering around and then he had a couple of drinks
and a bite or two to eat, and then he'd taken out the
card that the Korean cab driver had given him the
night before and called him. The Korean had picked
him up at the front door of Harrah's Marina and had
driven him to the Ram's Head, which was ten miles
away but, unlike the Islander, easy to find.

"The goddamn place," Ferlin said, "it looked like
the state capitol buildin' in Baton Rouge. Least it had
as much security. And it was lit up even brighter.
'Specially the parkin' lot. There were lights all over
the place. And all those limousines. I'm thinkin' the
captain of the state police is probably inside, havin' his
dinner. And those bodyguards out beside the cars
looked like they was all carryin' guns. I said, 'Now I
know this guy is crazy, thinkin' I could do it someplace
like this.'

"I never even got out of the cab. Just made the
circle around the parkin' lot. I said, 'Nice restaurant.'

The Chinaman said, 'You don't want to stop?' I said, 'Fuck, no, just take me back to the casinos.' "

"And then what?" O'Brien said. "You just wake up in the morning and go home?"

"Shit, he *woke* me up. Called my room at eight o'clock in the mornin'. And he wasn't happy. He wanted to know why the job wasn't done. I said, 'Man, you're crazy. That parkin' lot was filled up. There was no place for anythin' like that to happen. Besides, I didn't bring nothin' but a shotgun'—which, of course, I didn't bring no gun at all. I flew on the plane with walk-on luggage. 'I got to go back home, get what I need,' I said. 'You send me that other three thousand and I'll be back in a week or so.' He said, 'I'm bringin' her down to Harrah's Friday. Can you be back by then?' I mean, this guy was *determined*. There was no way he was gonna let that lady live."

Rob, of course, had sent the three thousand. It arrived in Shreveport only two days after Ferlin did, and again, Ernie Grandshaw was prevailed upon to pick up the money order.

"Then he started callin'," Ferlin said. "Marshall kept callin' and callin' and *callin'* Myers, and every time he did, Myers called me and said, 'The man appreciates that you have twelve thousand dollars of his money and you haven't done nothin' for him yet.' Andy was pressurin' me to go up and do what it was I'd agreed to do.' "

So, Ferlin said, he'd gone back up in July. More money was the major motivation. "As long as he was willin' to put it out, I was willin' to take it," he said. He had called Myers to say he'd be back in Atlantic City on July 17 and that Myers should pass the message on.

On the July trip, L'Heureux said, he'd brought a friend named Travis Greene, someone closer to the center of the bank robber gang. They'd left Shreveport at 9 A.M. on July 16 and had arrived in Atlantic City at seven o'clock the next morning. This time, Ferlin chose not to stay at Harrah's. He stopped instead at an inconspicuous motel near the airport called the Seacomber. It was Greene who signed the registration card.

Two hours later, he said, after a shower and another big breakfast, he'd left Greene sleeping in the room and had walked down the street to a pay phone outside the Airport Motor Inn and had called Rob Marshall at his office. He'd told Marshall to go out to a pay phone and call him back.

Ten minutes later, Marshall had called back. He'd said he would bring Maria to Harrah's Marina for dinner that night and then they would go to the casino for gambling. He told Ferlin, whom, of course, he was calling "Ernie Grandshaw," to meet him in the rear lobby of the casino at 9 P.M.

"He did meet me there," Ferlin said, "but I told him this job was requirin' a lot more money than I thought it would, that I would need more. Somethin' like this was expensive, requirin' stealin' cars and guns, involvin' other people, things like that."

"He must have been overjoyed to hear that," O'Brien said.

"Well, he said he was currently in the dinin' room havin' dinner but would come back in a little while, and he'd have more money then."

Which he did, bringing an additional seven thousand dollars' worth of chips. But having paid that, Rob insisted on immediate action. "To him it was supposed to be, you know, just right then. He was ready."

Rob said that he'd leave the casino and drive to an all-night diner that was located just before the en-

trance to the parkway. He'd park behind it, telling
Maria his favorite story: that his weak bladder necessi-
tated a trip to the men's room. He would try to see to
it that she wouldn't lock the door, but being as how
she was such a cautious, timid woman, she probably
would.

" 'If she locks the door, I can't get in,' is what I told
him. And he said, 'Well, then, you'll just have to
shoot her through the glass.' I tell you, he was on
edge. Much worse even than in June. That man was
driven. It was like he was gettin' down to where he
had to cover his money. He made some comment to
me that he only had so long to get the money that it
was that he needed. He was desperate to get this
done. It was like these underworld people, they had
the squeeze on him somewhere.

"Somebody was puttin'—either himself mentally or
someone else—was exertin' a lot of pressure on him
for a tremendous amount of money in a hurry and he
was at the point of jumpin' out the fuckin' window."

Ferlin said he'd always heard that casinos, like banks,
had cameras trained constantly on all areas where
financial transactions were made, and he did not want
to wind up on videotape. So he gave his friend Greene
the chips to cash in, while he waited at the bar.

Sitting there alone, he said, he looked casually out
upon the crowded casino floor. His eyes moved ran-
domly from table to table. It was sure some scene.
The plush carpet, the highly polished brass and silver
and wood, the bright green felt of the playing surfaces.
And all those suckers dressed to the gills, as if an
expensive wardrobe would guarantee gambling success.

Then, he said, his eyes fell upon one particularly
attractive and fashionably dressed woman, sitting at a
blackjack table with an empty chair beside her.

It was Maria Marshall.

He recognized her instantly from the picture Rob had handed him the first time they'd met. She was holding a long-stemmed red rose. Ferlin thought that she looked even lovelier in person than in the picture. And he wondered again about what desperation a man would have to be driven to in order to feel he had to arrange for the murder of a woman like that.

"She was just sittin' there by herself," he told the men from the prosecutor's office. "And she was holdin' that rose. Just holdin' that rose. I never will forget that."

He didn't kill her that night either, of course. "I took Greene back to the motel," he said, "and then I took a ride up toward the, ah, twenty-four-hour restaurant, where, ah, the murder was to take place, and thought that I might wait and see, ah, Marshall enter and see if he would go through with what he said he wanted done. But it was the kind of place where every cop in three counties must stop for a cup of coffee on their shift, and I only stayed there a short period of time and decided, what the heck. You know, it was more just a curiosity on my part.

"But I got to tell you somethin' else I always wondered about. I always wondered what they talked about all the way home. I mean, what do you say to your wife when she is already supposed to be dead?"

Back in Shreveport, he'd gotten a frantic call from Myers, saying Marshall was demanding to know why he'd failed to show up for their "meeting." That was when he'd invented the picaresque tale about the stolen cars and hitchhikers and auto accidents and missing guns—he couldn't even remember all the bullshit he'd put into that story.

In any event, it had not mollified Rob. "Myers called me back," Ferlin said, "and he says, 'He is upset. Please give this man a phone number so he won't keep calling and bothering me.' "

Finally, Ferlin had agreed to give the number of the Exxon station at Bunkam Road, just off Interstate 20, four miles from his house. He had told Myers to tell Marshall to call him there at 7 P.M. on July 24.

It wasn't until 9:49, according to Gladstone's records, that Marshall had made the call. But he had made it. To that number. Ferlin's story was checking out in every particular. That call had lasted four minutes.

"He wanted to know what had happened, what the problem was," Ferlin said. "Why I didn't take care of Maria. He had went inside the restaurant, he said, and he waited a good while inside, but he heard no gunshot. I said, 'Well, weren't you surprised?' And he said, 'Well, yes.' And I said, 'Well, all kinds of things happened. We stole the car and had a wreck and I had some other guys with me and two of them got arrested and, ah, we just had to get out of the area as quick as possible.' And he said, 'Oh, that's too bad. But we got to get this thing done.' "

Then Rob had told him that they'd be taking a vacation and he would not be back until early August. They arranged for Rob to call the same number—the pay phone at the Exxon station on Bunkam Road—on the evening of August 5.

But Rob had apparently lost the number because Ferlin had waited by that phone for hours and the call never came. Instead, Rob had called Andrew Myers, asking him to relay the message, Ferlin said, that if the "investigation" was completed by Labor Day, "there would be an extra fifteen in it for me."

At that point, however, Ferlin had begun to think that he might be pushing his luck. He'd made more than twenty thousand dollars for doing nothing and he'd had a little fun in Atlantic City besides. Maybe the time had come to leave well enough alone. Being an "investigator" had been kind of fun, and it had taught him that people in New Jersey had a lot of money to throw around and got themselves in some godawful messes and sure were stupid to boot, but maybe this was a time not to be greedy. Marshall was a little too crazy and desperate for his taste. Besides, he'd kind of liked Maria when he'd seen her in the casino that night. She'd looked so darned pretty, sitting there all by herself, just holding that rose.

"I just did not want to get on the road and come back up here," Ferlin said. So he'd told Myers to pass the message along to Rob that it would be a while before he could get to it.

Gladstone's phone records indicated that that call would have been made on Friday, August 31, a date that Myers later confirmed, saying he remembered it exactly because it was his birthday.

Within twenty-four hours, Ferlin said, he'd received a phone call from a man named Ricky Dew.

"He said, 'I need to talk to you right away.' I said, 'Well, I'm fixin' to go out to dinner, can it be later?' He said, 'No, it can't. I need to meet you now. Behind the McDonald's on Pines Road and I-Twenty.' I told him, 'Okay, I'll be up there in a minute.' "

Ferlin tried to explain about Ricky Dew. He'd known Ricky for at least fifteen years, since back when he was a cop and Ricky was an auto mechanic.

But Ricky wasn't just an auto mechanic. Ricky was into a lot of things. Rattlesnakes (which he hunted for recreation). Silver mining. And banking. It was just that Ricky's banking habits were somewhat unorthodox, Ferlin explained. Like he tended simply to go in and take the money.

His was a name that Gladstone had heard mentioned a lot in Shreveport, and Gladstone knew that, among other things, Dew was a prime suspect in more than fifty bank robberies that had been committed since 1981 in northern Louisiana, east Texas, Arkansas and Mississippi.

Ricky's was the gang that Ferlin was trying to be part of, while hinting about it to law enforcement authorities at the same time. Thus, it had not been comforting to hear that Ricky wanted to meet with him right away. Behind McDonald's.

"One thought I had was, they may be waitin' up there to take me out."

So, he said, he'd told his wife that they wouldn't be going out to dinner after all. Then he'd taken his .45 from the glove compartment of his Cadillac, where he normally kept it, and he'd laid it on the front seat and he'd headed for the golden arches to see whether it was shooting or talking that Ricky had on his mind.

As it happened, Ferlin said, it was both.

"What he said was, 'I hate to tell you this, but you are in a lot of trouble.' And I said, 'Is that right?' And he said, 'Yeah, a man out of Dallas has approached me. He wants you taken care of.' And I said, 'Why is that?' But, see, I kind of already knew why. I mean, I hadn't done anything up north.

"And Ricky said, 'He's put out a seventy-five-thousand-dollar contract on you.' Ricky told me that he understood that I had not fulfilled a contract that I had taken in New Jersey from a man and the man was willin' to lay the money out to have me taken care of.

"This went on for some time," Ferlin said, "and it was a little upsettin' to me. I didn't know that what maybe he did have those kind of connections."

"That's Mr. Marshall?" Gladstone asked.

"Mr. Marshall," Ferlin said.

Then Ferlin explained that a few years earlier a

mutual acquaintance had offered him five thousand
dollars to kill Ricky, but that instead of doing it, he'd
told Ricky about it. The thought occurred to him that
maybe Ricky was simply returning the favor. Then he
realized that Ricky wasn't really the favor-returning
kind.

What seemed more likely, as Ferlin thought about
it, was that Ricky figured if it was worth seventy-five
thousand dollars to someone in New Jersey to go
through a middleman in Dallas to have Ferlin killed
for not killing someone he was supposed to have killed,
then killing that someone might wind up being worth
even more.

"So he asked me, 'Why haven't you done it?' " Ferlin
said.

And that was a question that posed a problem for
Ferlin. The reason he hadn't done it was that he didn't
really want to kill Maria. Obviously, whoever had put
Rob in touch with Andrew Myers at the Riccio party
had expected that Myers would be able to supply a
man who could solve any sort of problem Marshall
might present for solution. And, just as obviously,
there were people in Louisiana—Andrew Myers apparently being among them—who had been confident
that Ferlin L'Heureux was that sort of man.

Yet it hadn't worked out. It had seemed so much
easier to Ferlin just to take the client's money and do
nothing. Especially when the client seemed so squirrelly
—wanting it done that very first night, in the parking
lot of one of the most crowded restaurants north of
Atlanta; and then the second time at an all-night diner
where half the customers had seemed to be cops on a
coffee break.

Besides, he'd looked at those pictures Rob had
showed him. The nice house, the good-looking kids,

the woman herself, who looked like the sort of wife a
man should kill to *get,* not kill to get rid of.

Hell, having their mother murdered was going to be
upsetting to those kids. And Ferlin liked kids. He had
six of his own of various ages and he tried not to upset
them any more than was absolutely necessary in the
conduct of his own personal business.

Then, once he'd actually laid eyes on the woman—
sitting all alone there at the table, twirling that red
rose in her hands. No way Ferlin had been going to do
it that night. Or probably ever, if the choice had been
left to him. Only now, it seemed, the choice was
somewhat different. It wasn't even so much a choice
anymore as it was a matter of self-defense. Because it
sure looked like somebody was going to die: the question was, would it be him or would it be Maria
Marshall?

Not that he'd wanted to get very deeply into that
with Ricky. Or even with these Ocean County people
now.

"So I said, 'Well, I—' See, I didn't say that I didn't
want to do it or anythin' like that. I'm not wantin' him
to think I'm chicken-livered. He had a habit in the past
of sayin', 'All you want to do is get the gravy. You
don't want to take any risks.' Shit like that. That was
the air surroundin' me.

"And, see, I knew that Ricky and them's got some
things goin' of their own, so I don't want to say I ain't
comin' up here to do this job—not goin' to go along
with this and then want in on somethin' else. If Ricky
thought I was comin' up here to maybe help him do a
hit, then I'd be invited on the next bank job.

"Ricky said, 'These things can be done. Let's go up
there and take a look at it. Let's get on the road. Let's
go do it.' So I led him to believe, 'Sure, let's go do it.'
I was maintainin' a front. And in my mind I'm thinkin',

'Well, hell, if Marshall's goin' to pay all that money, *somebody's* going to kill his wife for him, so I'll just introduce him to Ricky.' "

And so, Ferlin said, he called Myers and told Myers to call Marshall and say he was coming, after all, and would be arriving in Atlantic City on September 6.

He said he and Dew left Shreveport on the evening of Tuesday, September 4, in Ferlin's white Cadillac with the Texas plates and the .45 automatic in the glove compartment.

(Dew, on the other hand, would later tell authorities, and would maintain throughout his trial, that he'd had no involvement in the murder whatsoever, and that he'd never accompanied L'Heureux to New Jersey.)

Ferlin said they spent the night in a Comfort Inn in Jackson, Mississippi, and then drove straight through, arriving in Atlantic City just after dawn on Thursday, September 6.

He said he checked into the Airport Motor Inn under the name of Ernie Grandshaw, and, at just about 10 A.M., he called Marshall from the pay phone outside the motel and told him to go out to a pay phone and call him back.

The longer he'd spent in Shreveport in October, the more Bob Gladstone had been told the same thing. It didn't matter where he was, whom he talked to—the Shreveport police, the detectives, the Caddo Parish Sheriff's people, even the FBI—they all told him the same thing: Ferlin L'Heureux was not a killer.

At least not of a sleeping woman, shot in the back.

Ferlin was a weak man and a greedy man and even a vicious and *absolutely* immoral man, Gladstone was told, but Ferlin would not shoot a sleeping woman in the back. Not even, most likely, *any* woman, back or front, asleep or awake. Ferlin might be the one who set it up, and Ferlin might be the one to profit by it, and Ferlin might drive the getaway car, but Ferlin would not be the shooter.

And so Gladstone had been plagued all fall by the damp, chill fear that the man who'd actually pulled the trigger, the man who had shot and killed Maria Marshall, was somehow escaping their net.

So now, on December 14, when Ferlin L'Heureux finally reached the part of his story in which he introduced the name of Ricky Dew, it did not come to Bob Gladstone as a total surprise.

All fall, Gladstone had asked around Shreveport, "If L'Heureux wasn't the shooter, then who do you think it could be?" He was told there was no shortage of candidates, especially among the bank-robbing crowd that Ferlin was hanging with, but the name that had been mentioned most frequently—and in voices tinged with fear and awe—had been the name of Ricky Dew.

Ricky had been around Shreveport a long time, Gladstone was told. Since the late 1950s, anyway, when he was a teenager and his father had moved down from South Carolina, looking to make a little money out of the oil fields that were sprouting in northwest Louisiana and east Texas.

He was a man who kept a low profile, living back deep in the woods, disappearing for months at a time. But in Shreveport, his was a name well known to law enforcement authorities.

In the late 1960s, Gladstone was told, Dew had started looking at banks. That was also when he'd begun to travel with Ferlin, the sheriff's deputy who had not yet been dismissed from the force. "Back then," a Shreveport police official said, "you didn't get one without the other."

It was funny, they told Gladstone, to look at Ricky you'd never figure people had long since stopped count-

ing the number of murders he was supposed to have
committed. He was just an average, kind of scruffy,
middle-aged, down-home sort of guy. Six feet tall,
with red hair, long sideburns, a mustache and a craggy
face marked with small, X-shaped scars that supposedly had come from snake bites.

The one thing about Ricky that stood out was his
eyes. They were the kind of eyes, someone once said
to Gladstone, that you would sometimes see in Viet-
nam. Eyes with no feeling behind them. Eyes that
never smiled, not even when the mouth appeared to.
Eyes as opaque and uncaring as the ocean floor.

Dew had attracted some attention in November 1977,
when his first wife died in a boating accident. She had
been fishing with Ricky at the time, and what people
told Gladstone in Shreveport was that he had collected
quite a bit of money from her pension plan and that,
of course, he'd been considered a suspect—*the* suspect
—in her death. But there simply had not been any
evidence.

"Ricky's a pro, no doubt about that," Gladstone
was told. "He's a legend around here. What helps him
is he don't have any fuckin' conscience at all. I don't
think he could cry if he wanted to. And he could wash
his hands in your blood."

But the story that had caused Gladstone to pay the
closest attention, and the story that came back to him
now, as Ferlin L'Heureux continued to talk, was the
story of Linda Carlisle.

Like Maria Marshall, she had been blond and attractive, and like Maria Marshall, she had been shot
from the rear while seated in a luxury car that had just
pulled off a major thoroughfare. Her husband, like
Rob Marshall, had been at the scene when the fatal
shots were fired. Her husband, like Rob Marshall,
stood to benefit financially from her death.

She'd been killed on Halloween of 1981. Her husband, Steven Carlisle, who had been on the verge of bankruptcy, had pulled off a highway on the outskirts of Shreveport and had parked briefly behind an oak tree in a park.

She was killed by a blast from a .12-gauge double-barreled shotgun, fired from a distance of only two to three feet into the back of her head. The killer apparently had been waiting for her in the darkness behind the tree.

Her husband settled several debts, including the mortgage on his home, from the proceeds of her life insurance policies, Gladstone was told, but, for lack of evidence, he was never prosecuted in connection with the murder.

Her husband had been a friend of Ricky Dew's.

Dew wasn't charged either, although a number of Shreveport law enforcement officials suspected he had done it. Again, the reason was no evidence.

"Thing about Ricky," Gladstone was told, "is that there's never any evidence. Ricky don't leave traces behind."

All of this was much on Bob Gladstone's mind as Ferlin, in his narrative, began to re-create what had happened on the morning of September 6.

The story he told (which, of course, was contradicted in many particulars by Ricky Dew) was as follows:

At 10:07, using the coin box outside the 7-Eleven on East Washington Street, Rob called L'Heureux at the coin box outside the Airport Motor Inn. Their conversation lasted three minutes and twenty-three seconds. Rob told L'Heureux that he'd be bringing Maria back to Harrah's that night to get the job done, but that he wanted to meet L'Heureux in an hour at the Roy Rogers rest area on the parkway just below Toms

River so the two of them could go scouting locations. Rob said he had some good ones in mind.

Sometime between 11 A.M. and noon, L'Heureux pulled into the Roy Rogers parking lot, which was officially known as the Forked River Rest Area at mile marker 76. L'Heureux had told Rob to park at the north end of the lot. L'Heureux parked at the south end, left Dew sitting in the car, and walked to the north end to meet Rob, who was standing in the parking lot next to his Cadillac Eldorado.

Rob, as usual, was dressed in blue blazer, rep tie, and chinos. The day was sunny but unseasonably cool for that early in September. L'Heureux wore sunglasses and a leather car coat. At 250 pounds, he knew he cut a conspicuous figure standing there next to an ivory Eldorado in broad daylight in a busy parking lot just off such a heavily traveled highway, only ten miles from the town of Toms River, in which the man who was now smiling at him and shaking his hand was such a big shot.

L'Heureux looked around at all the busyness. He didn't like it. *This guy could kill his wife without me even knowing about it and frame my fucking ass,* he thought. "Say, Marshall," he said, "how about we get in the goddamned car."

Once they did, L'Heureux asked for the "extra fifteen" that had been promised. It was only three days after Labor Day and here he was and he wanted his money. Rob said he didn't have it with him then but would give it to L'Heureux at the casino that night. What he wanted to do now—and he didn't have much time because he was running a little late—was to select a site where the job could unquestionably be accomplished that night.

He pulled out of the parking lot at high speed, heading south along the parkway. (This would have been at just about the time Roby Marshall was waking up on Crest Ridge Drive and his mother was asking him if he wanted to join her and his father for lunch at the club.)

"He was drivin' eighty, ninety miles an hour," L'Heureux said. "Checkin' his watch the whole way. I said, 'Hey, Marshall, let's not get stopped.' "

They drove through two toll plazas and shortly beyond the second Rob made a U-turn across the median strip and pulled to a stop at the side of the road just where it made a slight bend.

"This is good," he said. "I could pull over here on our way back tonight and in a matter of minutes you could have it done and be gone."

"Marshall, you're *crazy!*" L'Heureux said. "Man, this is right out here in the daylight."

"But tonight," Rob said, "it will be dark. Late at night sometimes there are three or four minutes between cars."

"No way," L'Heureux said. "It's right out in the open, which is fine for you because when they start askin' you questions you can say, 'Listen, there's no way I'm gonna have my wife killed right out here in the *open*. But it ain't fine for me. Keep drivin'."

Rob continued north a few miles further until he came to a picnic area along the median strip. He pulled in and said, "How about this?"

L'Heureux did not like this site either. "The trees had been all trimmed up. You could see all the way through to the other side. I said, 'That won't do.' "

So they drove further north until they came to the thickly wooded Oyster Creek picnic area. Rob pulled in there and L'Heureux said, "This looks fine."

From there, it was less than four miles to the Roy Rogers where L'Heureux's Cadillac was parked. When they pulled in, L'Heureux could see Ricky Dew sitting on the front steps of the restaurant, taking the noon-day sun. (Back on Crest Ridge Drive Roby was asking Maria why his father was late and where he was and she was saying, "God knows where your father is these days.")

L'Heureux told Rob to keep driving to the north end of the parking lot. He did not want to introduce Rob to Ricky Dew. If anything ever went wrong, he figured, the fewer people who knew one another the better. He told Rob to meet him outside the back door of Harrah's, by the marina, at 9 P.M., just as they'd done in July. He told Rob to be sure to have the extra fifteen with him. He said the Oyster Creek picnic area looked like the right place, but he wanted to do a little further checking and he'd give Rob final instructions that night.

"We drove back down the parkway," Ferlin said, "so I could show Ricky the place I'd picked out. We stopped there for a bit, in fact we even took a leak in the bushes. I told him, 'This seems to be the only place to do it. The other places he showed me weren't worth shit.' And he said, 'This'll be all right. But let's get out of here now, we'll talk in the car.' "

On the trip back to Atlantic City, Ferlin said, Ricky explained how he wanted the scene arranged. He said L'Heureux should drop him off in the picnic area before the Marshall car arrived. That way, in the unlikely event that another vehicle—such as, perhaps, a state police patrol car, or a passenger car containing potential witnesses—pulled in before Marshall and was still present when Rob entered the site, Dew could just sit silently in the bushes and permit the Marshalls to leave without incident.

Should that happen, Rob was to continue north to the Roy Rogers parking lot. After L'Heureux retrieved

Dew from the bushes, they could make a second attempt there, if the lot were sufficiently vacant.

"Then you tell him," Dew continued, "if we don't
get her at Roy Rogers he should just drive on up and
when he gets to Toms River, just ease slowly into his
regular off-ramp and we can pull up alongside and try
her there. If that don't go, tell him to go home, you'll
talk to him tomorrow."

"He ain't gonna be happy with 'tomorrow.' He's
been hearin' that all summer long."

"Well, he ain't likely gonna hear it tonight. What
I'm tellin' you's just in case. We'll get the job done
right there at that picnic spot. But you tell him once
he pulls in there to get the hell out of the car. Make
like he's got engine trouble or tire trouble or something. I don't want her sittin' in his lap."

"He don't either, from what I can tell."

"Then, of course, I'm gonna have to shoot him,
too."

"What?" L'Heureux said.

"Not to kill him, just to wound him up a little bit.
Got to make it look good, you know. Like a robbery."

"Ricky, I can tell you right now, he ain't gonna like
that part."

"Fuckin' difference does it make what he likes?
We're the ones that's doin' the job."

"I'll tell him, all right. It's just that he don't strike
me as bein' too keen on personal discomfort."

"I'll make it a flesh wound. No kneecaps or nothin'
like that."

When they reached Atlantic City, Ferlin said, they
went back to the Airport Motor Inn and took a nap.
(Ricky Dew would later insist that L'Heureux's story,
insofar as it involved him, was a total fabrication.)

"I met Marshall there," Ferlin said, "just outside
the casino, out back by the marina part, at nine o'clock.

I thought the man had done come apart. He said, 'I just don't know how much longer I can *stand* it.' He was takin' his hanky out, you know, and wipin' his forehead. Said, 'I don't know how much longer I can go on.'

"But the first thing I said was, 'Where's the money? Where's the fifteen?' He said he didn't have it but he'd be drawin' it from this casino credit line he kept talkin' about and he'd *definitely* have it on him by the time he got to Oyster Creek.

"So I told him, 'All right. You stay here gamblin' until about eleven thirty, quarter to twelve. Then you just drive on up to Oyster Creek there, like we done this mornin', and when you pull in, pull *way* in, make that second left that goes down the lane there and then stop the car and get out. That's real important. Get out of the car.

" 'Go to the rear,' I told him, 'like you're checkin' a tire. Somebody will be there. He'll shoot you, but not too bad. Then he'll take care of your wife and I'll pull in and pick him up and we'll be gone. You give it a minute or two and then go out on the parkway—the *northbound* parkway, 'cause we'll be goin' south— and flag down a car and ask for help. All's you know is you've been shot and you've been robbed. And that'll be true, 'cause you be sure to have that fifteen thousand in your pants pocket. We'll take it off you there.'

"But I notice that Marshall's turnin' whiter and sweatin' more. He's got that hanky goin' a mile a minute, moppin' himself, but the sweat is just pourin' off him. He says, 'He can't *shoot* me. *I'm* not the one who gets shot.' And I says, 'Well, damn, we got to make this look like a robbery, we can't just leave you sittin' there listenin' to the Hit Parade while your wife is bleedin' all over your lap.' But he says, 'You'll have

to think of somethin' else. I don't want to be shot.'
And he's *still* sweatin'. Fact, I thought the man was
gonna faint right there at my feet.

"So I says, 'All right, but he's at least gonna have to
hit you on the head.' And he says, 'But not too hard.
Make sure you tell him not too hard. I don't want to
wind up as a idiot. I don't want to be a idiot the rest of
my life.'

"I told him, 'Don't you worry, you just kneel down
by your tire there. We'll give it the professional touch.' "

Ferlin said he and Ricky then left the casino and
stopped by a True Value hardware store and he went
in and bought Ricky a pair of rubber gloves. Then
they drove up the parkway to Oyster Creek.

At some point close to midnight, Ferlin said, he
dropped Ricky off, giving him the gloves and the Colt
.45 from his glove compartment. Then he pulled out
of the picnic area and headed south.

But he was nervous, he said, he was edgy. He had
never really thought it would come to this. He went
through the toll plaza just below the picnic area and
then left the parkway at the first available exit. He got
on again, heading north, and went through the toll
plaza again. He pulled to the shoulder of the road by a
bank of pay phones. Five minutes later, he started up
again and continued north, driving past the picnic area
in which Dew was waiting. He got as far as the Roy
Rogers where he'd met Rob that morning. He swung
through the Roy Rogers parking lot and headed back
south. He passed the picnic area one more time and
thought of pulling in to ask Ricky if maybe they
shouldn't just forget the whole thing. Then he figured,
shit, I'm the first car in there, he'll probably shoot *me*.
And there wasn't likely to be much other traffic, what
with big signs at all entrances saying "Closed After
Dark."

He drove through the toll plaza again—he had plenty of quarters, so he could use exact change every time—and once more exited the parkway and reentered northbound. This time, when he came through the toll plaza northbound, he pulled to the shoulder by the pay phones and just waited. Waited for whatever would happen next. He really hadn't wanted things to get to this point. She was such a pretty woman, after all, and it wasn't like *she'd* done any harm to anyone. All he'd been in it for was however many thousand he could squeeze out of her husband. He hadn't figured that the man would have connections. He hadn't figured on a contract out on *his* life. But now it didn't matter what he figured. It was too late to do a goddamned thing. Just sit there by the pay phones and watch the toll booths, waiting for that ivory Eldorado to come through. It was just one goddamned hell of a shame, though. And those three boys of hers—they were just bound to miss her like hell.

Then Rob came through the toll gate. L'Heureux was so deep in reverie he almost missed him. Besides, there was a lot of traffic for practically one o'clock in the morning.

It was about two miles from the toll booth to the picnic area. He waited for what he estimated as two minutes, in order to give Rob time to arrive. Then he pulled out onto the parkway. *Christ, there was a lot of traffic.* That fool Marshall had said that this was practically a deserted stretch of road at this time of night.

The traffic, in fact, was so thick when L'Heureux reached the ramp that led to the picnic area from the parkway's extreme left lane that he couldn't get to it and was forced to pull off onto the shoulder to the *right* so he wouldn't miss it entirely. Then he had to sit for what had to be another sixty or ninety seconds at least, waiting for the traffic to thin out, before he could cut across the parkway and pull into the dark and thickly wooded location that he'd helped to choose as the place where Maria Marshall would die.

"Okay, Ferlin," Gladstone said. "What happened next?"

"I pulled in and stopped and I could see Marshall's Cadillac parked at kind of an angle to me, the door on the passenger's side was open, and Marshall was layin' on the ground, kind of toward the rear wheel.

"Uh, Ricky came runnin' and I reached over and opened the door and Ricky put some things on the floor. He said, 'Just a minute,' and then he run back around, squatted beside Marshall's car and I could hear the air hissin' out of the tire. He run back to my car and got in and I eased out of the exit into the southbound lane.

"After we went through the toll, he turns on the map light and he begins lookin' through Maria Marshall's purse. He took out some money—it seems like there was twenty-dollar bills in there—and fumbled through there. I said, 'Man, get rid of that purse, get it out of the car!' I was hesitant about bein' on the parkway, because to me it was just a one-way road with gates every now and then and lots of police. So I made an exit. He asked me what the hell I was doin'. I said, 'Throw that purse out the window, let's get out of here.' He was complainin' that there was only, I think, four hundred dollars inside, and he said Marshall never did have the fifteen thousand in his pants.

"And, uh, in my nervous condition I had went the wrong way once I got off the parkway and after a while I seen the sign that said Toms River, three or four miles, or somethin', so I realized I was travelin' in the opposite direction of Atlantic City, so I pulled to the shoulder of the road and turned around, and, uh, I

don't know how I did it but I got back up on the
parkway, going to Atlantic City.

"At first, Ricky didn't want to throw the gun away.
He said, 'If some fuckin' cop stops us, we might need
it again,' but I guess he thought better of that because
when, uh, we come up on what looked to be like a
bridge with a lot of water under it, I assumed it to be
salt water, and I figured that was a good place to
throw the gun, Dew rolled down the window as we got
to what we thought would be almost the middle of the
water and heaved the gun out the window.

"Then we drove back to the motel and washed up.
And I'm wantin' somethin' to eat and he's wantin'
somethin' to fuck, so we go back downtown. He done
have a good killin' and he was ready to have some sex.
So we wound up in Bally's Casino there on the boardwalk, must have been about three A.M. by this time,
and I had me a plate of scrambled eggs that had a fly
in 'em, and then we picked up these two hookers on
Pacific Avenue and went with 'em somewheres and I
got a blow job with a rubber on for a hundred bucks.
Some old flophouse they took us to, and Ricky he
wan't up there any time before he's back bangin' on
the door, sayin', 'Let's go, let's go.' He'd always claimed
to be able to fuck for four or five hours so I figured
he'd be up there half the night.

"Anyway, we drive on back to the Airport motel
and didn't sleep but for a couple of hours and was on
the road early the next day and we drove straight
through all the way to Shreveport. We didn't talk
much about the incident at all, Ricky just said it went
smooth. He was sure in a good mood, though. Fact, I
even sold him a car on that trip home. He agreed to
pay me twenty-five hundred for an old '62 Nova that
I'd been tryin' to unload.''

Here, Ferlin actually laughed. "That damn car was

so sorry that it broke down before he even got it out from in front of my house. Fact, that was my last sight of him, down under that damn old Nova, still workin' on it when I walked through my front door."

(Again, it should be noted that Ricky Dew consistently denied any involvement whatsoever in these events.)

The only other questions the detectives had for Ferlin concerned Gary Hamilton and his real role in Louisiana. Ferlin said it was his impression that Hamilton had been sent down by Seely to help put together a story that would provide Rob with an innocent explanation for any documentable contacts he'd had with "Ernie Grandshaw."

"I wrote up a scenario," he said, "which I gave to my sister to type, right there in Garner's office. I figured nobody knew about me bein' up there in July, since Greene had been the one to register, and I figured that the fewer contacts between me and Marshall the better. If we could knock out one out of three, that weren't bad.

"For that last night when I met him in the casino, I put in that he paid me eight hundred in cash, 'cause what he was supposedly doin' was tellin' me he wouldn't be needin' no more investigation because everythin' with his wife and family had worked out so fine.

"The eight hundred was supposed to cover my extra time and expenses. Seemed like if we both had that same odd number in both our stories, it'd make them more believable.

"Even after I was arrested, Hamilton come to see me and I told him that if he would give me the address and location of the investigator's buildin' that Mrs. Marshall had employed, I could make up a story that said I came back to New Jersey in September in order to steal the investigator's file on Marshall and any photographs that might have been taken, so that Mrs. Marshall couldn't use it in a divorce proceedin'.

"That was all fictitious, too, of course. I didn't know whether there were photographs or whether there weren't. That's just what I was goin' to say. I just wanted to get it straight with Hamilton, so Hamilton could get the story to Marshall and Mr. Seely, so our stories would be the same at the time Marshall was arrested—*if* he was arrested.

"I just *assumed*, until you boys played me that tape, that Marshall was goin' to follow the scenario. Sonofabitch. I guess I *never* did understand how stupid and crazy he really was."

19

IT was a good story, Bob Gladstone thought, as those kinds of stories went. It checked out. The dates checked with the motel registrations. The trips checked with the phone-call activity. The payments checked with withdrawals made from Marshall's line of credit at Harrah's Marina.

Even the pocketbook checked. Maria's pocketbook had been found just where L'Heureux had said it was thrown from the window, and there would have been no way for him to have known that unless he'd been in the car at the time, because the prosecutor's office had never publicly disclosed any information about the pocketbook.

Best of all, Ricky Dew seemed plausible as the shooter. Everything Gladstone had ever heard about Dew made his involvement seem plausible, even if there were no actual proof.

L'Heureux's story was good enough to justify the deal. And as part of the deal he would testify against Marshall in court. And with L'Heureux's testimony, supported by that of Felice, and by the enormous amount of documentation that Gladstone and his men had so painstakingly accumulated over the preceding three months, there was no doubt in Gladstone's mind that the case against Marshall was strong enough to lead to conviction.

Only one aspect of the story posed a problem. That was L'Heureux's account of Dew's reason for having contacted him—the business about the seventy-five-thousand-dollar contract on L'Heureux's life, put out by someone in New Jersey through someone in Dallas because L'Heureux had failed to deliver for Rob Marshall.

That opened a lot of doors better left closed. It provided a link in a chain at a point where no further links were desired. Investigation of it could lead back to people who did not want to be part of the story.

The county prosecutor seemed quite content to take to court a case that accepted as pure coincidence Marshall's meeting with Myers at Riccio's party. The prosecution's case, as tried in court, would move forward, not backward, from that point. This meant it would not have to concern itself with John Riccio or his relatives, or Patsy Racine/Ragazzo, or—except insofar as she testified in the prosecution's behalf—with Felice.

No attention whatsoever would have to be paid to the possibility of any loansharking or drug connections or to the connections between different layers of Toms River society, such as friendships between influential political figures and adulteresses, particularly adulteresses suspected (at least, initially) of at least peripheral involvement in a murder plot.

And, moving forward from the Riccio party, the case was clean. The chain of circumstance was clear and well documented and entirely consistent with the eyewitness testimony L'Heureux would give.

Except for that one sticky point about Dew.

What would have been nice was if there had been some other way for Dew to have learned about L'Heureux's involvement with Rob Marshall, and if the whole story about the seventy-five-thousand-dollar contract put out on L'Heureux's life had just been, well, some sort of joke.

Suppose, for example, L'Heureux had mentioned to Travis Greene during their July trip that the real reason he was coming back and forth to Atlantic City was that he had been hired by a man to kill his wife for a lot of insurance money.

Greene and Dew were acquainted. Quite well acquainted, according to the Shreveport FBI. It would have been entirely possible that between late July and the start of September Greene could have mentioned to Dew that Ferlin was involved in a lucrative contract up north but was having a bit of trouble closing the deal. That alone could have been enough to have prompted Dew's call—nothing more than Ricky's desire to cut himself in on a piece of the action.

As an "alternative reason" that explained Dew's interest in the venture, it was not perfect. For one thing, in this version there was no money in the deal for Dew, save whatever share he might someday claim of whatever insurance proceeds Rob might eventually collect.

Would a casual mention by Greene—with no payment of any kind in advance—have been enough to prompt Dew to call L'Heureux with such apparent urgency, to fabricate the bizarre story of the contract on his life, and then to jump in a car and drive fifteen hundred miles in order to shoot a complete stranger in the back? Just on a whim?

No, the Greene connection was not airtight by any means. L'Heureux's original story, in fact, seemed more plausible in many ways. Unfortunately, it also seemed dangerous. It was the kind of story that might complicate the lives of a number of people.

The beauty of having the connection come, almost

accidentally, through Greene was that it kept unnecessary players off the field. Players who had managed to make it understood that they would prefer not to be players at all, in this instance, but only spectators. Or, better yet, to be able to pretend that they did not even know that this particular game was being played.

The other nice thing about the Greene connection was that no one stood to benefit from subjecting it to scrutiny or challenge. Thus, the whole messy notion of a contract put out on Ferlin's life because he had failed to deliver for Rob Marshall in New Jersey could just disappear—as long as Ferlin was able to remember to forget it.

L'Heureux signed his plea-bargain agreement on December 15, 1984.

Four days later, in Stanton, Louisiana, fifty miles southeast of Shreveport, half a dozen officers from the Ocean County prosecutor's office, the New Jersey State Police, the Caddo Parish, Louisiana, Sheriff's Department and the Federal Bureau of Investigation, clad in bulletproof vests and carrying fully loaded semiautomatic weapons, surrounded a hamburger stand called Jumbo's and arrested Ricky Dew, who recently had married the woman who owned the restaurant. Dew was charged with the murder of Maria Marshall and was held without bail, pending extradition to New Jersey.

At 2:30 that afternoon, as he was returning from Grog's Surf Palace in Seaside Park with a full load of expensive Christmas presents for his sons, Rob's car was stopped by police on Route 37.

Gladstone had received a report that Rob had been inquiring at a local travel agency about flights from Miami to Costa Rica, from which extradition might prove complicated.

Two uniformed officers and two in plainclothes approached the car and told him to get out and to stand alongside it, with his legs apart and his hands spread out on the roof.

It was raining, and Rob was not pleased at having to get wet while the policemen patted him down for concealed weapons. Also, it didn't look good. It was undignified, being arrested out in public like this, where clients, or club members, or maybe someone from Rotary might drive past.

"You couldn't have waited," he said. "You couldn't have waited one lousy week so I could have had Christmas with my boys."

"Hey, scumbag," one of the arresting officers said. "They don't get to have Christmas with their mother, why should they have it with you?"

Sal Coccaro had received a call that morning from the Dover Township chief of police. "They're taking him today, Sal," the chief said. "You may want to be there for the boys."

And so it was Sal who called Lehigh, Sal who drove to the mall and told Roby as he worked at Feet First, and Sal who drove to the junior high to tell John that his father was being arrested for having arranged the murder of his mother.

Rob was arraigned two days later, in Ocean County Superior Court. Roby, Chris and John were present. Their father wore a prison jumpsuit on which he'd stenciled I LOVE YOU in Magic Marker. He waved and smiled to the boys and gave them a "thumbs up" sign. Bail was set at two million dollars.

Three days after that, on Christmas Eve, Carl Seely appeared in court to argue that bail should be reduced. In opposition to his motion, the prosecutor's office produced a twenty-four-page sworn statement from Ferlin L'Heureux, which purportedly implicated Marshall in the murder.

After reviewing the statement in chambers, the presiding judge ordered it sealed. He also ordered that Marshall be held without bail.

At the same time, the prosecutor's office announced that it would seek the death penalty against Rob.

Sal Coccaro stopped by the Marshall house that evening. The Christmas tree was lit and presents were stacked underneath. Many of the presents said, "To Dad." An album of Christmas carols was playing.

"What happens now?" Roby asked. "Are we wards of the state?"

"What happens if he's convicted?" Chris asked. "Do you think they'd really put him to death?"

Not even Sal had any answers.

Later that night, alone in the house—and that's what it had become, their house in Toms River, no longer a home—Chris and Roby stayed up to talk.

"We've got to stand by him, Chris," Roby said. "One hundred percent. He's all *we* have and he needs us more than ever."

"I don't know, Roby. I'm not sure I can."

"You've got no choice."

"Yes, I do. We all do."

"He's your dad, too, Chris. Not just mine. And this is no time to desert him."

"Yeah, Roby, but Mom was yours, too. Not just mine."

They both fell silent. Then Roby spoke.

"You've gotta believe, Chris. You've gotta have faith."

"I wish I could," Chris said, "but I don't."

"Well," Roby said, "I'm backing Dad all the way, no matter what."

"That's fine, Rob. I'll never try to talk you out of that. But do me the same favor, too. Let me go my own way. Let me keep trying to figure it out. Don't try to make me join the team."

The two brothers sat looking at each other for a long time. Then they stood to say good night. This time, instead of hugging, they shook hands.

Part Three

THE TRIAL

20

SHORTLY before the start of the trial, a longtime resident of Toms River—a native, really, who had been raised in the town and had witnessed its transformation from the sleepy village by the sea it once had been to the urb-less suburban maelstrom it became—wrote a letter to an acquaintance who had expressed curiosity about a possible connection between the town's collective values and the story of Rob and Maria Marshall.

"Actually," the native wrote, "except that Rob Marshall happened to be there with his wife's dead body and he could hardly claim he'd never seen her before in his life, he's only functioning exactly the way the commercials tell him to behave. Get it, get it now, get it at any cost, and then get another one."

In this respect, the native suggested, he was not very different from a lot of other people in town. Which perhaps explained why the murder of Maria was perceived in Toms River as more than just a sensational event—one redolent with possibilities for scandalous gossip; indeed, with huge gobbets of such gossip being tossed up on shore with every tide—but as an episode that brought definition to a town where none had existed before.

By the time of trial, in January of 1986, the Marshall case had become the quintessential symbol of the consequences of a life-style that so many in Toms River had espoused if not embraced, or embraced if not espoused.

As such, it provided a graphic illustration of how fragile was the crust above the fault line, especially for married women in their forties.

"Maria," the native wrote, "was a person who only showed a certain side to the world: The Perfect Suburban Wife. Not only does she cancel herself out if she leaves, throws out, or in any other way terminates the marriage, she wouldn't be doing it because she's in love with someone else or she's been offered a vice presidency with W. R. Grace Co.; she'd be the forsaken wife. A forty-two-year-old has-been in a job where there's no thanks, no raises, and no promotions anyhow. Her life has been the house, Rob, the kids."

And then, of course, there was Felice.

"In her yearbook," the native wrote, "it says she wanted to be a lawyer. The staff chose 'nightclub entertainer.' They were pretty close. Picture Rob O.—the Superprep—he's so OP'ed he dreams in apple green and pink. When he finally 'falls in love' with one of his many mates, [she turns out to be] bespangled, wiry-haired, loud-mouthed, 'obnoxious' [and] disreputable. She came to Toms River when we were in the eighth grade, a bunch of kids out of tar-paper shacks and kerosene lamps by half a generation . . ."

And, the implication was, the town had never recovered.

Felice herself, on the other hand, seemed to have rebounded quite nicely by the time of trial. True, she had resigned her job at Seaview Regional, but she'd opened her own video store and was already thinking of expanding, and she and David had reconciled and were living together in the condo at the beach.

Those who called by telephone received a prerecorded message, in which Felice and David delivered alternate lines.

"This is Felice."

"And this is Dave."

"And we're trying . . ."

"Hard to be brave."

"We're out and about . . ."

"Doing our thing."

"Sorry we missed your . . ."

"Ringy-ding-ding."

Then, at the end, they both giggled.

For Rob Marshall's sons, however, the mood upon the eve of trial was somewhat less festive.

Roby had returned to Villanova shortly after his father's arrest and had successfully completed the spring semester. He'd spent the summer as a lifeguard at Ortley Beach and had returned again to Villanova in the fall.

Chris had stayed on at Lehigh, where he was compiling an outstanding record both academically and with the swimming team. He had worked the previous summer as a lifeguard at the country club pool, which put him directly in the line of sight (and within earshot) of those Toms River residents most addicted to gossiping about the case. He had taken the job, he'd said, just to prove that he didn't have anything to be ashamed of.

John had completed eighth grade successfully and had entered Toms River East in the fall. He was living at the house on Crest Ridge Drive, under the supervision of his father's mother's friend Tessie McBride, who had moved in just after his father's arrest to take charge of running the family.

Over the year that had passed since Rob's arrest, the two older boys had grown, if not estranged, certainly more aloof from one another.

Roby felt that Chris was not supporting their father openly or vocally enough.

Chris, on the other hand, despite his doubts, had visited and written to his father far more often than had Roby, and grew annoyed when his family loyalty was questioned, just as he was irritated by the thought of Roby being blindly led about by Tessie McBride instead of thinking matters through on his own.

And about Tessie McBride, there was no doubt: she was an absolutist. Absolute loyalty to Rob. Absolute scorn and contempt for the prosecutor's office. And absolute insistence that anyone who wanted to continue as a friend of the family proclaim the same absolute belief that Rob was innocent and that he would ultimately be vindicated.

This meant that there hadn't been much traffic through the house in recent months. The boys, under Tessie McBride's dominion, had become isolated from the friends and neighbors who'd been so quick to extend sympathy in the first weeks after Maria's murder. Even Sal Coccaro—*Uncle Sal*—who, like everyone else in town, had come to view Rob's guilt as undeniable, was no longer welcome at the house.

"People are too quick to judge," Roby said, during a conversation with an acquaintance who had asked him about his views. "I was at lunch with them that day, at the country club. Don't you think that if you were planning something like that you'd be a little shaky? But it was just a normal lunch. It was like the perfect afternoon with my parents. It was what I was used to for eighteen, nineteen years.

"The lack of allegiance is what bugs me," he said. "My dad's done everything for this town—the United Way, everything. And now they just turn away from him. They just don't know him. You'd have to have lived with him to know the kind of person he is, and I've lived with him all my life.

"The thing is, my dad was honest with us right from the start, as soon as this happened. He told us everything. Everything. So now we're never going to let him think we're going to doubt him. We're always going to let him know that we're going to stand behind him right to the end.

"And I think everything's going to be okay. There's a lot of positive energy and I just don't think it can go any other way. There's always a chance, I know there's a chance, but I just don't think of it. It's always in the back of my mind, like a movie—'what if *this* happens' —but then I always just stop it. I never let it go until the end. I just don't think of the bad things.

"You know," he said, "at the time my mom died we had everything you could ever imagine. And now we have nothing. We've gone from riches to rags. Literally. But I don't think God would put us through this much bullshit if it weren't going to be okay in the end."

Chris Marshall was not quite so optimistic about the outcome. He had decided, however, not to share his feelings with his father.

"He thinks that we're behind him a hundred percent and thus that we're a hundred percent sure he's going to be found innocent and life's going to continue the right way. He needs to think that in order to have something to live for," Chris said.

"Sure, I want to tell him how much I miss Mom so he knows it and knows how much I'm hurting—that it's not just him that's hurting. I don't think he realizes that enough. I want to tell him how John is hurting, too, but in the situation we're in it's better that he doesn't know, because it would just give him one more thing to worry about.

"I've never said, 'What if you're found guilty, Dad? What's going to happen to us?' because that would terrify him, I think, and I don't want to upset him anymore. Right now, he needs support. I'm not putting on an act. I'm just doing what I feel is right.

"I tell him that I love him, but—it's not a lie, I do love him—but it seems it's a kind of . . . temporary clause. That if he was involved, I'm not going to love him. But that's, you know—I don't know. It's just so confusing.

"It feels like there's this high-pressure thing that's inside me that I'm just trying to keep contained as best I can. It's like a burning feeling—no, that's not right. It's just—there's something there that I have to keep—either keep in until it's over, or just keep in, period. My only release, really, is nights where I'll just sit there and cry and just feel sorry for myself because I don't have my mother.

"I just want . . . peace in my mind. One way or the other. That he did or he didn't. I don't want there to have to be a question mark left. I want to know for sure, either way. Either hate him or love him, I guess.

"The hardest thing would be if there was a technicality and he was released and I wasn't sure. I don't know if I could hug him, tell him that I was glad he was back. I don't know if I could do that. And not know, for the rest of his life, whether or not I should go visit him for Christmas.

"Either way, I want it to be the facts. I don't want it to be some technicality. For me, that would be the worst."

* * *

Carl Seely, however, prior to trial, was attempting to have the case against Rob dismissed on just the sort of "technicality" that Chris feared.

Seely argued that the tape Rob had made for Gene Leahy was, first of all, a legally privileged communication between client and attorney and therefore not something the state was entitled to make use of. Second, he said, investigation by Gary Hamilton at the Best Western had shown that Rob had actually placed the envelope containing the tape *inside* a closed wooden mail receptacle in the lobby and that the retrieval of it by Detective Vandermeer was improper.

Not only should the contents of the tape not be permitted as evidence at trial, Seely argued, but to the extent that Rob's words on the tape had induced Ferlin L'Heureux to cooperate with the state, the entire indictment—based as it was, in large part, upon L'Heureux's testimony before the grand jury—should be dismissed.

Roby Marshall professed to be elated by this possibility. Chris was not.

"They had no right, Chris," Roby said by telephone from Villanova, where he had reenrolled. "Mr. Seely is going to prove that they had no right to take that tape in the first place, which means they never even had the right to arrest Dad, which means they're going to have to let him go."

"But don't you see, Roby?" Chris said from Lehigh. "Don't you see how that misses the point? That doesn't do a thing to prove that Dad's innocent."

"This is America, Chris, in case you've forgotten. A man doesn't have to prove he's innocent. The state has to prove that he's guilty."

"Not when it's Dad you're talking about. And not when it's Mom who's dead."

"Oh, Chris, come off the soapbox. Mr. Seely says this is the best chance we have."

"Then Mr. Seely must think Dad's guilty, too."

"No, Chris. I don't think so. Some of us have a little more faith."

"Yeah, you and Tessie McBride and Mr. Seely. Whoop-de-doo."

"You know, Chris, you can really be a pain in the ass. Here's a chance to get this whole thing blown out of the water and get Dad back home where he belongs and instead of being happy about it you're acting as if it's some sort of dirty trick."

"Look, I'm not arguing with Mr. Seely. His job is to get Dad off any way he can. But I'm looking at it a little differently. What I want to know is whether or not Dad hired L'Heureux and Dew to kill Mom. And all this bullshit about a tape in a mailbox has nothing to do with that."

"Yeah, but don't you see, if they illegally seized it, then L'Heureux's whole statement gets thrown out."

"So what? It gets thrown out. That doesn't mean it's not true."

"You know, Chris, sometimes I really wonder whose side you're on."

"Well, then, I'll tell you, Roby. So you'll never have to wonder again. I'm on Mom's side."

Seely lost his legal argument about the tape, but he had won an earlier motion for change of venue, on the basis of extensive pretrial publicity (much of which had been generated by himself).

The case was moved to Atlantic County, one county south, and would be tried in Mays Landing, the county seat, a nondescript village twelve miles inland from Atlantic City. The shift had at least three significant effects.

First, it meant that Rob would not be tried before a jury composed of people who had already decided he was guilty.

Second (and this was sorely vexing to many), it meant that anyone from the country club who wanted to take in the spectacle would have to drive for an hour to get there—which might look tacky—instead of being able to "just drop by" almost as if by accident, as they could have done if the trial had been held in Toms River.

Third, it meant that the presiding judge would be, instead of a member of the Toms River Country Club, Manuel H. Greenberg of Atlantic County Superior Court. Judge Greenberg was a short, trim, white-haired man in his midfifties who, in his fourteen years on the bench, had compiled the best record of any judge in the state in terms of how rarely his rulings were reversed by higher courts.

There was also a fourth, and somewhat ironic, effect: the jury would be composed of Atlantic County residents. What made this ironic was that Atlantic City was in Atlantic County, which meant that approximately half the citizens summoned for jury duty would be employed by a gambling casino.

Three casino employees eventually wound up on the jury. And one of them—in fact, she became the forewoman—was actually a blackjack dealer from Harrah's Marina. There to deal Rob his ultimate hand.

Rob and Ricky Dew were being tried together. Charges against Grandshaw had earlier been dismissed, and Myers—because his alleged involvement was not such that it could warrant the death penalty—would be tried separately, at a later date.

To try the case the county prosecutor had selected the most aggressive, experienced and loyal of his assistants, a thirty-nine-year-old Bricktown lawyer named Kevin Kelly.

Kelly had grown up in Newark. His high school was St. Benedict's, one of those old inner-city Catholic schools where corporal punishment was considered an integral part of the educational process.

Summers, he worked as a garbage collector for the city of Newark. Life among the flies and rats and stench of South Orange Avenue, with the clank of the big cans hitting the shimmering pavement and the sweet taste of Ripple from a brown paper bag at nine o'clock in the morning. There was a rumor that another white kid worked sanitation for Newark also, but if he did, Kelly never met him.

Kelly's marks weren't much at St. Benedict's, but he had developed that tough skin and can-do attitude the Benedictines approved of, and they sent him on to one of their colleges—St. Bernard's (now defunct) in Cullman, Alabama. After graduating from there, Kelly went to Cumberland Law School in Tennessee and then came back north to take the New Jersey bar exam.

While waiting, he taught seventh grade at Broadway Junior High School in Newark, which showed him that being a garbage collector wasn't the worst job in the world, or even in Newark.

After passing the bar, he went to work for Joe Lordi, the prosecutor in Essex County, which included Newark. He stuck it out there for four years, doing homicides mostly, so many of them coming so fast that often his first look at a case file was when he was riding the elevator up to the courtroom to try it.

He was good at the job: not a brilliant lawyer but a workhorse, and in the Essex County prosecutor's office, endurance counted for far more than genius. His days as a garbage man helped, too. More than once, at that point near the start of a trial when the judge would ask prospective jurors whether they were personally acquainted with any of the principals, a deep, black voice would rumble forth, "That Mr. Kelly standin' there. Him 'n' me was trashmen together." Kelly didn't lose many cases.

It got to him, though, the pace and the gruesomeness. Especially during the period of intramural warfare among various Black Muslim sects, when headless corpses (and corpseless heads) began piling up in basements and stairwells all over town. When he found himself bringing some of the photos along to show to young women he was dating, Kelly knew it was time to get out.

His father, like almost every other white man in North Jersey, had acquired a small summer place down at the shore. In this case, Bricktown, that vague agglomeration of sand and scrub and rusted-out cars that had existed unnoticed for years just north of Toms River and then, in the boom years, had suddenly become a giant parking lot.

Kelly's father died in 1975 and Kelly converted the Bricktown summer house into an all-weather home and found himself a job as a part-time assistant prosecutor in Ocean County.

In conjunction with another part-time assistant, and with a great deal of assistance from the prosecutor himself (in Ocean County all assistant prosecutors were part-time, devoting one third of their hours to the prosecutor's office and the remainder to their private practices), Kelly opened his own office right on Brick Boulevard, specializing in real estate closings.

Not long afterward, he had a visit from Rob Marshall. Rob, apparently, had worked a deal with the local bar association by which they would tip him off whenever a new lawyer moved into the area, so Rob could get there first, offering life insurance, mutual funds and retirement plans.

He swung by one day at about noon, picking Kelly up in a Mercedes. But that was where the opulence ended. Rob took them to a nearby restaurant named Mr. Steak (in fairness, Bricktown was not big on opulence), and even before the menus had arrived, he had his briefcase open on the table.

"None of the niceties," Kelly recalled. "No 'Where are you from? How do you like it here? Someday, let's take a ride in my boat.' None of that kind of shit. Just bang-bang, straight to business. And once he'd signed me up—I don't know what it was, some goddamned thing, some mutual fund where I'd send in fifty or a hundred bucks a month—once that was over, it was, slam! Snap the briefcase, get the check, sign that Amex slip and out the door. I still have half my fucking hamburger on my plate and he's out in the parking lot with the engine running. The guy could fit in three or four lunches a day, the way he hustled."

Kelly had brought his Newark personality with him to Ocean County. He walked into a courtroom as if he were ready to sling a City of Newark trash can across it. He went after defendants the way the Benedictines had gone after him (except he stopped short of whipping them with a strap). He was, in short, a tough kid from the city ready to kick ass down at the shore. And nothing galled him more than to see these rinky-dinks waltzing around a nowhere town like Toms River flaunting what appeared to be pretensions.

Pretensions! To Kelly, that was one of the most vulgar words in the English language. When Kelly worked out (which he did often, for he was proud of his weight-lifter's build) he worked out at Lou's Gym on Brick Boulevard. None of these Toms River "health salons" with tinted glass and carpeted floors that looked like a car dealer's showroom. And none of this jazzercise crap, either. You work out, you work up a sweat, you go home.

"At Lou's," Kelly liked to brag, "they don't even have a shower." He showered at home, and he showered the way his father had taught him: the military shower. You turn the hot water on and once you're wet you turn it off. Then you soap yourself up. Then you turn the hot water on again to rinse off. Then you're done. That's it. Next. In a house with eight kids you learn fast not to waste the hot water, and even now that he was a thirty-nine-year-old bachelor living alone (though with a steady female companion who lived only ten minutes away), Kelly still showered that way.

And if somebody gave him a million dollars, he wouldn't move to Toms River from Bricktown. Bricktown. Kelly even liked the name of the place. No way anybody was going to get pretentious living in a town with a name like that. It sounded like a slum neighborhood in Belfast. He could picture skinny, pale Catholic kids tossing a bomb through the door of a Protestant pub and then running like hell to get away. Tough kids. Smart kids. Like himself. All they needed was a little red meat, a little time with the weights, build themselves up. Kids like that, they ever came over here, you could be damned sure it'd be Lou's Gym they'd work out at, not one of those faggoty Jacuzzi joints where the country club ladies went to wiggle those extra inches off their fannies. And you could be damned sure it would be Bricktown they'd live in, not Toms River.

The most hilarious article that Kelly had ever read in the newspaper in his whole life, he thought, was the one in the Asbury Park *Press* about the fortieth birthday party held for some dame named Rosenberg who was the daughter of Fred Frankel the car dealer. He remembered reading the story and laughing out loud and then passing the paper over to his girlfriend, Alice.

"Hey, Alice," he'd said, "Take a look at this. What a bunch of smackers."

He also remembered reading the story in the *Press* about the murder of Maria Marshall. It was a Saturday morning and he was sitting on his back deck, overlooking a marshy section of the bay in which he'd just placed several crab traps. His mother and his brother were coming down that afternoon and he was looking forward to plenty of crabs and beer.

The story was on the front page. It took him a minute, but then he remembered the name. "Hey, Alice," he said. She was inside, fixing breakfast. "Hey, Alice, I know this guy. This is that flamer that sold me that mutual fund the first month I moved to town."

"What are you talking about, Kevin?"

"This story here in the paper. About the murder. Didn't you read the paper this morning, Alice?"

"No, Kevin, you took it right out there with you on the deck before I even saw the front page."

"Yeah, well, wait a minute, wait a minute. Let me finish reading this." So he went back to his deck and sat in the sun and read the rest of the story.

Then he stood, and stepped into his kitchen and tossed the newspaper on the table.

"Hey, Alice," he said. "Read that. I'll tell you right now—that guy's story is bullshit."

Which is pretty much what Kevin Kelly's mother said later that afternoon when he showed her the story. "My mother," he said later, "you got to understand. You could sell my mother the Brooklyn Bridge. But she took one look at that story and she said, 'Baloney.' Then she said, 'The guy did it, what do you think, Kev?' "

And Kevin Kelly had said, "Yeah. With a story like that he had to have done it. Just wait and see. I'll bet there are going to be two things coming out in this story. One, the guy had a girlfriend. Two, I bet there's a shitload of insurance on the wife."

So when it finally came time for the prosecutor to explain to Kevin Kelly what this case was that he'd be trying, there were not too many things he had to say twice.

The Marshall case would be Kelly's last as an Ocean County assistant prosecutor—he was about to leave the office to devote full time to his private practice. And it was the first one he'd ever asked to try.

To him, Rob Marshall personified all that Kelly found loathsome about the life in Toms River he scorned: the snobbery, the pretentiousness, the phoniness, the shallowness, the greed. He thought it would be a kick to get Rob Marshall convicted for murder. And so, for the first time ever, he went to the prosecutor and asked for a case. The prosecutor gave it to him willingly. For one thing, Kelly was the best trial lawyer on his staff, and, for another, Kelly understood the concept of loyalty and all that it could sometimes entail.

Through the late fall and early winter of 1985–86, Rob Marshall became the focus of Kevin Kelly's life, and the more he learned about the man and his activities the more he came to detest him.

More than ever before in his career as an assistant prosecutor, Kelly would be taking with him into the courtroom not just a sense of outrage at the crime that had been committed, but genuine revulsion for the criminal. At least for one of them. Toward Ricky Dew, he felt indifference. Dew, in his view, was simply a gun for hire. A professional. If it hadn't been Dew it would have been someone else. It was Rob

Marshall who had knowingly caused the death of his wife, and he'd done it for the basest of motives: lust and greed.

Kelly intended to make him pay.

And still, despite all that buildup of emotion, it was not until the morning of January 14, when he walked into the courtroom and laid eyes upon Marshall for the first time since their lunch at Mr. Steak years before, that Kelly felt the full force of his hatred for the man.

For there he sat, in blazer and khakis, pale, subdued, quite a bit thinner, his hairline having receded even further, but *wearing his gold wedding band!*

There was something so cynical, so unfeeling, so blatantly manipulative about that act—*after what he'd done to her, that he could sit there in court and wear the ring she'd placed on his finger on their wedding day just to try to milk sympathy from the jury*—that Kelly had to choke back the impulse to walk over to the defense table where Marshall sat and tear the ring from Rob's finger himself.

Instead, he said to himself, *You'll pay for that, you son of a bitch. Along with everything else, before this is over, you'll pay for that.*

Two weeks later, however, after the jury had finally been chosen, when the time came for him to make his opening statement, Kevin Kelly had gotten a much firmer grip on the anger he felt toward Marshall. Indeed, in his opening remarks he seemed subdued to the point of indifference. He wore his glasses and a dark necktie and a very conservative suit and he stood straight and still, as if he were back at St. Benedict's and had just been called upon to recite a poem to the class.

This was, of course, a carefully calculated pose.

Kelly knew that juries liked to sympathize with lawyers they felt just a little bit sorry for, and, once he'd observed his opponent, he had decided to play his off-the-rack look for all it was worth.

Carl Seely had spent the two weeks prior to trial in the Caribbean and thus brought to court not only the slicked-back hair and shiny gold Rolex and the suit that looked as if it could have cost a thousand dollars, but also a tan that was the envy of every New Jersey resident—jurors included—who could not afford a winter vacation.

So Kelly delivered his half-hour opening in a monotone and riddled it with all the confusing dates and names and places and insurance policy amounts and didn't even try to explain what anything meant. He wanted it to seem, at this point, as if maybe he didn't quite understand what he was doing; as if, perhaps, he'd been thrust into this courtroom and this case on short notice, maybe because a more senior man had taken ill, and he was just going to try to do the best he could, but, really, nobody should be expecting very much.

But there was one point he did want to make clear right from the start. A deal had been made in this case. The state had made a deal with Ferlin L'Heureux.

Making deals with accused murderers who are willing to talk in return for lessened punishment is a practice that some might view with disapproval. Kelly wanted to be certain that the jury understood the need for it in this case.

The murder of Maria Marshall, he told them quite unemotionally, had been "a terrible, terrible act." It had also been the result of a conspiracy. "Normally," he said, "conspiracies are shrouded in secrecy, silence and furtiveness. Rarely, if ever, does anyone outside the circle of conspirators become privy to its details."

In order to find out the truth about what had happened to Maria Marshall, he said, that circle had had to be broken. The state had done it by making its arrangement with Ferlin L'Heureux.

There. He had finished reciting. He sat down. A nice boy, certainly, but clearly not the brightest in the class.

Carl Seely might not have been the brightest either, but he would definitely have gotten the gold star for good grooming. He wasted no time going after what he perceived as the weak link in the case against Rob: the plea-bargain arrangement with L'Heureux.

"A pact with the devil," he called it. "And but for that pact, Rob Marshall, who was a respected member of his community, would not be here. And I want to tell you one other thing now at the outset. Rob Marshall will take the stand and Rob Marshall will testify. I will tell you right now, and I will honor this commitment and so will Rob—he will get on this stand and he will testify and he will tell you how he, too, in addition to his wife and his three children, is a victim of the treachery of Ferlin L'Heureux."

It had a nice ring to it: respected family man versus the devil. Rob Marshall as a victim, too.

"Now, to get into Rob a little bit," Seely went on, "Rob was born on December sixteenth, 1939. He is now—"

But Kelly was on his feet with a pained expression on his face. "Excuse me, Judge. I'm sorry to interrupt. I just wish we'd get into the facts of this case. I mean, 1939 . . ."

Judge Greenberg was possessed of both a calm demeanor and a quick mind. He had about him the reassuring aura of the pediatrician you were never afraid to go to as a child. If he had bad news to give or an unpleasant procedure to perform, you knew it really would hurt him more than it hurt you. Indeed, he seemed as if he'd have been very comfortable residing in a Norman Rockwell painting, one of those suffused with the spirit of fairness and kindness and warmth. On the bench, he was a man who never raised his voice, because he didn't have to.

"Well," he said now, displaying also a gift for understatement, "it would not be impermissible to show the age of a defendant, so that comment is not beyond the bounds of propriety. I'll overrule the objection."

As, of course, he had to. Kelly could hardly deny Seely the right to tell the jury how old his client was, but Kelly had known that before he stood. His purpose had been twofold: to let Seely know that the part-time prosecutor from Ocean County, even if he acted like a schoolboy to the jury, wasn't going to let the slick Philadelphia lawyer skate all over him, and, second, to distract everybody for a moment, so that the notion of Rob as a victim just like Maria would not take hold.

If Kelly had had L'Heureux as the albatross around his neck for the opening, Seely had one, too: Felice. And so, after giving Rob's date of birth and fifteen minutes of further biographical detail, he confronted it.

"Rob was involved in an affair," he said. "We're not proud of it. Rob is certainly not proud of it. But that is a fact that we are not going to deny. Felice Rosenberg, I anticipate, will be a witness in this case and will, in essence, confirm that which we now admit, and that is that she and Rob had a relationship. What we are denying, most vehemently, is that Rob had anything to do with the death of his wife."

*　　*　　*

Ricky Dew had his own lawyer, a man named Nathan Baird, who had been one of New Jersey's leading criminal defense lawyers for twenty-five years.

Baird was a tall man of ample girth. He had a jowly face, a quick wit, a powerful voice and an extensive vocabulary. White-haired, in his early sixties and attired always in a rumpled three-piece suit, Baird looked the part of the old warhorse, whose many battles before the bar had left him seasoned, mellowed, perhaps scarred just a trifle, but possessed of both tolerance and wisdom in full measure. Not that he couldn't be a mean son of a bitch, too, if the occasion required.

And there sat Ricky Dew himself, dressed in suit and necktie for purposes of the trial, and utterly blank-faced. He stared straight ahead expressionlessly as if this whole enterprise did not concern him in the least.

Baird stepped forward to intone: "A famous patriot once said, 'Give me liberty or give me death.' In the case now before you, Ferlin L'Heureux has said, 'Give me liberty and give *them* death.' "

He proceeded to point out, briefly but clearly, that all the evidence the state had accumulated in the case, all the phone records and insurance policies and casino credit reports and American Express bills and motel registration cards and everything else—all of it—concerned only one of the two defendants in the case and it did not happen to be Ricky Dew.

The whole story, Baird said, could well be true. He didn't know. Maybe Marshall had conspired with L'Heureux to murder Maria Marshall and maybe the conspiracy had led to her death. Maybe it happened that way and maybe it didn't. But either way, Ricky Dew, this mild-mannered, well-dressed family man and auto mechanic, had nothing to do with it and there wasn't one shred of evidence to prove he did.

If you *want* a killer, Baird suggested, you need look

no further than L'Heureux. He'd had the motive, he'd
had the opportunity, he'd had the car, he'd had the
gun, he'd had it all. The only reason *he* wasn't on trial
for murder, Baird said, was that the state needed his
testimony in order to win a conviction against Marshall. And they couldn't make a deal with him if he'd
been the shooter. So he'd had to invent a shooter for
them. And for some reason unknown to any man on
earth but Ferlin, he'd fixed upon Ricky Dew.

Well, said Baird, one unsupported statement of a
proven liar who had, in this instance, every reason to
lie, didn't seem much of a reason to drag a man fifteen
hundred miles away from his home and lock him up
for fourteen months until they could get around to
trying him. But nobody ever said life was fair. What
would be fair would be this trial. And in a fair trial
there was no way that the guilt of Ricky Dew could be
established.

"I am *astonished*," Baird said, "truly astonished at
the paucity of evidence against my client. And I suspect that you will be, too."

21

ROBY had been present for the opening statements, but Chris had remained at Lehigh. They spoke by telephone that night.

"What did you think?" Chris asked.

"I think I wish Dad had Mr. Baird as his lawyer."

"If he's innocent, Roby, it shouldn't matter."

"Don't start the civics-class bullshit again."

"But what about the prosecutor? What about Kelly?"

"Oh, he looks like a real jerk. A zero. He just stood up there and rattled out a lot of mumbo-jumbo."

"Somehow, Rob, when I pick up the Philadelphia *Inquirer* tomorrow morning, I don't think that's what they'll say."

"It's just a lot of phone bills and receipts, Chris, just like Dad always said. It's all circumstantial. And that's all it will be. Until they drag out their paid liar, L'Heureux. You know, Chris, it would have been nice if you could have been there."

"Why? To hear a lot of mumbo-jumbo?"

"No. For Dad. To show some of your famous support."

"Roby, every day since he's been in jail I have written Dad a letter. Every day. And do you want to start counting how many times you visited him last

summer compared to me? No. No, you were the one
with the big party over at the beach that couldn't wait.
And I was the one who had to go down there and tap
on the glass. 'Hi, Dad, it's me, Chris. Just like old
times. Except they've got you so locked up I can't
even hug you, I can only kiss the six-inch-thick bullet-
proof-glass window in the steel door they've got you
locked up behind. And I can only talk to you on this
shitty little intercom phone. And that may be the way
it is for the rest of my life.' And then I go home and
sit up with John while he cries. While you spend the
night on the beach, drowning in six kegs of beer."

"Let's not start that again," Roby said. "I was there
today, Chris, and I'm backing Dad all the way."

"Yeah. You and John and Tessie McBride. And the
rest of the world is wrong, including our former Uncle
Sal—remember Uncle Sal, Roby? He's no longer welcome in the house, is he? Just because he hasn't joined
the team. Just because maybe, like me, he's interested
in what the facts turn out to be."

"Chris, I love Sal. I'll never forget how he helped
me. But he just lost faith in Dad. He just lost faith.
Like you're losing faith. And yes, you're right. Tessie
doesn't want him around."

"And all of a sudden it's what Tessie wants that
matters. It's Tessie who's running our lives."

"You have to admit, Chris, since she moved in at
Christmas she has been a tremendous help."

"She's been a tremendous pain in the ass is what she's
been. All this 'Trust in the Lord' shit. After we'd seen
her, what, maybe once in five years before Mom died?"

"So? She and Mom didn't get along."

"That's because Mom had good taste. And now that
she's dead Tessie has moved right in to take her place.
Just like Mrs. Rosenberg was supposed to. If you want
to know the truth, Roby, it gives me the creeps."

"Then I guess you're not going to want to hear the latest."

There was a pause. After a certain point, you come to feel that all the unpleasant surprises are already out of the bag, and when someone says to you, "You aren't going to want to hear the latest," it gives you a chill down the spine and a dry mouth and a rapid increase in heart rate all at once, and you know instinctively that, yes, that's correct, you are *not* going to want to hear the latest.

"What is it, Roby?" Chris asked in a soft voice.

"Brenda Dew is living at the house."

It took more than the usual minute for this to sink in. Brenda Dew was the wife of Ricky Dew, the man accused of the actual murder of Maria. The charge against him was that he had stood over her in the front seat of the Cadillac and had fired two shots, close together, into her back, turning a loving mother into a corpse within an instant.

And now his wife was living at their house? *Their* house? *Mom's* house? *Brenda Dew?*

"Roby, is that a joke?"

"No joke. Tessie McBride invited her. Said she was up here all alone, had no place to stay, the trial might last for six weeks, it was an act of Christian charity, Tessie said. She also said it was what Dad wanted. That he and Mr. Dew are on the same side now, and we've all got to stick together through this."

Chris felt dizzy and nauseated. He felt the same way he'd felt when his father had first walked into his room, sixteen months earlier, saying that he had some bad news.

"Roby. You can't mean this. You can't mean that *Ricky Dew's wife* is living in *our* house?"

"Chris, she's not a bad person once you get to know

her. She's really not. She's got kind of a neat sense of humor."

"Where is she sleeping, Roby? In Mom's bed?"

"No. You know Tessie is sleeping there. Brenda's down in the guest room. Listen, Chris, I know it sounds weird, but John likes her, she's really good with him, and with neither of us around much, it's—"

"Stop, Roby. Please. You said Dad knows about this?"

"I think it was actually his idea."

"But, Roby, doesn't anybody realize that even if Dad is telling the truth—even if Dad is innocent— Ricky Dew might still have been the one who shot Mom?"

"How could that be?"

"Say L'Heureux *was* just hired as an investigator. But then he found out about all the insurance on Mom. And he told Dew. And the two of them came up to kill her and then figured somehow they could blackmail Dad, because—because—"

"Because he'd hired an investigator? That doesn't make any sense, Chris."

"Well, I don't know why. There's a lot we don't know. But I do know that Ricky Dew is on trial for murdering Mom and it seems a little too weird to have *his* wife staying in our house during the trial."

"Hey, Chris, lighten up. You know what they say— it's a small world."

Kevin Kelly plodded through the first week of trial, the nuts-and-bolts week, presenting the testimony of various state troopers who had been at the scene, the crime-scene photographer, the pathologist (who said it appeared to him that Maria Marshall had been sleeping when she'd been shot), the Korean cab driver who had driven L'Heureux to the Ram's Head in June, and others whose words and documents provided the foundation upon which he'd be building his case.

To start the second week, he called Ferlin L'Heureux to the stand.

Fourteen months of confinement, most of it solitary, had taken much of the spring from Ferlin's step and a good deal of the glitter from his eye. There wasn't much of the wheeler-dealer about him now. Still paunchy, though he'd lost twenty pounds to jailhouse cuisine, and having acquired a mustache and goatee, he presented an odd mixture of the satanic and the saturnine. Indeed, he brought with him to the witness stand the morose air of a man who'd seen things go just about as wrong as they could go, and who, in addition, had pissed away the last of his integrity and self-respect by ratting on a friend to save himself.

Kelly handled him as if he were radioactive. He ran L'Heureux through his story as if the two of them were playing *Beat the Clock*. There was a smattering of pathos, as when Ferlin described his July visit: "Maria was sitting there by herself," he said in a soft-spoken drawl, "and she was holding that rose. I guess the one that she had gotten in the restaurant. Just holding that rose. And I never will forget that."

But the overwhelming impression created was that Kelly wanted from L'Heureux the barest, most unadorned possible recitation of the facts.

He made sure, however, to bring Travis Greene into the story.

"Would you tell us," Kelly asked, "whether or not on the way back to Shreveport you told Greene about Marshall and his conversation and plans?"

"I had pointed out Maria Marshall to Travis. And just told him, you know, 'You see those two people? I will tell you later.' Just like that. And on the way back to Shreveport, I made the comment to him, I said,

'That fella is crazy.' He said, 'What are you talkin'
about?' I said, 'The man wants to have his wife murdered.' And Travis made a comment about, you know,
she was an attractive lady. And I said, 'Well, he is
willing to pay good, you know, to have it done.' And
he asked me how much. And I told him he was willing
to pay fifty thousand dollars. That's the last conversation Travis and I had about it."

When he got to L'Heureux's meeting with Ricky
Dew, Kelly quickened the pace even further.

"Ricky told me," L'Heureux was saying, "he said,
'I understand that there is a—there is a contract out
on you.' That he had been offered a contract on me
from some people out of Dallas for seventy-five thousand dollars."

"Did you ask him why?"

"Well, I kind of knew why. You know, I mean—I
knew that I hadn't done anything up here. I just took
the man's money. So it had me shook up, you know.
And we carried on there for a while. And finally he
said, you know, 'Our friend told me about it. And I
talked with him about it.' "

"You mean Greene?" Kelly prompted.

"No," L'Heureux said. Then he said, "Yeah."

"Greene had told him about what you were doing in
New Jersey?" Kelly asked, in as leading a fashion as
possible.

"Right."

"All right" Kelly said, and never asked another
word about the supposed "contract" from "some people out of Dallas."

The entire direct examination of the state's key witness in the murder case against Rob Marshall and
Ricky Dew took only two hours to complete. It was as
if someone had told Kelly that there would be a bonus
if he could finish before lunch.

John Marshall was the only one of Rob's three sons present in court to hear L'Heureux's testimony. He was sitting in the front row, between Tessie McBride and Brenda Dew, directly behind his father's position at the defense table.

As L'Heureux described his first trip to Atlantic City, quoting Rob as saying, "I want to get rid of her, I want her done away with, as soon as possible," John Marshall started to cry.

Rob turned and looked at his son. "You all right?" he said.

John nodded, his eyes wet with tears.

"Don't listen to him," Rob whispered. "Don't believe him. This guy is lying."

An hour later, at the lunch break, John jumped up and ran to the railing that separated him from his father. He reached across, hugged Rob tight, and kissed him firmly on the mouth. Sheriff's deputies stood by awkwardly, knowing that physical contact with a prisoner was not permitted, but not wanting to interfere.

Returning to court for the afternoon session, Rob caught John's eyes and asked, "Are you going to be here all week?"

John said he would.

"Good," Rob said. "I want you to be here for the rest of the week so you can hear the other side of this."

John smiled.

On his second day as a witness, with Carl Seely cross-examining, L'Heureux asserted that he had been "constantly trying" to talk Rob out of his plan to have Maria murdered. "I had no intention of fulfilling my end of the bargain," he said.

In fact, he went so far as to claim that even on the morning of September 6, after he and Dew had al-

ready arrived in Atlantic City, he still did not intend
that Maria would die. It was not, he now said, until
"after my meeting with Marshall at Harrah's, and my
being in need of money, and Ricky in need of money,
it was agreed that we would carry out the murder.

"I guess I was having a fight with my conscience,"
he said.

"In other words, you had a pang of conscience at
that point?"

"Well, somewhere in there, you know, we crossed
over. I felt Robert Marshall would pay the money if
Maria Marshall was murdered."

"So what you are really saying," Seely asked, "is
that in terms of your motivation, and your conscience,
it was money that motivated you, right?"

"The whole thing was motivated by money," L'Heureux said. "Money was the only motivation that I had,
and I believe—well, I don't—" But there he stopped
himself.

Suddenly, he was perspiring heavily and his voice
sounded as if his throat had gone dry.

"Do you need a glass of water or anything?" Seely
asked.

"Please."

"I noticed you lifted your collar. It gets a little warm
in here," Seely said.

L'Heureux nodded, but said no more about the
motivation of anyone other than himself.

On the afternoon of the second day, Nathan Baird
took over the cross-examination.

"Mr. L'Heureux," he said, rising like a great lum-
bering bear awakening from a nap, "do you remember
my telling the jury that I was going to demonstrate
that you had a great motive to lie?" The very timbre
of his voice—that rich bass quality—seemed intimi-

dating. Particularly when one recognized that this was the confrontation that would quite likely determine whether Ricky Dew returned to Louisiana and freedom, or faced lethal injection while strapped to a table in a locked room somewhere in Trenton.

"I don't recall that particular statement," L'Heureux said.

"Do you have a great motive to lie about this case?"

"Do I have?"

"Yes."

"I guess from all signs it would appear that I do," L'Heureux conceded.

"There is nothing more precious to you than saving your life, is there?"

"That's correct."

"That is part of the motive you have to lie about what happened out on that highway that night, isn't it?"

"If I were lying."

"Well, we are just talking about motive now. We will talk later about whether you *are* lying. For the moment," Baird said, speaking slowly and pacing just as slowly, back and forth, in front of L'Heureux, "I would like to explore the size and enormity of your motive. Do you agree that you have a very, very substantial motive to lie?"

"That's correct," L'Heureux said.

"As a matter of fact, you have made a plea bargain with the state of New Jersey, is that correct?"

"That's correct."

"And in the plea bargain, when it says that you are not the shooter, that was something that was negotiated between your lawyers and the state to make it clear that you were not the shooter, isn't that so?"

"That's correct."

"Because the state made it clear to you through

your attorney that if you were the shooter they weren't going to give you the wonderful deal they gave you, isn't that true?"

"Only by telling the truth," L'Heureux said.

"Sir," Baird intoned sternly. "We will deal with the subject of truth—which we hopefully have been dealing with throughout your testimony—later. Right now, answer my question, which is, did you understand as a result of what your attorneys told you that the state would not give you this wonderful deal if you in fact were the shooter?"

"That's correct," L'Heureux said.

"Okay. So in order to buy freedom from the death penalty, and the other things you got in this deal, you had to say that you did not shoot Maria Marshall, isn't that true?"

"That's correct."

"And whether it was true or not, you wanted very badly not to receive the death penalty and to get this deal in the alternative, didn't you?"

"I think had it not been true," L'Heureux said, "I would have said so."

Nathan Baird took a step backward and rolled his eyes toward the ceiling of the courtroom. "You mean," he said incredulously, "you wouldn't tell a little teeny lie to save your life?"

"I don't believe so," L'Heureux said. "Not at someone else's expense."

"Mr. L'Heureux!" Baird thundered. "Your whole life is a history of lies, is it not?"

"I object," Kevin Kelly shouted.

"Objection sustained," Judge Greenberg said quietly. "The jury will disregard it."

"You want this jury to believe," Baird persisted, "that to save the life of Ferlin L'Heureux you would not tell a lie to the extent of saying you weren't the shooter?"

"Not at someone else's expense."

"Is that because of your conscience?" Baird asked.

"It's my conscience that would have kept me from being the shooter."

"Well, your conscience didn't keep you from being involved in a conspiracy to commit murder, did it?"

L'Heureux shrugged. "That's true," he said.

"Your conscience," Baird suggested, "is somewhat of an elastic thing, isn't it? The elasticity depending on how many dollars are involved?"

"It seems to have a battle there."

"So I take it different degrees of money accomplish different things with your conscience."

"At the time I needed some money," L'Heureux said.

"Let me ask it this way: would you lie about where you were at night to your wife for fifty dollars?"

"I might for zero dollars," L'Heureux said, and for the first time all day there was laughter in the courtroom.

Baird himself had no choice but to grin. "As a great statesman once said," he said, "now that we have settled the issue, let's talk about the amount. Do you have different values for different lies? Some are hundred-dollar lies, some are two-hundred-dollar lies?"

"I don't think so."

"Do you have different values for different other bad acts besides lying, some things you do for a hundred dollars, some for two hundred?"

Finally, Kelly was on his feet. "I object and ask he stick with the facts the witness testified to."

"Judge," Baird responded, "this is cross-examination. His credibility and morality are at stake in judging his truthfulness in this courtroom."

"Well," Judge Greenberg said patiently. "The question, I think, is overly broad. It really is getting into what he would do in a hypothetical situation. It is not calling for a factual response."

"I withdraw it," Baird said, and then turned quickly to confront L'Heureux again: "How much money would it take to ease your conscience in terms of incriminating an innocent man in a murder?"

"I don't think there is any amount of money that could ease my conscience," L'Heureux said.

"How much money do you think your life is worth?"

"Had I committed the murder—"

"Just answer that question!" Baird shouted. "What value do you put on your life? A million dollars? Five million dollars?"

"I object again," Kelly said. "It's argumentative."

"Sustained," Judge Greenberg said.

Baird now walked across the courtroom until he was standing very close to Ferlin L'Heureux. "Do you agree with me," he said softly, "that living is worth a tremendous amount of money?"

"Yes."

"Living is worth enough money that it would ease your conscience in lying about Ricky Dew, isn't that so?"

"No," L'Heureux said, but he did not sound terribly convincing.

"Anytime you can be involved in murdering somebody and be sure you are not even going to do three years in jail, that might make an impression on your conscience in terms of pleading, don't you think?"

"Are you looking for a response?" L'Heureux said.

"Yes, I am."

"I don't think so."

Baird turned his back to L'Heureux and walked away, shaking his head. From the far side of the courtroom he spoke again. "Tell me something, sir, is there a way in which the jury can tell—something you know about yourself that will help them know when you are telling the truth and when you are lying?"

"Objection," Kelly said.

"Objection sustained."

"I don't understand why, Judge," Baird said.

"It's not calling for a factual response," Judge Greenberg said.

"Well, for example, Judge—if I know I have gas every time I tell a lie, I can answer that question."

"It is not calling for a factual response," the judge said evenly. "It's also calling for an opinion or conclusion on the part of the witness, it's calling for conjecture, so I will sustain the objection."

Again, Baird spun—surprisingly quickly for a man of his bulk—and confronted L'Heureux.

"Did you see the movie *Pinocchio?*" he asked.

Kevin Kelly, who had been tapping lightly on his table with a pencil, now tossed the pencil into the air and jumped to his feet. "That's wonderful," he said, with a full complement of sarcasm. "I object."

"I will withdraw the question," Baird said before Judge Greenberg could even rule.

Baird took another step closer to L'Heureux.

"Does your nose get longer when you lie?" he asked.

"I object again, Your Honor!" Kelly shouted.

"I will sustain the objection," Judge Greenberg said. And then, with just the barest trace of annoyance in his voice, he added, "Furthermore, Mr. Baird, I will instruct you at this time to refrain from facetious questions. I realize that in this trial, as in most trials, things happen that are humorous, but I think it is up to counsel when they are posing a question to do it in a professional manner."

"Thank you, Your Honor," Baird said.

Then, through further questioning, Baird established

that it was L'Heureux's gun that had been used to shoot Maria Marshall, that it was L'Heureux who had purchased the gloves intended to conceal the finger-prints of the person holding the gun, that it was L'Heureux's car that had been used to transport the shooter to the scene, and that L'Heureux was the only person known to have received any money from Rob Marshall in connection with the shooting, and that L'Heureux himself had acknowledged being present at the scene.

"I think you were there," Baird said, "I think you were there and you shot that lady to death. Isn't that what you did?"

"No."

"Just think for a second," Baird continued, "about something you said yesterday. You said, 'I will never forget her sitting there holding the rose,' and you made a gesture of the lady holding it at about the middle of her chest. A beautiful picture of a beautiful lady, was it not?"

"That's correct."

"And the reason you will never forget it is because of the way it contrasts in your mind—that peaceful-ness, that beauty, that serenity—with the violence that you saw done to that body in the car as you shot it. And that's the reason you will never, ever forget that, isn't it?"

"My part of that," L'Heureux admitted.

"The only reason you won't forget is that just as we in life see something beautiful and then see it de-stroyed, you saw something beautiful and you were a party to its destruction, too, weren't you?"

"I was a party to it," L'Heureux said.

"As a matter of fact, you were *the* party to it: your gun, your rubber gloves and your car."

"That's true, it was my gun. I had purchased the rubber gloves. But I did not shoot Maria Marshall."

"Sir," Baird said. "I'm telling you that the state had a good case against you, and the reason they had such a good case against you was because you were the shooter, and you put Ricky Dew as the shooter because you knew that as long as you were the shooter you couldn't make a deal."

"They had no case on me as the shooter," L'Heureux said.

"They have no case against Ricky Dew as the shooter either," Baird said, "except you."

The next morning, as Rob Marshall was led into court by the sheriff's deputies who transported him from his jail cell each day, he spotted his son John and gave a big grin. Then he held up the folder in which he carried his paperwork back and forth from courtroom to jail cell each day. On the side of the folder, he'd printed the words I LOVE YOU in purple Magic Marker.

A photographer from the Asbury Park *Press* took a picture. John looked embarrassed. Rob looked very pleased with himself.

Baird kept L'Heureux on the stand for two more days. Occasionally, he employed ridicule to make L'Heureux's story (in regard to Dew, at least) seem less believable.

"Now tell me about these gloves," he said. "You say they were the kind that you use to wash dishes. That is not personal knowledge on your part, is it?"

"I have washed a few," L'Heureux said.

"Okay. Do they come in sizes?"

"I don't know."

"What size did you buy?"

"I asked the girl there."

"What did you say, 'I got a fellow, Dew, out there in the car and I want a pair of gloves that will fit him?'"

"No, I just bought a pair of gloves. I was looking for a pair of rubber gloves and I bought a pair of gloves."

Later, Baird asked L'Heureux about the hours that followed the murder.

"You went to bed at two o'clock?"

"Yes, about then."

"And you slept until six o'clock?"

"Well, I didn't do much sleeping, but I slept."

"You didn't do much sleeping? Do you mean you were still troubled by this experience?"

"Yes, sir."

"Or do you mean you were in the process of fornicating?"

"In the process of doing what?"

"Fornicating," Baird said. "You know what that means, don't you.

"No, sir."

"You don't?"

"Oh, I know what that means, but no, sir, I wasn't."

"Didn't you say in your statement that after this happened you went out and picked up a couple of prostitutes and brought them back to the motel and had sex with them and then went to bed?"

"Yes, sir."

"Well, now, was the problem that interfered with your sleeping being with a woman or being upset about the crime?"

"Being upset about the crime."

"Did that spoil the pleasure of being with a woman for you?"

"It wasn't my desires," L'Heureux said.

"Oh, she forced herself on you?"

"No, sir."

At this point, Kelly objected, but Baird had already made the point he'd wanted to, and one he would come back to in closing argument: that according to L'Heureux's story there were at least two eyewitnesses, the prostitutes, who could have placed Ricky Dew in New Jersey at the time of the murder, but the state had not been able to produce them.

Although he made L'Heureux's motive to lie a constant theme, and continued to criticize the entire plea-bargain arrangement, Baird's closest scrutiny was reserved for that portion of L'Heureux's original statement in which he had first implicated Dew.

"Let me suggest something to you," Baird said. "And that is that the story that on the way home in July you told Greene about Marshall wanting his wife killed is an integral and necessary part of your entire statement. Because when you concocted the idea that Ricky Dew was going to be identified as the shooter, you had to somehow bridge the problem of how Dew would know anything about it.

"And I submit to you that if you did not say in your statement that you told Greene on the way home that Marshall wanted his wife killed, there would be no way you could explain how Dew would ever have approached you. *That is an absolutely key part of the story*. It is the underpinning."

With that in mind, Nathan Baird figuratively held a magnifying glass to the sworn statement L'Heureux had signed at the prosecutor's office on December 21, 1984, as part of his plea-bargain agreement.

"You say," Baird said, " 'Upon my arrival there at the McDonald's, Ricky told me that he had received word from somebody out of Dallas who wanted to put a contract on me for seventy-five thousand dollars.' Is that what Ricky said?"

"Yes, sir."

"Did you say, 'That is a handsome sum'?"

"I might have."

"And you did say, in fact, 'What the hell for?' "

"That is correct."

"Well, now, when you testified on your direct examination, you said you kind of knew why. If you kind of knew why, why would you ask, 'What the hell for?' "

"Well, you know," L'Heureux said, "even though I said, 'What the hell for?' I kind of knew why."

"Well, let's continue on," Baird said. " 'He [Ricky] said that he understood that I had not fulfilled a contract that I had taken in New Jersey from a man and the man was willing to lay the money out to have me taken care of.' Now did you believe, at that moment, that somebody who had given you at that point twenty-two thousand dollars was going to pay somebody else seventy-five thousand to kill you for not doing the job?"

"He was the only one I could think of that might be doing that."

"Who is the 'he'? Marshall?"

"Yes."

"And did you ever have any suggestion that Mr. Marshall would know somebody in Dallas who would be a contract killer for him?"

"I had no knowledge of who he knew where."

"I see. Okay, then you say in this statement, 'I didn't know that what maybe he did have those kind of connections,' and the 'he' you are referring to there is Marshall, is that right?"

"That is correct."

"Let's turn to the next page, which curiously enough is not numbered but since it is between fourteen and sixteen we will assume it is fifteen, okay? And you

say, 'And, uh, finally Ricky said, uh'—and then there's
an underlined blank—' "You know, our friend told
me about the deal," which I assume was Ricky, uh,
Travis.'

"Now, do you think the name Travis, or Travis
Greene, was supposed to go in that blank?"

"My thought at that time was that Travis Greene
had mentioned it to Ricky," L'Heureux said.

"This is very specific, though. Are you saying in
your statement, in that sentence, are you saying that
you *thought* Travis Greene told Ricky, or are you
saying that Ricky *told* you that Travis Greene told
him? Which are you saying?"

"I am saying that is what I thought."

"So, Ricky did not, as the sentence reads—Ricky
never said anything about Travis Greene telling him
about that at all, correct?"

"That is true."

And with that, Nathan Baird had succeeded in getting Ferlin L'Heureux to contradict not only his direct
testimony (in which he'd told Kelly that Dew had
mentioned Greene's name), but also the sworn statement he'd given in December in return for the drastic
reduction in charges against him.

The Greene "underpinning" had collapsed. The "integral and necessary" part of L'Heureux's statement—
the part that served to keep all those reluctant players
off the field—had been invalidated, leaving in place
only his original story: that Dew had been offered a
contract to kill him just one day after he'd passed
word through Andrew Myers that he would not be
coming north again.

But the telling of that story wouldn't help anyone,
and there was no telling whom it might hurt.

22

CHRIS called Roby from Lehigh. It was the middle of the third week of trial.

"Mrs. Rosenberg testifies tomorrow," he said. "Are you going?"

"Hell, yes. I want to sit close enough to spit."

"Remember the night of my prom, when Dad made us go over to her house just so she could see how nice we looked?"

"I sure do. Just one more happy snapshot from the old family album."

"Well, I just thought of another. Remember the night of Mom and Dad's twentieth-anniversary party, right after Christmas two years ago?"

"Yeah, it was like Dad had invited the entire population of Ocean County."

"But it was a surprise for Mom, right?"

"Yup. Dad loved surprises."

"Everybody they ever knew was there, right?"

"Yeah, I even remember Raymond DiOrio showing up."

"So do I. In fact, he was wearing a brown tweed jacket. For some reason, I even remember that."

"Probably because you liked it so much you wanted to ask him where he'd bought it."

"And you remember when Dad brought out the bouquets?"

"Are you kidding? I think we've got that on video-tape. He gives her the big bouquet of white roses, twenty of them, and says, 'One for each year of our blissfully happy marriage,' or some bullshit like that."

"Right. And everybody claps and cheers."

"And then he gives her the three red roses—'One for each of our three magnificent sons whom she's raised to the threshold of adulthood.' Yeah, I remember. I thought it was kind of cool that he called me magnificent. Six months later when I got bounced from Villanova, that wasn't what he was calling me."

"But do you remember Mom, Roby? Do you remember Mom when he gave her those flowers and made that speech and then he leaned over and kissed her?"

"Yeah, I remember. She was crying."

"Right. Tears of joy. Isn't that what you thought?"

"Of course."

"Think again."

"Oh, my God," Roby said. "The affair had already started by then!"

"It had been going on for six months."

"In fact, Mom had already hired her detective! Oh, my God, Chris, this is awful. That was one of the few happy memories I had left."

"Sorry to be the Grinch who stole Christmas, Roby, but I'm into reality these days. Do you remember who else was at that party? Standing right there clapping and cheering with everyone else?"

"Mrs. Rosenberg," Roby said quietly.

"How could she do that?" Chris asked.

"I wonder how the bitch could even walk through the front door," Roby said.

"At least you know now why Mom couldn't stop crying, even when it got to be embarrassing."

"I guess they weren't tears of joy," Roby said.

While he was in jail, awaiting trial, Rob had written a memoir of his affair with Felice. He began with the moment, at Jerry Mitchell's party, when he had first sensed the limitless possibilities.

"She walked onto the patio deck on that hot day early in July," he wrote, "looking around for the approval she knew she would get. Her curly jet-black hair fell onto her shoulders, complementing the red jumpsuit which clung to her thin frame. Our eyes met with a smile as she walked toward me under the yellow and white tent canopy. All the playful sexual innuendo that had been going on between us for years came to a head that afternoon."

It was exactly this sort of impact that Kevin Kelly did not want when he summoned her to the stand on Thursday afternoon during the third week of trial.

"I can play it any way you want it," she had told him. "I can be a schoolmarm or else I can Felice it up."

He had strongly advised the schoolmarm image, and that was what he got, as she appeared wearing an ankle-length gray suit and a red blouse securely clamped at the throat by a demure silver brooch.

The sixty-five-seat courtroom was hushed and, for the first time since the trial had begun, filled to capacity. To hear Felice—or, rather, in anticipation of watching her squirm—many of the Toms River matrons had managed to overcome the sense of propriety that had heretofore kept them away from Mays Landing.

Felice had told Kelly that she was worried about several things, among them any references to previous extramarital affairs. But mostly she seemed worried about Patsy Racine's name coming up publicly.

"She did not want to have to mention his name," Kelly said.

On the stand, Felice was stoic and composed, the fires of passion thoroughly damped for the occasion. She didn't even seem as if she'd be much fun at a game of Trivial Pursuit.

Refusing to look him in the eye, or to look anywhere near him, Felice said she'd known Rob for "fifteen or sixteen years" and that they "moved in the same social circles."

Throughout their affair, she said, "We had many discussions about the debts that he had," including one in which "he made reference to the fact that if [Maria] were not around, the insurance money would definitely take care of the debts."

She said Rob had been "very upset at his home situation, very frustrated," because Maria "was pulling in the reins. She was hovering over him. She was aware that there was some problem between them, and she was suspicious that there was a relationship between us. She was bombarding him with these suspicions to the point that he was very upset, and in a conversation with me said something like, 'I swear if there were a way that I could either "do away" or "get rid of" her, I would.' And he asked if I knew anyone that would do such a thing."

"What did you say, ma'am?" Kelly asked.

"I didn't think he was serious," she said coolly, "and I told him that there was only one other person who I even knew who had any kind of dealings with the law, and he wouldn't even consider doing such a thing and that the idea was absurd and out of the question and I could have nothing to do with him if he even considered pursuing it."

Kelly did not ask her who that person was.

Then, in his questioning, he reached the morning of September 6. All relevant phone calls from that day were listed on a large chart that had been placed at the front of the courtroom.

Kelly pointed to the 9:46 A.M. call from Rob to her and her return call from a different telephone two minutes later.

"Do you recollect that scenario, as to what happened and why?"

"Yes."

"Could you just explain that to us?" he asked, almost deferentially.

"I was interviewing a candidate for a teaching position," she said, "and was interrupted by a secretary to say that there was an urgent call, an urgent call that had been made to me by Mr. Marshall. I went into the principal's office and received the first call for one minute and twenty-seven seconds [a duration reflected on the chart] and after concluding that call and excusing myself from the interview, went, I believe, to a pay phone and called him back."

Kevin Kelly did not ask Felice a single further question about those calls. Indeed, he never referred to them again.

In regard to their in-person meeting that afternoon—after Rob and L'Heureux had already chosen the site where Maria would die—Felice said only that Rob had seemed "subdued." Not, she said, his "normally quite enthusiastic and outgoing and happy-go-lucky—not happy-go-lucky, that's wrong—confident" self.

She added, "I do remember him telling me that he was annoyed because he was going to be going to Atlantic City that night. He didn't really want to go, but his wife insisted."

She said she had been "just appalled by the deception" when she'd learned of Rob's lies to her concerning his relationship with Myers and L'Heureux.

"Was your relationship with him based on honesty and trust?" Kelly asked.

"Yes. That was sort of a foundation," she said.

And that was it. Kelly was finished with her in half an hour.

Carl Seely, who did not propose to be finished in half an hour, began his cross-examination cautiously. Indeed, some of his early questioning was almost comical in its courtliness.

"Would you agree with me," he said, "at least that in regard to your contact with him and your feelings about him, and his reputation in the community, that Rob was a decent type of person, a decent man?"

"Yes."

"And can we at least assume had you not at least felt that and believed that, you certainly would not have permitted yourself to get involved in any type of relationship with a man other than someone like that?"

"That's true," Felice said.

"Now, the relationship, I think you indicated, began sometime around July of 1983. Do you recall where you first met?"

"I'm not sure. I think it was the Smithville Inn."

"Some type of prearranged meeting or was it spontaneous?"

"No, it was prearranged."

"How did you happen to set it up?"

"I don't recall."

"You were both members of the same country club, correct?"

"Yes. We belonged to the same country club. He played tennis. I played tennis. My husband played tennis."

"Well, do you recall whether or not the first contact was in a restaurant, for example?"

"The first contact?"

"The first contact where you and he met for the first time and the start of this relationship outside of your respective marriages began. That was certainly an important moment, wasn't it?"

"I have already told you, we met at the Smithville Inn."

"Okay. What I'm trying to find out is, how did it come to be that you met there?"

"There was a phone call," she said, "but I don't recall who made it."

"Were you going there for dinner?"

"No, we were meeting there and we were going somewhere afterwards. We were going to a motel, Mr. Seely."

"Well, obviously, before you got there you knew what the purpose was and you knew where you were going to end up."

"Unquestionably."

"Well, had you had any discussions before that date about doing this, or was it one of those whirlwind kind of things and you decide to run off to the Smithville and go to a motel?"

"Yes, there were discussions."

"On that day, or the day before?"

"I don't remember."

"Who initiated the discussions?"

"Who initiated? Mr. Marshall initiated the discussions."

"When did he first call you?"

"Sometime early in July."

"And was that at home or in the office?"

"In my office."

"Well, how did he get your office number, just looked it up in the phone book?"

Finally, Felice let some impatience show. "Are you asking me whether he asked me about this at a party? Is that what you are aiming at? Is that what you want? Yes, there was a party at which he came up to me and discussed this and asked for my phone number. That's where he got it."

"The Smithville," Seely said. "How far is that from where the two of you lived in Toms River?"

"About an hour away."

"Was the purpose of going there the hope that no one would see the two of you?"

"Yes."

"You had a certain image and certain, if you will, identity in the community, did you not, that you wanted to, you know, continue with?"

"Yes."

"And it's a small town, isn't it, Toms River, at least in terms of the town itself and the people who know one another? It's somewhat of a tight-knit little group, isn't it?"

"Yes."

"And isn't it true that you had a sensitive enough position as vice principal of a school so that certainly you didn't want to be in the position where some type of scandal or some type of allegation about your conduct would reflect on your ability to be an administrator?"

"Absolutely."

"Because it certainly is a very sensitive position, where you supervise young people. Right?"

"That's correct."

"And can we assume at least that the standards of the school are such that if they thought you were doing something which would cause damage to the reputation of the school, they might want to fire you?"

"That's true."

"So when Maria became suspicious of you, did you take steps to try to be more discreet?"

"Absolutely. In fact, there were at least two times when as a result of suspicions that I was becoming aware of, I backed away from the relationship."

"When was the first time?"

"It was in late fall 1983."

"When would the second time have been?"

"It was in 1984, early spring."

Apropos of late fall, Seely asked Felice if she could "pin down exactly" when the conversation had taken place in which Rob had first mentioned hiring someone to murder Maria.

"No, I can't," she said. "Closest I can pin it down is November, December or January '83, '84."

"Do you remember where you were? Were you, for example, in a motel room or restaurant, or in his car?"

"To the best of my recollection it happened in a telephone conversation. I was at school."

"I assume he called you?"

"I don't remember."

"You don't remember whether he called you or you called him?" Seely had a hard time containing his amazement. The purported topic of the conversation, after all, had been the murder of his client's wife.

"The likelihood is he called me," Felice said, "but I can't pinpoint the conversation enough to know for sure."

"Can you estimate about how long the two of you were talking during that particular conversation?"

"No, I can't."

"Do you recall anything else that was said?"

"I know that we changed the subject shortly after that part of the conversation and went on to other things. It was dismissed as being an outburst that was bizarre, outrageous, not to be taken seriously."

"And do you recall whether or not it was more likely that the conversation took place at the end of '83 or beginning of '84?"

"I would say the end of '83."

"So that would mean it was probably sometime in December."

"Very possibly."

That would have meant also, though Seely did not explore this, that the conversation in which Rob first mentioned having Maria murdered would have come at a point in time very close to the twentieth-anniversary party at which he presented her with the bouquets— the party that Felice attended.

In addition, it would have meant that Rob's first mention of the possibility of "doing away with" or "getting rid of" Maria, would have come quite soon after the first occasion in "late fall," when Maria's suspicions had caused Felice to "back away" from the affair.

But this was not a cause-and-effect relationship that Carl Seely was eager to establish. He turned his attention instead to the second occasion on which Felice had "backed away," and to what had preceded it.

"Now, you mentioned that you and Rob and many of the people in the Toms River area traveled in the same social set and have friends in common. Is it not true that one of these people is a lawyer named Tom Kenyon?"

"That's correct."

"It's true, is it not, that Mr. Kenyon was a close friend of yours? In other words, he was a close friend of *yours* and really did not have that type of close relationship with Rob Marshall or Maria?"

"That's correct."

"And do you remember attending a function at the Toms River Country Club where you had discussions with Tom Kenyon with regard to your situation as it related to Rob?"

"Yes, I do. It was probably March of 1984, perhaps February, and it was a dinner dance at the club, and Tom Kenyon, while he was dancing with me, told me that Maria had come to see him regarding her suspicions about Rob's infidelity."

"He recommended to you that you cease the relationship, didn't he?"

"Yes."

"He also suggested, did he not, that Maria may have hired an investigator, may have hired counsel?"

"He may have said that, but I don't remember."

"Did you at any time after that have any further conversations with Tom Kenyon with regard to your relationship with Rob, or Mrs. Marshall's retention of an attorney and an investigator?"

"To the best of my recollection, no. However, it's possible—no, I'm sorry. I correct that. It seems to me I called him. I did. I called him the following week after Rob and I had discussed what had happened. Rob was not at that dinner dance and we agreed that I should call Tom back and get more specifics on what it was he was trying to tell me that night. So I did call him back. But I don't remember what he told me that night versus what he told me in the phone conversation."

Whatever he had told her, however, seemed enough to cause her, as she testified, to once again "back away" from the affair.

Whether that in turn caused Rob to intensify his efforts to find someone to murder Maria was not a question anyone in the prosecutor's office had ever explored.

It is a fact, however, that the meeting with Myers occurred in May, soon after Felice's second episode of "backing away" from the affair, just as the conversation in which she'd given Rob the name of Patsy Racine (a name she was determined not to mention publicly) had taken place soon after her first such episode.

One might infer that Rob reacted strongly to any displays of recalcitrance on Felice's part.

In any case, they soon passed. By summer—after Rob had spoken to Myers and after L'Heureux had begun his travels north—Felice's attitude toward the relationship underwent a significant shift.

"I made a commitment to myself," she said, "to choose the life in which I could be honest, and no longer feel the push and pull of the ambivalent feelings that were plaguing me. By then, Rob and I had made a commitment that somewhere down the line we were going to be together permanently."

"But," asked Seely, "wouldn't you agree with me, at least, that one of the things Rob was trying to do and one of the things you were certainly trying to do was to maintain the social status that you both had in the community?"

"I have a problem answering that as a yes or no, Mr. Seely," she said, "because implicit in our relationship was the knowledge that the social status that we may have enjoyed together or independently was going to be tremendously disrupted. We were very aware of that. Our entire social status would undergo a total upheaval once we left our respective spouses."

"But that would only have occurred, would it not, if at some point he left and you left and then the two of you went together. Until then, certainly neither you nor he would have wanted your circle of friends, or anyone for that matter, to know about the relationship, isn't that a fair statement?"

"Only in the beginning. As time went on we became more committed to one another and less committed to our respective spouses to the point we were ready to go public."

"In fact, that time never did come, did it?"

"It would have come," she said.

But murder came first.

So Seely tried to show that Felice had a motive for trying to hurt Rob through her testimony. He contended the obvious: public awareness of the affair and its link with the murder had forced her not only to leave her thirty-thousand-dollar-a-year vice principal's job, but had pushed her out of the field of education altogether.

"Without question," she agreed, "my perception is that I would not be a welcome addition to most educational staffs."

"You sound a little bitter. Are you still bitter about this?"

"I'm not happy about it. I'm not happy about appearing on this witness stand."

Seely then proceeded to make her a little less happy, asking about her encounter with the Ocean County prosecutor's office on the day of the murder.

"You were a little concerned, weren't you, whether they thought you had anything to do with anything?"

"I really don't remember," she said.

"You *don't recall* whether or not you may have asked them whether or not they thought you may be some type of suspect or target?"

"I might have asked that question, but I really don't remember."

"But you were concerned, weren't you, on Septem-

ber seventh, 1984, after the police processed you, fingerprinted you and took your photographs, that they
may have suspected that in some way you may have
had some involvement in whatever went on here?"

"Yes."

"And was that concern sufficient to keep you from
seeing Rob for at least the next few days?"

"I didn't see Rob from September seventh to September fourteenth."

"In other words, a whole week went by when you
didn't see him?"

"That is correct."

"Then you continued to see him after the fourteenth, didn't you?"

"That's correct," she said. "By that time my position had been clarified, according to my lawyer, and I
was no longer concerned about any involvement in the
suspicion that existed."

"You were certainly very concerned on nine seven
eighty-four," Seely said, "because it's not often that
one ends up getting fingerprints taken and photographs
taken by the authorities and questioned by the authorities in a case that may be a potential homicide. Right?"

"That's true," Felice said.

The very next day, she had retained the Trenton
lawyer, Anthony Trammel. This was the same day on
which Rob met with Raymond DiOrio, although
DiOrio's bill reflects that he'd actually started work on
the case the day before.

On Sunday, she'd driven to Trenton to meet with
Trammel and an associate.

"Did you get any assurances at that time," Seely
asked, "from your lawyers, that at least in their opinion they felt that the prosecutors were not looking at
you as any type of target in any criminal investigation?"

"No, I did not," she said. "They caused me to feel

that I clearly could be considered connected to this case if Rob were—if the finger were pointed at Rob."

But then, within a week, and for no apparent investigatory reason, Felice's position had been "clarified." That week, of course, coincided with the period of Ray DiOrio's involvement in the case.

Seely tried to probe this a bit. In regard to her first meeting with Rob after the murder, he asked, "This was supposed to be a clandestine or secretive type of encounter, right?"

"Yes. That was a sensitive issue. His wife had been murdered, and for me to appear with him publicly was a totally insensitive thing to do."

"Nevertheless, you voluntarily made arrangements to see him, didn't you?"

"Yes, I did. I called him. I asked him to come to my house."

Seely stared coldly at her from across the courtroom and paused before asking his next question.

"Did the prosecutor's office or your lawyers or anybody ever suggest to you that at some point in time you contact Rob, so you could talk to him, find out whatever you could about—"

"Absolutely not," she interrupted.

"They never did that?"

"Unquestionably not. I called him because at that point I had been isolated from my family and my so-called friends. I was alone and was feeling very much in need of his support."

"You have a lot of other friends besides Rob, don't you?"

"Not anymore."

"Do you have other friends?"

"Not anymore."

"You lost all your friends because of this?"

"Most of them."

"You are right now with no friends?"

"I didn't say 'none.' "

"But in other words, the one person on this earth that you could contact for some kind of emotional support on September fifteenth, 1984, you are telling us, was Rob Marshall."

"That's absolutely correct."

"So you reached out for him to help you?"

"Yes, I think I asked him to come over to my place at the beach."

"Did he do it?"

"Yes, he did."

"How soon after you called him?"

"I think it was quickly."

"He came running, right?"

"To the best of my recollection, yes."

"When he came running to you on nine fifteen eighty-four, did you then sit and chat?"

"I don't remember."

"You don't remember?"

"No, I don't."

"You don't remember what happened?"

"No, I don't."

"You remember how long he stayed over?"

"I don't think it was very long, but I don't remember."

"Did you confide in him what the nature was of your problems and your concerns and what was worrying you, and your feelings?"

"I probably did, but I am not sure."

"Did you ever ask Rob, 'Hey, Rob, did you have anything to do with the death of your wife?' "

"I don't know. I doubt it, because at that point I didn't think it was possible."

"Did you ever ask him that question?" Seely demanded.

"I really don't know, but I might have."

"You *might* have?"

"I might have."

"You *might* have," Seely repeated. "Did you tell the prosecutor's office about the visit and what you talked about?"

"I'm sure I told them about the visit, but I didn't—I don't remember telling them anything we talked about."

The day ended with Seely still in the midst of his cross-examination and with Felice appearing as unperturbed as when she'd begun and with her memory's extraordinary selectivity still intact.

Because of scheduling necessities and the Presidents' Day holiday, Felice would not be returning to the stand until the following Tuesday. That gave her a long weekend to spend at home, reading the papers.

23

THERE were front-page close-up photographs in the Ocean County *Observer* and the Asbury Park *Press* (which even used color).

Headlines like FELICE: ROB WANTED TO "DO AWAY WITH" WIFE, and worse, far worse—in fact she could not believe this when she read it—a report of how Carl Seely had told the judge, prior to her being summoned to the stand, that he intended to question her about past love affairs because he considered that to be "a fertile area."

She called Detective McGuire on the telephone. She was not happy. She said Kevin Kelly had promised her this wouldn't come out. She said Kevin Kelly was a liar. She said she wanted Kelly to call her right away.

She called McGuire for the first time on Friday night. She called him again Saturday morning and then again Saturday afternoon. McGuire called Kelly, pleading with him to call her and calm her down. Kelly said she was getting what she deserved. McGuire reminded him that she was still his witness, facing additional hours on the stand, and that a loss of control on her part could conceivably jeopardize, or at least complicate, the case.

Finally, at 8 P.M. Saturday, Kelly called her. She
wasn't home. He left a message. She didn't call back.
From her point of view, it is probably a good thing she
didn't. Kelly was sick to death of Felice Rosenberg.
To him, she and Marshall were exactly the same phony
country-club type and it was the one type he most
despised. Now she was frightened: well, too goddamned
bad.

The first time he'd met with her, before the trial
started, Kelly had been very frank. He'd said, after
asking Gladstone and O'Brien to leave the room so he
could talk to her privately, "I've heard all the rumors
about the affairs. I really don't care if they're true and
I don't care who else might be involved. I don't want
to embarrass you up there and I want to assure you that
I don't intend to ask you about any affairs other than
Marshall, and I'll do my best to protect you if Seely
starts."

Now, according to McGuire, on the basis of Seely's
comment as reported in the papers, she was accusing
Kelly of going back on his word.

He did reach her by phone late on Sunday afternoon.
She yelled at him. She called him a liar. She said,
"You promised me this wouldn't come out!" Then she
put her husband, David, on the phone. David told
Kelly that he had to prevent questioning about past
love affairs. "There's children involved," David said.

That line proved too much for Kevin Kelly.

"Who the fuck do you think you're talking to?" he
said. "After all the bullshit that's gone down around
here for a year and a half, you've got the balls to tell
me *there's children involved?* You want to talk about
children involved, pal, show up at the fucking courtroom one day and take a look at Marshall's three kids
sitting there like they're still at their mother's funeral.
Don't tell me about children involved. In fact, don't

tell me about anything. I told her I would protect her
and I've been protecting her and I'm going to keep on
protecting her next week. Now what the fuck else do
you want to talk about?"

David put Felice back on the phone. "You've left
me totally vulnerable," she said.

"You could save yourself a lot of headaches," he
said, "if you'd just stop reading the fucking papers.
You let me take care of what happens in court."

Now, her tone shifted, the anger replaced by self-
pity. "But you read that in the paper on Friday. You
must have known how I'd feel. But you didn't even
call me. You didn't even call to say, 'Felice, it's Kevin.
I know you're hurting.' "

"Hey!" Kelly shouted. "Who the fuck do you think
I am? You think I'm David? You think I'm Rob
Marshall?" He shifted to an imitation of Rob's voice
on the tape. "Hello, babe. This is Kevin. I know
you're hurting." Then he went back to his regular
voice, which at this point was close to a bellow.

"Listen! You be the witness and I'll be the lawyer
and we'll get through the rest of this fine. But don't
even start with that 'hurting' shit. I'm not one of those
ass-kissers from the country club. You just show up on
time Tuesday morning!"

Felice was not the only nervous person Kelly talked to
that long weekend. Other phone calls were received
reporting that other people from Toms River had been
equally startled by Seely's comment about a possible
public probe of the "fertile area" of Felice's past romantic life.

More than once, Kelly was reminded that much was
at stake. That it was essential that he stifle any attempt by Seely to introduce extraneous names into the
public record.

In Toms River, it appeared, there were a lot of people with a lot to lose and many of them were acquainted with Felice.

And so it was that on Tuesday it was not so much what Felice said as what she didn't say—what Seely was not permitted to ask her—that caused the sighs of relief that raised the air temperature from Mays Landing all the way to Trenton.

He did question her on her attitude toward Maria Marshall. "You didn't like her, did you?" he said.

"I can't say that," she replied.

"You can't say that?"

"No."

"Does that mean that you did like her?"

"It means that she was not someone whom I needed to like or dislike," she said with an edge to her voice. "She was an acquaintance."

Her unnerving weekend had left Felice somewhat pricklier than she had been during her first day of testimony.

"When you say someone that you needed to like or dislike, is that how you determine whether or not you are going to like somebody, whether you *need* to or not?"

"No, what I was trying to say, Mr. Seely, is, we did not have enough contact for me to characterize our relationship as, in my opinion, my liking her or disliking her. We had contact on a very limited social level in such a way that our conversations were not extensive and it was not necessary for me to like or dislike her. She was not a close friend."

"Well, just so I understand how you categorize your relationships with people, there are obviously people whom you like. There are people who are your friends, and then I gather there is another category, people who are your acquaintances. Is that how you define your relationships with people?"

"I'm not sure I can answer that broad a question," she said, "because I suspect that there is going to be some follow-up that's going to try and turn that around."

"Are you anticipating I'm trying to trap you?"

"Yes, exactly."

Seely began to grin broadly and to look around the courtroom as if expecting to see that everyone else was as delighted with him as he was delighted with himself.

"Can I assume then," he said, still grinning, "that at least since Thursday, that you, in your own mind, have been trying to anticipate the little traps I may have been trying to lay out?"

"No," Felice said coldly. "I have been much too busy for that."

"So you have been at least busy enough in other matters, I guess with your video stores. Have you been busy with them?"

"Is that relevant?" Felice said.

Kelly jumped to his feet and pointed his finger at Felice. "Listen," he said. "You answer the questions. I'll do the objecting."

"How did you learn that word, 'relevant'?" Seely asked.

"Time out," Kelly said. "I'm going to object."

"Sustained," Judge Greenberg said.

Seely, however, soon reached the two areas of inquiry that prompted Kelly's most serious and energetic objections. The first concerned drugs; the second, sex.

At side-bar, out of the hearing of the jury, spectators and press, Seely said, "Based on information that I have recieved from my client, there was a time period when Felice was down in the Caribbean with her husband and she was detained and under arrest, from what I understand, with her husband, for carrying drugs and contraband out of the country and she was, at least as far as I understand—when she was down there, she was under detention by the authorities. And what ultimately happened was, they confiscated whatever drugs were in their luggage and then after a period of—I'm not sure how long, you know, an hour or so—they ultimately allowed the two of them to clear customs and enter the United States."

Seely pointed out that Felice had said her questioning by Ocean County authorities in regard to the murder of Maria had been her first encounter with law enforcement personnel.

"I would like to be able to impeach her with the fact that that was not her first encounter, because she had been, in fact, detained and she did encounter customs officials."

"Where is your information?" Judge Greenberg asked.

"The information is based on what my client has told me about conversations she has had."

"I would like to see something of a record," the judge said. "Either a report—"

"I don't have a report."

"I have to see something. When did this happen?"

Seely left the bench momentarily to confer with Rob and returned to say, "My client says that it happened about three years ago, in the Caribbean, and there were drugs that were confiscated in the luggage."

"Was there an arrest?" Judge Greenberg asked.

"From what I understand," Seely said, "and, once again, I'm getting this from my client, because I wasn't able to get records from the Caribbean, from what I understand she was detained by customs. In other words, they detained her and her husband. So, in essence, they were not free to leave. So, in a sense they were under arrest. They were certainly not free to go. They were in a custodial setting. I think they missed their plane. From what I understand, they then, through some type of an arrangement worked out with the customs officials that they would confiscate the contraband, they ultimately were released."

"See," Kelly said, "the problem is this is all coming from Marshall. He has nothing to back it up."

"I would say this," the judge said. "Your client, with all due respect, could say anything."

"Well, Judge," Seely said, "the problem is that he doesn't have anything in the way of a document."

"Even if this did occur," the judge said, "what does it have to do with this case?"

"Well," said Seely, "we have received information from our own defense investigation that there has been an ongoing federal investigation into the Toms River area involving conspiracy to possess and distribute various types of drugs. This includes people from an auto dealership in the Toms River area and there was a recent indictment of about thirty-some people from the Toms River area.

"That's true," Kelly said, "but how was she involved in this and how are you going to establish that?"

"Well, from what—"

"She wasn't even arrested," Kelly said.

"She may not have been arrested," Seely said, "but at least from what we have been able to find out on our end, she may at least be some type of subject of *that* investigation, if not a target of *this* crime and I would like to know whether or not there were any understandings or agreements with her, either by state or federal authorities in that area in return for her coming in here and testifying."

"Absolutely not," Kelly said.

"Then," the judge said, "I just don't see how it has any relevance to any issue in this case."

"It goes to credibility," Seely said.

"It might," the judge said, "if she had been arrested and charged with an offense, put in jail and convicted of that offense, yes. I agree with you. But what you have told me is so tangential it doesn't seem to have any significance. She left within an hour, isn't that what you said? She was free to leave in an hour?"

"She may be able to give you more detail," Seely suggested. "She was detained and they searched all the suitcases and luggage and there was something worked out."

"I don't know what was worked out or what wasn't worked out," Judge Greenberg said, "but a mere detention, if somebody looks through your luggage, is innocuous. The same thing happened to me one time. I came through customs and I happened to be traveling light and I had one small bag with me and I think they were suspicious as to why a person would be going with one bag, so they detained me. They took that bag apart, and you could say that I was detained."

"It's just so remote," the judge concluded. "It seems to me it's simply an effort to get something into the case to besmirch the witness with no legitimate objective."

Seely then proceeded to his second area of potential besmirchment, which was the one that had caused most of the weekend's dry mouths in Toms River.

"It deals with the prior affairs and relationships that the witness has had," Seely said. "Based on our investigation and based on conversations that the witness has had with my client over the time period that they were together. It's fairly obvious that she has had other meretricious relationships, which—"

"Not to interrupt you," Kelly said, "but so has Marshall."

"What is the relevance?" Judge Greenberg asked Seely.

"The implication now in front of the jury," Seely said, "is that this was a relationship between two people who were going to leave their spouses and then live together. And the theory behind the killing of my client's wife was to collect life insurance proceeds and also, in essence, to put her out of the way so my client could continue a life with this particular woman.

"The historical track record, if you will, of this particular witness over a period that goes back almost fifteen or twenty years is replete with a series of relationships outside of the marriage where they never resulted in her leaving her husband permanently. She always returned to him. And he, being the kind of person that he apparently is, was willing to take her back notwithstanding the fact she had done these things.

"I think it's relevant to show the lack of seriousness with which she used this type of relationship. It is also relevant because it shows, I believe, clearly a course of conduct. It shows a scheme, a mode of operation, if you will, that she has engaged in over a very long period of time where she will engage in a relationship with someone for a lengthy period of time, she will get whatever benefits she can from that, and then she will break the relationship off in some fashion and return to her husband.

"Because over all these years, some twenty-odd years, she has never divorced him and he has never divorced her and yet she has continued in the Toms River area to engage in meretricious relationships with various people. She has been doing this for quite some time, and it certainly is probative because it goes to what her state of mind was and what my client's state of mine was and what his intentions were."

"How many liaisons, if that's the word, would you say occurred?" the judge asked.

"I can tell you this, Judge," Seely said. "I got a phone call yesterday in my office from a woman who demanded that she be allowed to come to court today. She said that almost twenty years ago the same thing happened to her, where her husband ended up in a relationship with this witness and gave her various things and almost ruined her marriage until she confronted her. It goes back over a number of occasions. This is not an isolated incident."

"But we have to bear in mind," the judge said, "that the issue here is whether Marshall, as to the murder of his wife, what *he* was thinking, what *his* actions were and why he took those actions. It seems to me in regard to this witness what you are offering is simply character evidence—that this person is of such character she shouldn't be believed. Because the only issue here with regard to her is whether she is telling the truth or not. Not anything else.

"And it seems to me that if you allow this type of evidence to come in, you would be allowing evidence that's going to distract from the issues of the case. What the jury would get from this type of evidence is simply that this is a bad character, a Jezebel, or whatever the word is, and whatever she says you can't believe her.

"Therefore, it seems to me that the prejudicial impact and the capacity to distract the jury from the main issues in the case would substantially outweigh any probative value and I don't, quite frankly, see any probative value to it. I'll sustain the objection."

Now that he'd lost both arguments at the bench, not much remained for Seely but some final sniping to cover his retreat.

"You mentioned Thursday," he said, "among other

things, that you and Rob traveled in the same social circles in Toms River. And you mentioned, among other things, that as a result of this you have suffered the loss of a number of friends and acquaintances, isn't that true?"

"Yes."

"You say 'this.' Does 'this' refer to the fact that your situation with regard to Rob Marshall has now become a matter of public record in your town, in Toms River, and thereby has subjected you to a certain amount of scorn and criticism?"

"Are you simply clarifying the pronoun 'this'?" she asked. "Is that the point of your question?"

"Yes, I'm trying to clarify, to use your word—are you an English major, by the way?"

"No, I'm a math major."

"What I'm trying to determine is this: did this disassociation by your friends and acquaintances occur because they heaped ridicule upon you because of the fact that you had an extramarital relationship with Mr. Marshall?"

"I really can't read the minds of my friends," she said. "I simply know the facts are that I found myself isolated once this became public."

"Do you blame Rob Marshall for that?"

"No. I blame myself."

"So, therefore, you have no bitterness towards him whatsoever, is that correct?"

"No, that's not correct."

"Well, then, you're bitter towards him?"

"I don't think 'bitter' is the best adjective," she said. "Would you like me to explain?"

But even if she wasn't an English major, Carl Seely had had enough.

"No," he said.

And Felice's testimony drew to its close, with just

one final declaration about how she and Rob had hoped to handle the delicate matter of leaving their spouses and children.

"Part of our plan," she said, "was that we would try to make it as—'painless' isn't the right word, but we would try to minimize the amount of pain we were going to inflict on people."

"Damned nice of her, don't you think?" Roby whispered to Chris.

"She's all heart," he agreed.

Then they went back to their separate schools, while Felice—liberated from her schoolmarm pose—headed home to David so they could put a new message on their answering machine, this one promoting her video stores.

"This is Felice."

"And this is Dave."

"And this is the office of Video Village, Inc."

"If you wait for the beep . . ."

"Before you begin to speak . . ."

"We'll call you back . . ."

"As quick as a wink."

Then they chanted in unison: *"And we mean business."*

24

IT was nine o'clock Monday night, February 24, and Roby Marshall was lying on his bed in the dark listening to a Mötley Crüe tape when the phone rang in his off-campus apartment near Villanova.

Chris was calling. It was the night before their father was due to testify.

"How you doing?" Chris asked.

"Hah! Listen to this," Roby said, jumping out of bed and switching on the light. "You're not going to believe this. I'm in advanced expository writing today, right? And this teacher, my God, I couldn't believe it, you know, it's a pretty big class and I don't think she really knows who I am, but she says, 'Okay, here's the assignment for this week: write an essay about the worst experience of your life.' Can you believe it? I said, 'Hey, lady, where do I start?' "

"Did you really?" asked Chris, who would never say "Hey, lady" to a teacher.

"No, but I did go up to her after class and explain that, like, maybe I was still in the middle of the experience, you know, and I was still having a little trouble figuring it out."

"So what did she say?"

"Well, when I told her Dad was going to start

testifying tomorrow she almost had a stroke. She started that 'oh, you poor boy' stuff. So I wound up getting a week without an assignment."

"You going to be there on time for once?"

"Yeah, yeah, I'll be there on time. But remember, I don't have a big sturdy Jeep to drive like you do. All I've got's the same crappy old yellow Mustang. That would've been the best thing about Dad committing suicide. Maybe I really would've gotten a new car."

The boys had reached that stage where they could joke with each other about anything.

"Hey, Chris," Roby said. "How do you think things are going?"

"Oh, gee, Roby, you know—" he said, his voice full of mock enthusiasm. "Just like Tessie says. Everything's great. There isn't any evidence. The detectives are dumb. Kelly's falling flat on his face."

"Yeah, but then how come every time I go down there everything I hear from the prosecution makes sense?"

"That's just a minor difficulty you're having, with perspective, brother. You should come study architecture, like me. You'd learn all about the different ways in which perspective can affect your sense of what you see."

"How about my perspective on what I'm hearing?"

"And what sort of perspective is that?"

"That it doesn't sound good."

"Yeah, well, like Tessie says, that's only been their side we've been listening to. Our side hasn't even gotten the ball yet."

"Hey, Chris?"

"Yeah?"

"Are you as sick of Tessie's bullshit as I am?"

"Yes, and not just Tessie's, either."

"Who else's?"

"Dad's. All those 'I love you' signs. And always wanting us to hug him whenever he sees a cameraman around. What I want to say to him is, 'Don't be such an asshole. If you're innocent, you're innocent. And if you're not, all this bullshit isn't going to change a thing. It just makes us all look like jerks.' "

"Yeah, Tessie called me before. She says, 'Now make sure when you walk into the courtroom tomorrow to give Kelly an *extra-dirty* look.' Like that's really going to shake him up. A bad look from Tessie McBride. Or from some lame Joe College like me."

"The thing is," Chris said, "despite all that, I still want Dad to do well tomorrow."

"I know. I've just been lying here in the dark thinking about it. I want *so badly* to believe him. He's *got* to be telling the truth, Chris. He's just *got* to be."

"Yeah, but why would all of those other people lie?"

"Well, Mrs. Rosenberg would lie just because she's a dirty bitch and she'd do anything to hurt Dad because she's not going to make a million dollars out of their affair the way she'd hoped to."

"And L'Heureux?"

"Just like Mr. Baird said, Chris. He's got the biggest motive to lie—to save himself. And you should hear Brenda Dew get started on L'Heureux. She paints him like the devil himself."

"I suppose I would, too, if I were her. It's her husband as well as Dad he's trying to ruin. And with her husband there isn't even any evidence."

"You mean, like, with Dad there is?"

"There's sure a lot of phone numbers and dates and bank records and insurance applications and other crap. I just hope . . . I just hope Dad can get up there tomorrow and tell the truth and make it so obvious that it's the truth that not only you and not only me but everybody in the courtroom will know it right then and they'll call off the rest of the trial."

"That ain't going to happen, Chris."

"I know the calling-off-the-trial part won't happen. But the truth? So we really can feel it? Wouldn't that just be the greatest thing in the world?"

"Yeah. I might even feel happy again for the first time in a year and a half."

"Me, too."

"But you know what worries me?"

"What's that?"

"If all of a sudden he's just going to tell the truth and have it make sense, how come it hasn't made sense up until now?"

"I don't know," Chris admitted. "That worries me, too."

"You know what would be really weird?" Roby asked.

"What's that?"

"If he told such a good story that the jury believed him—because he's such a good salesman, you know— but you and I still weren't sure. Then he'd be acquitted and we'd never, ever know the truth."

"Don't even say it, Roby. I'm still having nightmares about that."

It may not have been Kevin Kelly's chief motivation, but by the time he had finished his cross-examination of Rob Marshall on the afternoon of Wednesday, February 27, one thing was certain: he had cured Chris (and almost all others who were present) for all time of the possibility of ever having a nightmare about not being certain of the truth.

But before that happened, Carl Seely gave Rob the last, best chance he'd ever have to tell his own story his own way.

And Rob's story, really, was very simple. He was a
good family man who'd happened to fall in love with
another woman. He'd been planning to tell his wife all
about it, and then to leave her, except that she'd
unfortunately been murdered before he ever got the
chance.

"Our plan was," he said, "to leave our respective
spouses and to live together and then eventually get
married. It was to be done in such a way so as not to
give the impression that we were having this relationship before I left Maria, or before Felice left her
husband. I was to leave first, then she was to leave,
and we were to meet sort of after the fact, thus giving
the impression—to my children, at least—that this relationship wasn't going on before I left Maria.

"I was also concerned," Rob went on, "for two
other reasons, of course. One, she was in a very sensitive job position and if news of a relationship like
ours, with people who were somewhat well known in
the community, were made public, it would hurt her
image as an assistant principal, and mine to some
extent as an estate planner with my own clients, possibly potential clients. So we were concerned with that."

Seely inquired about the phone call in which Rob
allegedly had asked Felice for the name of someone
who could help him "dispose of" Maria.

"It did not happen on the telephone," Rob said.
"We were together in a motel room. We were having
a conversation about why didn't we go to lunch, why
didn't we have dinner together. It seemed as though
we spent all of our time together in motel rooms.

"We couldn't go public because we were too well
known. She knew people in every walk of life, I knew
people in every walk of life. It was just our luck if we
went to a restaurant for lunch somebody would follow
us."

So it was in a motel, Rob said, that the subject—*the* subject—was first broached. And it was *Felice*, he said, who'd done the broaching. "She said, 'Wouldn't it be great if Maria and David were out of the picture?' "

"David!" Roby said to Chris. "Holy shit, do you think anyone ever mentioned this to David?"

"If I were David," Chris said, "I think I'd change my beneficiary."

"And I said to her," Rob continued, " 'I bet you know somebody who would do that, too.' And she said, 'Sure, I do.' And that was it." The whole thing, Rob said, was "a joke."

Regarding his meeting with Andrew Myers at the Riccio party, Rob spoke as if nothing could have been more natural. He and Maria had arrived late and all seats at tables appeared to be taken, so they had seated themselves at the bar. Then, he said, "Mrs. Riccio introduced Andy to both of us."

That was odd. That was not what Myers had said. And that was not what the wife of John Riccio had said either, when she'd been called to testify, oh so briefly, earlier in the trial. She had said that she recalled Myers "sitting at the bar most of the night," but when asked, somewhat trepidatiously, by Kevin Kelly whether she'd ever seen Myers speak to Marshall, she had said, "I don't remember." And Kelly had not pressed.

Now, as Seely guided Rob along the somewhat circuitous but (they hoped) clearly blameless path that led from May to September, he asked, at one point, why—especially after it had come to seem likely that L'Heureux was simply ripping him off—Rob had continued to place such reliance upon the recommendation of a man like Andrew Myers, who was, after all, merely a hardware clerk whom he'd met only once at a party.

"Because," Rob said, "of his relationship with the Riccios."

The trouble was, no matter how he told it—and this version was accompanied by a dabbing of the eyes with folded handkerchief at every mention of Maria's name—Rob's story just didn't make sense.

Not even when he explained as well as an insurance man could why it was economically sound for a non-working spouse to have her life insured for $1.5 million.

Not even when he explained that his signing of Maria's name was not really a problem because he and Maria had always had a clear understanding that he could sign her name to any document he chose.

Not even when he stressed that it was his innate sense of discretion—and, really, it was for the sake of Maria's reputation as much as his own—that had caused him to employ an "out of town" investigator.

And, especially, not when he tried to explain that last ride up to Oyster Creek.

"Just prior to the Barnegat toll plaza she had put her head in my lap," he said. "Prior to that we were talking about the plans for the next day. We were talking about our win at blackjack. We were enjoying ourselves, listening to the radio on the ride home. And then we ran out of things to talk about. She put her head on my lap and tried to sleep, or did. I'm not sure.

"As we approached the Barnegat toll, I slowed down. She sat up, she woke up, and we went through the toll. That's when she said. 'You'd better hurry, it's getting late.' She looked at her watch or the clock in the car. So I accelerated to sixty-five and that's when I felt something different about the car, about the tire performance. It felt to me the way a tire feels when it's going flat, lower than it should have been, lower air pressure than it should have been.

"I looked for a place to stop and I saw a sign that said either 'Picnic Area' or 'Oyster Creek Picnic Area' or a symbol for a picnic area sign, and I moved into the left lane and went up the ramp and went in, made another left, turned my high beams on and stopped the car.

"I looked for a flashlight. We have map cases sewn into the seats and I spent twenty or thirty seconds looking for a flashlight that I thought was there that was not there. So I got out of my side of the car, and I walked to the rear and that's when I noticed another car pulling in.

"As the car came to a stop, his headlights went off. Nothing else happened that I noticed. No car door was opened. So I looked at the driver's side rear tire and it appeared to be okay. I walked around the rear of the car and I saw at that point Maria had opened up her door and the light from her door gave me something— enough light to see the rear tire of my car."

"Would you describe how that tire looked at that point?" Seely asked.

"It was—it had a bulging on the bottom like it had lost air. It was not totally flat."

"What happened next?"

"Well, I had squatted down and I was looking at the car—at the tire—and I said, 'Pop the trunk,' and I was hit on the head and as I was hit, I heard her cry out, 'Oh, my God.'"

At this point, Rob had to pause in order to compose himself. The jurors watched him, dry-eyed.

". . . and when I woke up," he continued, "I don't know how long it was, I found myself—my head in a pool of blood and I immediately went to her and she was lying across the front seat of the car . . ."

Seely's final question was: "Did you have anything to do with the death of your wife?"

"Absolutely not," Rob said. "She was the mother of my children."

"What did you think?" Roby whispered to Chris.

"Like Tessie always says, let's wait until we hear the other side."

They did not have long to wait. Kelly was on his feet even before Seely had returned to the defense table. And as Kelly sprang forth, a strange thing seemed to happen to Rob Marshall. It was as if he physically shrank in his chair, as if he were somehow, in that instant, forever diminished—the last trace of the insouciance, the smugness, the arrogance, gone even before Kelly began.

Rolling his weight-lifter's shoulders, Kelly hammered out his first question like a punch. "Sir, did you hear me tell this jury in opening statements that at or about the time of your wife's death you were in debt in excess of three hundred thousand dollars? Did you hear me say that?"

One had the impression that had Marshall replied in the negative, Kelly would have had him by the throat. He was the all-powerful Benedictine with the leather strap in his hand now, and Rob Marshall was the quivering freshman who'd been caught whispering a dirty joke.

Within five minutes Kelly had a list of numbers up on a chart representing every known debt Rob Marshall had accumulated as of September 6, 1984.

Just once, Rob tried to explain away one of the figures. "It was First National's practice," he said timidly, "to let me renew the note, so I didn't have to pay it off."

"Just a minute!" Kelly shouted. "Did you ever renew the note?!" He took two steps closer to Marshall. *"Did you ever renew the note?"*

"Judge," said Seely, "he doesn't have to yell at him."

"Please don't, Mr. Kelly," Judge Greenberg said.

But Kelly was almost finished with his numbers. "Grand total"' he said, "three hundred thirty-four thousand, seven hundred twenty-eight dollars and ninety-two cents. Do you accept my math on all these numbers?" he challenged.

"I have to," Rob said, "because I haven't been adding it as I went along."

Then Kelly sped through a list of what supposedly had constituted Rob's assets. "If you add it all up," he said, "you have a minus two hundred forty-seven dollars cash on hand as of the date of your wife's death, and in July of '84 you went to the First National Bank of Toms River and asked for a twenty-thousand-dollar short-term note and they refused, isn't that correct?"

"In July of '84?"

"Right. July sixth."

"I would have to rely on your records, that's true."

Kelly swarmed all over him all afternoon.

". . . Because you wanted the application right away, isn't that correct?"

"And there was a reason for that, which I'd like to explain."

"You can explain when your lawyer has an opportunity to come back on redirect." And Kelly pressed on.

"It's just a *coincidence*, sir, that you took out a one-hundred-thousand-dollar policy on your wife's life on September sixth, the last day of her life. Is *that* your testimony? Is *that* what you're telling this jury?"

"Yes," Marshall said, tonelessly. Then, after a pause, he tried to explain. "Our portfolio was constantly changing—"

"There's no question pending!" Kelly said sharply to cut him off.

"There was a question pending," Seely said.

"He answered the question," Kelly said. "We can take a break now." Even Judge Greenberg, for the moment, seemed governed by the force Kelly was exuding.

Back from the break, Kelly drove on. That Rob had taken out additional insurance on Maria on June 18, "the day Ferlin L'Heureux says you hired him to kill your wife, are you telling us that *that's* a coincidence?"

"I did not hire L'Heureux to kill my wife," Rob said feebly.

"I understand that," Kelly said derisively. "But the fact that you sent that letter out the same day that he says you hired him, putting in your wife's coverage in full force and effective immediately, is that a coincidence, then?"

"If you want to characterize it as that, I suppose it is."

And then he jumped to July, when the same sequence of events had occurred.

"Is *that* a coincidence, sir?"

"If you wish to characterize it that way, I suppose it is."

"And you say that you were not the big spender, but even the night of September twenty-seventh, when you checked into the Best Western you were still, in effect, spending money. I mean, you talked about a used Porsche—'nothing too outrageous.' Do you recall saying that on the tape?"

"Yes."

"And a Mustang convertible, do you recall saying that?"

"Yes." Rob's eyes were downcast, his voice barely audible anymore.

"And since you've been in custody, as recently as a few months ago, you tried to buy a new car. You called the dealer up on the telephone, told him to have it ready for the end of February, didn't you do that, sir?"

"That call," Rob said wearily, "was to purchase a used car for a close family friend named Tessie McBride, as a Christmas present for her in the way of thanking her for all of the help in the past year."

"*A Two-eighty* Z-X?" Kelly asked incredulously.

"Used," Rob said.

"A Two-eighty Z-X?" he repeated.

"Yes."

And then he went to work on the alleged forgeries. And when everything was added up, he said, "Total insurance on all these policies and counting the one that was mailed inadvertently, one million, five hundred eighty-three thousand dollars. Would you accept that figure?"

"Well, I don't think we ought to count that one that was mailed inadvertently."

"Well, subtract that one," Kelly said magnanimously.

"Made it a million, four hundred thousand," Rob said.

"More than sufficient insurance, to quote Felice Rosenberg, to cover your debts—three hundred thirty-four thousand. You would agree with that, would you not, sir?"

"More than to cover my debts, yes. More than was necessary to cover my debts."

"With about a million-one left over for pocket money."

"I wouldn't characterize it that way, Mr. Kelly."

Kelly had his glasses off, his suit coat unbuttoned, and he was pacing. He gave off that aura of menace, of being just on the vege of losing control, that had graven fear into the hearts of young men just like him at St. Benedict's and, quite possibly, just like Rob Marshall, too, during those long-ago days at Monsignor Bonner, back when being unprepared for an English exam seemed the most dreadful fate that could befall a mortal, back when being on trial for the murder of one's wife was something that happened only in the movies one might occasionally see on a Saturday night.

"After Maria's funeral," Kelly said, "during the week that followed, did you ever once walk over to the prosecutor's office and say, 'Is Lieutenant Gladstone around?' and ask for Lieutenant Gladstone and ask him how the investigation was going?"

Rob remained silent, head down.

"Did you do that *once* during the week after Maria's death?"

"No."

"Ever pick up the telephone at any time during the month of September and call the prosecutor's office and say, 'Hey, fellas, how's the investigation going? Any leads?' "

Again, Rob remained silent.

"Did you ever do that?" Kelly demanded.

"No. I was told not to."

"Sir, for the month of October, the entire month, did you ever contact anybody in law enforcement, being a concerned spouse, a widower—"

But now Carl Seely was on his feet, a concerned corner man waving a towel, seeing his fighter defenseless on the ropes.

"I object to this," Seely said, "because of the fact that he was represented by counsel then, and Mr. Kelly is obviously trying to create some type of negative inference which is not fair with regard to the witness."

To say that Kelly was trying to create a negative inference was like saying that a charge of dynamite tries to create an explosion. But on the basis of the fact that Seely had formally advised the prosecutor's office as of September 24 that he was representing Marshall and that any contact with Marshall should be through him, Judge Greenberg sustained the objection as it pertained to any activities of Rob's after September 24.

"All right," Kelly said, hitching up his pants at the waist. *"Before* September twenty-fourth did you ever contact any law enforcement authorities *even once* to ask them how the investigation was going?"

Lamely, Rob tried to answer. "On the twenty-first of September, when Mr. McGuire and the other gentleman came to the house, I asked them how things were going."

Kelly shook his head in disbelief. "My question was, sir—"

"Did *I* contact?"

"Did you ever take it upon yourself to contact law enforcement and ask them how the investigation was going?"

"No. Upon advice from other attorneys, I did not."

"Did you ever go down to the prosecutor and say to him, 'The heck with these other attorneys, I hear all these rumors and suspicions going around, I had nothing to do with it, the trail's getting cold, you'd better go start looking in another direction?' Did you ever do that?"

Again, Carl Seely got to his feet. "Your Honor," he said, "I object for two reasons. Number one, he's badgering the witness, which he has no right to do, and number two, this is an improper attempt to create some kind of inference with the jury in a situation where an individual has been represented by counsel.

The prosecutor was and is right now and has at all times been aware of the fact that Mr. Raymond DiOrio had represented Mr. Marshall. Mr. Marshall testified on direct examination that he consulted Ray DiOrio. To suggest that he should be doing something when he has a legal representative is totally improper and totally unfair and infringes on Fifth Amendment rights that he may have."

"To save some time," Kelly said, "I'll move on."

"All right," Judge Greenberg said. "We'll consider it withdrawn."

But Kelly couldn't leave it alone. "On September eighth," he said, "the day after your wife died, you came to your office and you found a copy of the search warrant, did you not?"

"Yes."

"You know that the police officers had searched your office on that date?"

"Right."

"Did you go down to the prosecutor's office and say to the prosecutor, 'I have nothing to hide, why are you suspecting me? You'd better go off and look in another direction because the trail's getting cold'? Did you do that, sir?"

"Your Honor, I object again," Seely said, "because this suggests a certain duty upon a citizen to take certain actions and also that their failure to do that should lead to some negative inferences. That's not the law, that's totally improper."

Judge Greenberg sustained the objection, but Seely, by now, felt that so much damage had been done that he asked the judge to give a special instruction to the jury, which the judge agreed to do.

"One of the principles in law," Judge Greenberg said, "is that when a person is being investigated for allegedly having committed a crime, that person does not have a duty to go to or speak to the authorities about it, and you can't draw any inferences of guilt against that person if the person doesn't go to the authorities or doesn't talk to the authorities."

For Kelly (extending the boxing analogy), that was like being penalized the loss of a round for low blows when he was already ahead twelve rounds to none and the low blows in question had left his opponent unable to continue the fight.

Kelly walked back to his table and, putting his glasses back on, paged through some notes he'd made on yellow paper. Then he turned again to Marshall and spoke in a much softer voice.

"Did you ever tell any of the police officers that Maria sat up in the car, as you just told this jury—that she sat up in the car and you heard her yell, 'Oh, my God'? Did you tell *any* of the officers that the night of the murder, sir?"

"They didn't ask me," Marshall said, "They never asked me whether or not she said anything."

Kelly had been holding a pencil. He let it drop to the floor and did not stoop to retrieve it. Instead, he removed his glasses once again.

"Didn't those officers, not one, not two, but *five* different officers ask you to tell *exactly* what you remembered happening from the time you left Atlantic City? Didn't they say that to you, sir?"

"Yes, I think they did."

"Did you ever tell any one of them that you heard Maria say, 'Oh, my God'?"

"No, I never did."

"Sir, that woman was sleeping, was she not?"

"No, she was not."

"And when you pulled into that picnic area, if she did awaken ever so slightly, you told her you were going in there to relieve yourself, didn't you, sir?"

"No, I didn't."

"You saw the photograph of her body on the front seat, did you not?"

"Yes, I did."

"You know that her arms were folded under her head in a lying-down or sleeping position—"

This time, it was Nathan Baird up to object. "The photographs speak for themselves and they're in evidence," he said, "so I don't think they should be characterized by counsel."

"I'll withdraw it," Kelly said.

He put his glasses back on and walked back to his table. It was very late in the afternoon, very close to the time that the trial would recess.

"You pulled onto that ramp," Kelly said. "You made a left-hand turn and then you made another left-hand turn and you disregarded a Do Not Enter sign, is that correct?"

"Yes, that's true."

"And it was pitch black, wasn't it, sir?"

"There were no lights there. That's correct."

"It was so dark that the only description you could give of the car that pulled in was that it was a dark-colored sedan. Now, let me ask you this: when you pulled in there and you saw this car pull in, weren't you concerned at all about what these people were doing there? I mean, you were there with your wife. Did that concern you at all when they pulled in?"

"No, it didn't," Marshall said. "I thought they were coming to do what you suggested I was going to do." This was to urinate, although there was a rest room less than four miles further up the road.

Kevin Kelly stood with his arms at his sides, looking Rob Marshall squarely in the eye.

"Is that right?" he said softly.

"Yes," Marshall replied.

"And as you stood there in the darkness of night, you didn't hear a door open? Is that your testimony?"

"That's correct."

"And as you stood there some sixty feet away from that car, did you hear someone run towards you?"

"No."

"You were looking at this tire that was bulging at the bottom and not hearing anyone coming in your direction, not hearing a door open, the next thing you remember is hearing Maria saying, 'Oh, my God,' and you're hit over the head."

"That's correct."

"The only damage found on that tire was a slit in the sidewall. You heard that testimony, did you not?"

"Yes."

"There were no other holes or tears or rips or leaks of any kind found that would allow air to escape gradually from that tire. Did you hear that testimony?"

"Yes."

Then Judge Greenberg said, "Mr. Kelly, I don't like to interrupt. We're past our normal time. I don't know whether you could conclude now or not."

"No, sir," Kelly said, again gazing directly at Marshall.

And on his way out the door, nostrils flaring, he said to one observer, "This wasn't anything. Just wait till tomorrow. Tomorrow, the gloves are coming off."

25

THAT night, back in Toms River, Roby and Chris stayed up late, talking.

"What do you think?" Roby asked.

"I think," Chris said, "that I wish I didn't have to be there tomorrow."

"But I mean, what did you think about today?"

"I think Kelly made Dad look like a fool."

"He's such a mean, sarcastic prick, that Kelly. I'd like to just deck him. One punch. Boom! Down he goes for the count."

"Roby, he's just doing his job."

"Oh, bullshit. He can ask questions without all that macho routine."

"He is asking questions, Roby. And you were listening to the answers."

"Yeah, well, listen, I still believe in Dad, so if you're going to start—"

"No, no, it's not that. It's just one thing in particular I can't get out of my mind."

"What's that?"

"This business of whether or not Mom was sleeping. Ever since it happened, I've been wondering what her last seconds were like. You know? How scared was

384

she? Did she know what was happening? Why didn't she try to get away?"

"I always just assumed she was asleep."

"Why?"

"I don't know. I guess that's always been the impression I got from Dad. Every time I've pictured it, I've pictured Mom just lying there asleep, never knowing what happened. That's been something I've really been clinging to, Chris. That it was peaceful. It was quick. She didn't know a thing. She didn't suffer. She just went to sleep and didn't wake up."

"But Dad says she sat up and yelled, 'Oh, my God!' What made her yell, Roby?"

"Chris, I don't like where this is going."

"Neither do I, but let's get it there or else it will be bugging both of us forever. If she's awake and she looks out the window, the only thing that could make her yell is if she sees somebody who's not supposed to be there."

"Yeah. Whoever hit Dad on the head."

"Right, and then what does he do? He comes at Mom."

"*Chris!* Let's not take this any further."

"*We've got to, Roby.* We've got to know, in our minds, what it was like."

"Chris, she had to be asleep. They said she was lying down just like she was sleeping and then somebody just leaned in and shot her in the back. No way, if she was awake, Mom would ever have laid down and said, 'Shoot me.' She had to be sleeping."

"Unless it was like Dad said today, and then whoever knocked him out walked up to the car and said to Mom, 'Don't worry. Your husband will be okay. And you won't be hurt. This is a robbery. Just give me your pocketbook and lie facedown on the seat. Don't move for at least—' ten minutes, twenty minutes, something

like that. The guy's got a gun. But he didn't shoot
Dad, he only knocked him out. There's no reason why
he'd want to shoot her. So she does what she's told.
She lies down, with her head in her arms, just like
Kelly showed in court. And then—"

"And then some cowardly cocksucker shoots her in
the back!" Roby said.

"That's right."

"So instead of it being peaceful, Mom was probably
terrified."

"Think about it, Roby. She couldn't have been asleep.
Even forgetting what Dad said today. Just think, the
car is going along at sixty, sixty-five, and then suddenly he pulls off the road and onto that ramp and
then comes to a complete stop in the woods, and tries
to find a flashlight, and opens the door and starts
walking around the car—there's no way Mom would
sleep through that."

"You're right, Chris. You're right. Ah, shit. This
just keeps getting worse and worse."

"I know."

"I'd always liked to think that maybe she was dream-
ing. Maybe at the moment she died, Mom was having
a happy dream about us." Roby's eyes were filling
with tears.

"Roby, in this story there's no room for happy
dreams."

Roby thought about it overnight and decided not to go
to court the next day. Between what Kelly had done
to his father on the witness stand the day before and
the late-night talk with Chris about his mother's last,
probably wakeful and terror-filled moments of life,
there was too much confusion and pain in his mind.

He had never before seen his father the way he'd
been Wednesday. *Cowering.* That's what it had been.

His father, always in command, always so sure of himself, always taking charge in every situation, had sat there *cowering* while that bastard, that cheap bully Kelly walked all over him.

It had been, Roby thought, as if the man on the witness stand had been someone else entirely, not his father. This even went beyond the question of guilt or innocence. This raised the question of whose son was he, anyhow? The son of Rob and Maria Marshall of Brookside, the most admired and envied couple in Toms River?

Or had that family never really existed? Had that, too, been just a happy dream, like the one he'd tried to imagine his mother having at her moment of death?

He got up early, slipped down the hall, and went in to tell Chris he was going back to school instead of to court.

"Roby, you've *got* to be there. Dad will *shit!*"

"Dad has already turned to shit, in case you haven't noticed. It's too early to talk. Call me tonight. I'm out of here."

And so it was only Chris and John (along with Tessie McBride and Brenda Dew) who had to sit through what Kelly did to Rob on Thursday.

The gloves were off all right, replaced by brass knuckles.

Afterward, Kelly said it had been the wedding band that had triggered his fury. Kelly had been looking at it every day and thinking more and more what a *desecration* it was for Rob to wear it, knowing as he did, as they all did, the role he'd played in the murder of his wife.

Mockery. Marshall was mocking the memory of Maria by wearing the ring. Well, mockery was a game that Kelly knew a little about, too, and on Thursday morning he decided to play it for a while. He started with questions about the "investigator."

"Page two," he said, and on this day he didn't even try to suppress the anger and contempt in his voice, "of your tape-recorded farewell message, Best Western, you state: 'Because of Maria's actions over the past four or five months, I felt compelled to hire someone who I thought had a good reputation, was out of the town, didn't mind coming a distance.' You will agree that fifteen hundred miles from Toms River is out of the town. You would agree with that, sir?"

"It didn't matter to me where he came from as long as it wasn't Toms River."

"Well, you were the one who emphasized spending less, isn't that a quote?"

"He told me he would work for the same price that—a reasonable rate is what he told me. Two hundred and fifty dollars a day, plus expenses."

"Weren't you the one emphasizing the importance of spending less? Yes or no."

"Yes."

"Did you contact any investigators in North Jersey, Essex or Hudson County?"

"No."

"To compare rates?"

"No."

"Page fifteen. 'This was a guy that was recommended by this guy Andrew Myers, was supposed to be a very good investigator.' Before you sent twenty-five hundred dollars sight unseen to Louisiana, sir, did you make any inquiry of, let's say, the Shreveport Police Department to see if this guy was legitimate? Did you do that?"

"No."

"Did you contact the Better Business Bureau in

Shreveport to see if he was bona fide? Did you do that?"

"No. I relied on Andrew Myers."

"And so you're telling this jury that *sight unseen,* on June thirteenth, 1984, you sent down twenty-five hundred dollars to a man that you spoke with over the telephone, correct?"

"That's correct."

"When you went to the Western Union office on June thirteenth, you paid cash for the money order, did you not?"

"Yes."

"Do you have the receipt?"

"No."

"Well, sir, you've been a businessman for how long?"

"About seventeen years."

"And as a matter of fact, you took *nine* or *eleven* extra courses to become a Certified Life Underwriter, isn't that correct?"

"That's correct."

"You expected, did you not, that sometime in the future you would receive a bill from this investigator. Is that a fair statement?"

"Yes."

"And it didn't *dawn* on you, as a *businessman,* as a *CLU,* with these extra college courses, 'Perhaps I should keep this receipt just in case there's some question when he gets to the bottom line on his final bill.' That never dawned on you?"

"The issue was twenty-five hundred dollars," Rob said, "and that was to be it. There was never any mention of any additional fee or required money, just twenty-five hundred dollars, come up once. That was it."

"As of June twenty-fifth," Kelly said, "the date of the second money order, had this investigator pro-

vided you with any written reports as to the work he
had done?"

"No."

"Had he provided you with any photographs as to
the work he had done?"

"No."

"Had he provided you with any oral reports as to
the work he had done?"

"Other than the fact that he told me—"

"He wanted more money," Kelly said.

"That he hadn't completed the investigation and
wanted more money. But that was through Andy Myers,
anyway."

"As of June twenty-fifth, had he provided you with
any oral reports?"

"No."

"As to the work he had done?"

"No."

"And so, on June twenty-fifth, after sending him
twenty-five hundred dollars, you now sent him three
thousand more. Correct?"

"That's correct."

"Where's that receipt?"

"I don't have it."

In the front row of spectators, as Tessie McBride
glared furiously at Kevin Kelly, Chris Marshall sat
with his head in his hands. He envied Roby, back in
school, probably sitting in class, not hearing this. On
the other hand, he was glad, for Roby's sake, that
Roby was not here.

"Did you ever tell Gene Leahy that you wired money
to Louisiana to pay off a bet? Yes or no."

"I may have."

"Well, did you or didn't you?"

"I'm not sure. Things were very confused."

"Confused?"

"My wife had just been killed. Yes, I was confused."

"On the tape," Kelly said, "you mention that this guy who was 'supposed to be a very good investigator' came up here twice. June the eighteenth, you agree with that date?"

"Yes."

"And he came up the night Maria was killed."

"Yes."

"*Nowhere* on this tape do you mention that July nineteenth–twentieth visit of Ferlin L'Heureux. Do you, sir?"

"No."

"And that's because when you made this tape on September twenty-seventh, if you were to have put in that second meeting in July, it would not have been in accordance with Ferlin L'Heureux's phony scenario that he gave Gary Hamilton, isn't that a fair statement?"

"No, it's not."

"You do agree, do you not, that the day before you checked into the Best Western and made this *farewell* tape, you spoke with Gary Hamilton on the telephone. Isn't that correct?"

"That's correct."

"And not only did you talk to Gary Hamilton on the twenty-sixth of September, you spoke with him for forty-five minutes. Isn't *that* correct?"

"No, I didn't speak to him for forty-five minutes."

"Well, how long did you talk to him? I wasn't there. How long?"

"Approximately thirty-five minutes."

Kelly, who had been standing directly in front of Rob, now turned and walked back toward his table, shaking his head. Just once, he looked back over his shoulder as he walked. Now, standing as far from Marshall as he could get, he shouted his next questions across the courtroom.

"And during that telephone conversation, isn't it a fact that Gary Hamilton read to you over the telephone Ferlin L'Heureux's phony scenario that set forth his meeting with you on two occasions, in June and September? Isn't that a fact?"

"No, it's not."

"And so, sir, the next day you check into the Best Western and you, in effect, regurgitate everything that Hamilton gave you, so that when the police found the tape and when L'Heureux was arrested, your stories would jibe. They would apologize and you and Felice would ride off into the sunset. Making a quick stop to pick up the insurance, of course."

Carl Seely spoke next. "That sounds like a summation to the jury rather than a question, quite frankly."

"I'll withdraw it," Kelly said. But now he strode quickly forward across the courtroom until he was once again directly in front of Rob Marshall. He spoke quickly.

"When you made this tape about meeting with Ferlin L'Heureux on two occasions, June and September, you lied, didn't you? You never talked about the July twentieth meeting."

"Mr. Kelly," Rob said, "I would say that that evening was probably one of the foremost traumatic moments in my life, and I can only tell you that I was—I overlooked it. It was not intentional."

Kelly walked back to his table. Chris Marshall stared at him in fascinated horror. Every time he turned another page on his yellow pad, Chris thought, it was as if he were reloading a weapon. And Chris didn't like to think about weapons.

"You hired an investigator, Gary Hamilton, to go down to Louisiana, correct?"

"Indirectly. Mr. Seely advanced whatever expenses would be incurred."

"Which you realized you had to pay for eventually."

"Of course."

"Did you say, 'Wait a minute, why am I sending an investigator to Louisiana? I'm a taxpayer. There's police officers in my town. There's *seven* of them investigating this crime right now.' Did you ever say that? Did you ever say that?"

"No."

"Well, would you explain to me, sir, what were you trying to do: impress the *country club* by beating the police to it and solving this crime yourself?"

And with no more scorn can a man imbue any two words in the English language than did Kevin Kelly when he uttered the words "country club."

"Is that what you were trying to do?" he said.

"No," was all that Rob Marshall could say.

"And when you checked into that Best Western, isn't it a fact that all you did was stir some mixture, according to you, with your finger, and put it in your mouth, and then you fell asleep? Is that what happened?"

"I had done that to determine whether or not I could swallow it. Yes, that's what I did."

"And you fell asleep?"

"Yes."

"And you never took any of those pills?"

"That's correct."

"What, were you tired from all your dictation?"

From there, Kelly covered Rob's meeting with Andrew Myers, extracting from him the statement that John Riccio's wife had introduced Myers to both Rob and Maria. He ridiculed Rob's statement that the subsequent calls to Myers, many of which were one minute or less in duration, had largely to do with trying to sell the hardware clerk an IRA plan.

"I never met an insurance man that couldn't talk for

forty-five minutes. And that's before he even opens up his brochures," Kelly said.

"That's a question?" Nathan Baird said. "I think I've been advised against making statements and I wonder if it applies to the prosecutor as well?"

"Yes, it certainly does," Judge Greenberg said dryly. "That was a statement and it should be disregarded." But most members of the jury had already laughed.

"Oh, look," Kelly said, pointing to a chart of the Louisiana phone calls he had placed on an easel. "On June twenty-fifth here's two calls, one in the morning and one in the afternoon. One's for four minutes and one's for two. Were you having a sale on IRAs that day?"

"What I believe—if my memory serves me correctly, I had to hold and wait for Andy to come to the telephone. He was busy with a customer or something. He couldn't get to the phone right away."

"How about July third? That was a real busy day. Here you have a call from your office to the hardware store at 10:04 A.M. Here's another one, from the hardware store to you at 9:07. Did you talk business?"

"The first call, I wasn't in my office, so he maybe left a message for me to call back when I got in, and at 10:04 when I got to the office I called him."

"Well, on September third, we have three phone calls, 9 A.M., 9:02, and then one more in the evening. Things must really be hopping on September third."

"I object," Seely said.

"The comment will be stricken and disregarded. As I said before, counsel should not make comments. Only ask questions."

"On September fifth," Kelly said, "the day before the last day of Maria's life, there's three telephone calls."

"Well—"

"Were you close to making a sale on an IRA that day?"

It went on that way all morning, exposing to ridicule every detail of Rob Marshall's story and leaving the man himself without the slightest trace of credibility.

But there might still have been a whiff of injured dignity, and Kelly wanted to be sure that he obliterated that as well, leaving no traces, so that when the time for deliberation came, it would not be possible for even a single juror to sympathize with Rob Marshall on any level.

He started softly, like the most dangerous snows. "In your tape, sir, you say, 'It didn't matter. She wanted to start over. It didn't matter. She loved me, she would forget everything. And when I think about that now, how incredible she was, how much she loved me, and how foolish I was to walk away from her, I miss her so. And as each day goes by, it gets worse and worse.' You recall saying those words on this tape?"

"Yes."

"This woman, Maria Marshall, had documented evidence for eight months before her murder that you were having an affair with another woman. You agree with that?"

"Yes."

"But it didn't matter to her, did it? She still loved you. Do you agree with that?"

"Yes."

"She still kept the house clean, took care of the kids, made your meals, and slept with you. Isn't that correct?"

"Yes."

"She wanted to start over, to forget everything. Isn't that correct?"

"Yes."

" 'How incredible she was,' to use your words. She got up every morning early, dressed and showered, to feed both kids, is that correct, before they went to school?"

"Yes."

"She didn't want a divorce, isn't that a fact?"

"We never talked about divorce."

" 'I miss her so,'—page three—'and as each day goes by it gets worse and worse.' "

"Yes, that's true."

" 'I miss her so.' " Kelly repeated, his voice almost a whisper. Then he placed the transcript of Rob's taped message on his table. He took off his glasses, folded them, and put them inside the breast pocket of his suit coat.

"Isn't it a fact," he suddenly shouted, "from the day she died, for weeks and weeks and weeks to follow, all you talked about to your friends was *Felice, Felice, Felice,* and never once mentioned the fact that you loved your wife, you missed your wife, or you wanted to see the people responsible for her death apprehended? *Isn't that a fact?*"

"That's not true," Rob said, his lips scarcely moving.

"You agree with me that Felice, within a few days after Maria's death, was at your side? Do you agree with that?"

"Yes."

"In fact, after your wife's murder and the rumors that you mentioned in the tape, David Rosenberg kicked Felice out of the house, didn't he, sir?"

"Yes, he did."

"And you agree with me that there came a point in time, about September twenty-fifth, where she walked away from you and left?"

"Yes."

"And isn't it a fact the reason why she did that is

because she caught you lying to her? Isn't that a fact?"

"I don't know what her total motives were."

"Prior to that date, you both had a relationship based on honesty and trust, isn't that a fact?"

"Yes."

"You left a tape-recorded message to Felice after she left you. Isn't that correct?"

"Yes."

"And you still wrote her letters, did you not, sir?"

"Yes."

"Asking her to come back to you. Isn't that correct?"

"The motive was to have her come back, yes. I don't believe I specifically asked her to, though."

"You left tape-recorded messages on her tape machine to get in touch with you, did you not, sir?"

"I may have."

"And all of these messages and tapes that were sent to her were all done in an effort to get her back because *you missed her* and not Maria Marshall. Isn't *that* a fact?"

"No, it's not."

"Didn't you tell her on a tape, October seventeenth, that you could not accept her discarding her relationship with you? Didn't you say that on a tape?"

"Possibly."

"Didn't you tell her that nothing was important except your love for her? Didn't you tell her that on a tape on October seventeenth?"

"Possibly."

" 'There's a hole in my life since you left me.' Didn't you tell her that on that tape, sir?"

"Possibly."

"You also told her on that tape that the reason you lied to her was because you were in, quote, 'a corner.' Didn't you say that to her on that tape?"

"I don't remember saying that."

"Well," Kelly said, "do you want me to play the tape?"

Carl Seely spoke up. "We'll stipulate to the contents of the tape," he said. "It's no secret."

"Are you lying now," Kelly said, "because you are, quote, 'in a corner'?"

"No."

"On that same tape you also were critical of her, telling her, quote, 'You could have been a hero, a goddamned hero, if you stuck by me.' Didn't you say that on that tape?"

"If you're stipulating that that's what was on there. It's been a year and a half. Possibly I said it."

Kelly's voice now dropped to a near-whisper again. "Yet you would have us believe, sir, that you missed your wife and you loved her."

"Terribly," Rob said, eyes downcast.

"Hold up your left hand!" Kelly barked.

Rob did, instinctively, as if, left-handed, he were pledging allegiance to the flag.

Kelly walked toward him, pointing. "Is that the wedding ring that Maria gave you?"

"Yes."

"Who told you to wear that ring to court, Seely or Hamilton?"

"Your Honor," said Seely, "that is—"

"I'll sustain the objection," Judge Greenberg said.

As if paralyzed, Rob was still holding his left hand in the air.

"Is that ring," Kelly said, softly again, "a reflection of just how much you love and miss Maria?"

"Yes, it is," Rob said, still with his hand in the air.

"Then can you explain to me, sir, why her ashes are still in a brown cardboard box in a desk drawer at the funeral home?"

The courtroom was utterly silent. Rob looked as if he'd been slapped in the face. Ever so slowly, and much too late, he lowered his left hand until the wedding ring was out of sight.

Then Seely objected. And Judge Greenberg called counsel to the bench.

"Judge," Seely began, "there are a litany of cases where it's very clear that if a prosecutor tries with inflammatory statements or tries to unduly inflame the jury, and I suggest this is what's being done here—"

"The relevance," Kelly interrupted, "is that he's told this jury several times that he misses his wife, he loves his wife so terribly, and I think that's proper impeachment."

"Ashes in a box?" Seely said.

"He loves her so much he never even bothered to take her ashes," Kelly said.

"He's also been in jail for over a year," Seely said.

"He's been out. He wasn't arrested until December. And I think it's highly relevant."

"Well, I can conceive that it has relevance," Judge Greenberg said. "I mean, the man has testified as to his undying love for his wife. And under these circumstances it seems to me his treatment of the remains is something that might be logically relevant."

"Judge," said Nathan Baird, "you just can't bully this poor man and beat the hell out of his—"

"That's not true," Kelly interrupted. "It's my turn."

"Well," the judge said, "in his direct the witness has testified to undying love, it's in the record. And it might be reasonable to assume that if one had feelings about a person like that, he would want to make some arrangement to either claim ashes or have them deposited in the normal way. I see nothing wrong with this, I don't find there's any prejudicial impact. I'll overrule the objection."

                              *   *   *

As Kelly resumed questioning, nearing the end now of
what had been more an annihilation of a human personality than a cross-examination of a defendant, Chris
Marshall shut his eyes tight. He was wishing he could
also shut his ears. What he was really wishing was that
he could get up and walk out of the courtroom and
never come back, never see his father's face again,
never again have to listen to the sound of Kelly's
voice.

But he could not do that. He was as trapped as a fly
stuck in amber. From the beginning, he'd promised
himself that he would offer his father support until the
end. And it wasn't the end yet. Not quite. Although
Chris began to pray that there might be some way to
hasten it. Even a farm animal would be mercifully shot
to end this kind of misery.

"You do acknowledge the fact, sir," Kelly was saying
in what was now a tone of perfect calmness, "that
Maria Marshall's ashes are still sitting in a brown
paper box. You never bothered to pick them up. You
acknowledge that?"

"I don't know what container they're in," Rob said.
"The reason that her ashes have not been buried is
because we were trying to decide where to bury her. It
was a family decision. We hadn't reached a decision
and then I was arrested."

"Sir. This murder happened September seventh, 1984.
You were not arrested until December nineteenth,
1984. Correct?"

"Yes."

"You had the rest of September, October and November, during this mourning period, to dispose of
her ashes. Correct?"

"It was a decision," Rob said, "whether we should

bury her in Florida, which was at one point what she had expressed to me that she wanted to do. We had planned for the family to go to Florida during the Christmas break, the school break, so the boys would be off and we all would go to Florida. One consideration was, we would bring the ashes with us and bury the ashes. We never got to that point."

Chris could not believe he was hearing this. Not once had he ever heard a word spoken about his mother's ashes being buried in Florida.

But Kelly seemed glad that Rob had brought it up. He smiled, and walked across the courtroom with a fresh spring in his step.

"Let's talk about Florida," he said. "After your suicide attempt on September twenty-seventh, you went to Florida for three or four days, isn't that correct?"

"That's correct."

"Who did you go there with?"

"A friend. I didn't go with anybody. I went to see friends."

"Who did you meet down there, sir?"

"Friends."

"Did you have a girlfriend at the time?"

"Objection," Seely said.

"Judge," Kelly said, "he opened up the door about undying love and affection for Maria."

"I'll overrule the objection," Judge Greenberg said.

"Terri," Kelly said. "Does that name ring a bell?"

Rob was just shaking his head, as if in disbelief that things could continue to get worse.

"What was the name of the girl you were with in Florida?" Kelly pressed.

"I went down to see a woman I had met by the name of Terri," Rob said wearily.

"And that was, let's see—Maria died September

seventh, September twenty-seventh was your suicide attempt—*when* did you go to Florida?"

"I don't remember the dates."

"September, end of September?"

"I don't remember the dates."

"Was it October?"

"I think it might have been November, frankly, but I don't remember the dates."

"And where did you stay when you went down there?"

"I stayed in a hotel—a motel."

"Did you visit Jim and Molly Stevens?"

"Yes."

"Now, sir," Kelly said, and here he paused to heighten the effect he knew this question would have, "isn't it a fact that *you are now engaged to marry Molly Stevens?*"

"That's not true." Rob said this with a bit of snap to his voice.

"Did you not," Kelly said, "request as recently as two months ago to have a contact visit with a woman whom you were engaged to marry?"

"I did make that request, yes." The snap was gone.

Kelly put his glasses back on. He was holding a piece of paper in his hand. "This is a letter," he said, "that you wrote October nineteenth, to Captain—what's the name?"

"Heddin," Rob said.

Kelly started to read. " 'I am writing to request a contact visit on a date early in November, probably Wednesday, the sixth, with a woman who will be my future wife.' "

"This is November 1985," Rob said. "I'm talking 1985."

"Who was that woman?" Kelly asked.

"The woman that was coming up was Molly Stevens, but I was not engaged to her."

"Is the woman you're referring to in that letter the Molly Stevens who's married to your friend Jim Stevens?"

"She's separated from him now, but yes, that's the same woman."

Kelly put the paper down, took his glasses off, and scratched his head, as if he were truly bewildered. "So you go to Florida in October and November of '84 with a girl named Terri, you meet Molly Stevens, and now as of ten nineteen eighty-five you're going to marry Molly Stevens?"

"I'm telling you," Rob said impatiently, "I was not—"

Kelly pointed to the letter. *"Does that say 'future wife' or not?!"*

"Yes, it does. It was an attempt to get a contact visit and I used that as a reason, because they don't give contact visits to anyone but family or your wife or someone like that."

"What did Jim have to say about that?" Kelly asked.

"Objection," Seely said.

"Objection sustained," Judge Greenberg said.

Kelly took three quick steps forward until he was standing as close to Rob as the witness box enabled him to get. *"Didn't you tell your kids,"* he said, "that 'Molly Stevens is just like Mom. You're really going to like her'? *Didn't you say that, sir?"*

"Didn't I say what?"

Now Kelly's voice began to boom, filling the courtroom, and filling Chris Marshall's head with a sound he felt would never go away. *"Didn't you tell your kids that they're going to really like Molly Stevens, she's just like Mom. Didn't you say that?!"*

"I may have," Rob said meekly. "Over the telephone."

Kelly walked away from him, his face screwed up in

distaste, as if he'd been exposed to a bad odor. He was finished now. He was ready to stop. But he couldn't resist a final dig.

"When you were in Florida with Terri a couple of months after Maria's death, did you buy her a car down there? Terri? The girl?"

"I gave her a thousand dollars so that she could buy a car, yes."

"What was that," Kelly said, "a used Porsche or a used Two-eighty Z-X?"

"I think it was a 1961 Oldsmobile," Rob said.

"But Maria was the big spender, sir. Not you. Is that your testimony?"

"I didn't say that," Rob said.

Kelly threw up his hands. "Fine. That's all I have, sir. Thank you."

At lunchtime, all Chris wanted to do was to get into his Jeep and drive as far away as he could as fast as he could. He didn't want to hear one word from Tessie McBride or from Brenda Dew or even, at least for a while, from his brother John.

"It was like," he said later, "if they ever do carry out the death penalty, it wouldn't matter if I was there to see it or not, because I'd already seen it. What Kelly did to my father . . . what Kelly did . . . it was like that eliminated the last trace of any living father I might have had. From then on, Dad was just as dead to me as Mom was.

"But in a way it was even worse than that. Because Kelly didn't just wipe out my father. He wiped out everything my father had ever been. The father I'd always thought I had—at least until I started doubting him about the murder—he *never* existed. There never had been any such man. Everything, every smile he'd ever smiled at me, every hug he'd ever given me, every word of encouragement I'd ever heard—all false. All part of the big lie with nothing underneath.

"See, it came in three phases. First, my Mom got killed. Bad phase number one. Then, I came to doubt my father's story. Bad phase number two. Then, I learned I never even had a father to begin with. That was bad phase number three and that was all the work of Kevin Kelly.

"To have to sit there through something like that— when it's the only living parent you've got left who's being destroyed—I just felt empty, like I was falling through space, that soon there wouldn't even be a *me*, I'd just dissolve. There would just be a hole where I had been.

"And then they came out to me and told me I was going to have to testify that afternoon."

The strategy was obvious, if not especially humane. Put the boys up on the stand as quickly as possible to try to win back from the jury some of the sympathy that their father had lost.

Roby wasn't there, but they could throw Chris and John into the breach. (Or whatever it was. It seemed more like the hole left by a nuclear explosion than a breach.)

To do it now, when both boys were so stunned by the savagery of the morning, might be particularly effective. The jury could see them with wounds still fresh, could feel the raw pain they still suffered. Then maybe, just maybe, the jury would want to give them back their father at the end, whatever he'd done.

John was called first to the stand. He was there only ten minutes and all he said was that his father had called him at home on the evening of September 27 and had sounded "really depressed." But it didn't really matter what he'd said. He was someone upon whom the jury could take pity.

"Mr. Kelly, do you have any questions of this witness?" Judge Greenberg asked.

"Yes, I do," Kelly said. He stood up. "Where do you go to school?" he asked John.

"High School East," John said.

"Okay," Kelly said, grinning. "That's all. Now you can tell everybody you're cross-examined."

Chris was called next. He said that his father had sounded "nervous" when he'd called on the night of the twenty-seventh. That wasn't quite good enough. So, after Kelly said he had no questions, Nathan Baird stood up and asked, "Did he sound like he was saying goodbye?" Chris said, "Yes." Then he stepped down.

And at Lehigh that night, when Roby called to ask how badly the day had gone, Chris found that he had no words to describe it.

"Well, come on," Roby said. "You must be able to tell me *something.*"

"Just be glad you missed it, Roby. It's one less nightmare to live with for the rest of your life."

"You mean it was even worse than yesterday?"

"Roby, the one feeling I had was that they should've just given him the injection right there. It would have been more merciful."

There was a long pause on the line. Then Roby asked, "So you don't think Dad has a chance?"

"Roby," Chris said. "I don't think there *is* a Dad. And I don't think there ever was."

But half an hour later, Roby's phone rang. Sure, there was a Dad. It was him on the phone.

"I hear it was a rough day," Roby said.

"Listen, Roby, you've got to testify tomorrow."

"I don't know, Dad, getting somebody as handsome

as me up there after they've been looking at you most of the week might be too much of a shock."

"Roby, I don't have time for any jokes. This is a very serious phone call. This may be the most important conversation you and I will ever have."

"Okay," Roby said. "No jokes."

"Your testimony, son, is going to be *very, very* important. Do you understand what I'm saying?"

"Actually, I don't, Dad. I don't see how I can do much more than go for the sympathy vote, like Chris and John did."

"Roby, you're not listening. *Your* testimony is vital. *Your* testimony can turn this whole thing around."

"What do you want me to say, Dad? That *I* pulled the trigger?"

"This is the last time I'm telling you, son, *this is no time for jokes.* Now, just listen to me for a minute."

Roby began to get an eerie feeling, as if he were somehow outside of himself, watching himself have this conversation. As if it were some kind of sci-fi flick.

"Son, do you remember that morning in September? The day we had lunch at the club?"

"Yeah, sure, I do. Mom woke me up about eleven and asked me if I wanted to go with you guys and then she said I'd better hurry because we'd be leaving as soon as you got back."

"Roby. Think carefully. Can't you remember that I actually *was* in the house at that time?"

Roby had been standing up, walking around the room as he spoke, twirling the long phone cord with his fingers. Suddenly, he felt weak and faint, as if he'd just taken a hard right hand to the belly. He carried the receiver to his bed and sat down.

"Dad," he said. "You weren't there. You were out. I remember asking Mom where, and she said, 'Oh,

God knows where your father is these days.' Yeah, Dad, I remember it pretty clearly, now that you mention it."

"Think about it some more," Rob said. "Maybe you can remember it a different way. I'll call you back in an hour." Then he hung up.

Roby set the telephone on the floor and lay all the way back on the bed. This was sci-fi for sure. This wasn't real. This wasn't happening. Not this, on top of everything else.

For an hour, he lay on his bed and looked at the clock on the other side of his room. The first call had been at seven. He knew that at eight o'clock the phone would ring again. Suppose he just didn't answer it. Suppose he just let it ring. That would be simplest. Or he could just leave the room and go out somewhere, stay out for a very long time. That way, he wouldn't even have to hear it ring.

But he lay there, on the bed, unable to move. And when the phone rang at eight o'clock he answered it.

"Have you given it some thought, son?"

"Yes, I have, Dad. And you were not in the house."

He could hear his father taking a deep breath. Then Rob spoke. "Would you have any trouble saying I was?"

There it was, what he'd been fearing, what he had known was going to come. It was out in the open now, right there in front of them, like some kind of sci-fi monster let loose in his room.

"Dad," he said. "That would be a total lie."

"I know," Rob said. "And I hate to have to ask you to do it. But it would really help me out. In fact, it's crucial. You're the only person whose testimony can discredit L'Heureux. Listen—don't answer now. Just think about it. My whole future—*my life*— depends on this. Stay there for an hour. I'll call back." And then Rob hung up again.

This time, Roby got up and paced. He didn't leave his room but he didn't stop pacing, either. He thought about a lot of things. He thought about his mother. He thought about his father. He thought about his own immortal soul, and the fate that would befall it if he committed the sin of lying under oath. He thought about how long an hour was. He wondered if this would be the longest hour of his life. He wondered if this still *was* his life, or whether, really, his life had not ended with his mother's, or at the moment on that night when he awoke to see his father's hand fumbling for the light switch in his room.

Maybe this was purgatory, Roby thought, and after a while longer here he'd get to heaven and be with his Mom.

Or maybe this was hell. And he would be here forever—alone—waiting for the hour to pass and for the phone to ring again.

"Well?" his father said at nine o'clock.

"Dad, you always told us if we just told the truth we'd never have anything to worry about."

"Can you help me out?"

"So if you're telling the truth, how come you have so much to worry about? *If you're telling the truth, how come it's me who has to lie?*"

"You've got to help me out, Roby. You've just got to grit your teeth and do it. For me."

This time, it was Roby who hung up.

And the next day, when he testified, he told the truth.

26

WHILE all had raged about him, Ricky Dew had just been sitting silently, emotionlessly, expressionlessly and almost invisibly through four weeks of trial.

When his turn finally came, he took the witness stand and quietly said he hadn't killed Maria Marshall. Then six other witnesses, including his brother, his teenaged son and his wife, Brenda, testified that they remembered that Ricky had been down in Louisiana during the whole time all that stuff was going on.

Dew also said he'd never heard from either Travis Greene or Ferlin L'Heureux about any plot to kill Maria Marshall. And Greene, who was one of the witnesses testifying in Dew's behalf, said that while he had accompanied L'Heureux to Atlantic City in July, he'd never seen either Rob or Maria Marshall at Harrah's Marina or anywhere else, and said L'Heureux had never told him anything about any plot to murder anyone, and so, obviously, there was no way he had passed any such information along to Ricky Dew.

There wasn't much that Kevin Kelly could do with that, nor did he try especially hard. (Lurking in the background, after all, was the nagging question of who, if not Greene, had put Dew into the picture, and that threatened to spill over into the question of—or become the same question as—who in New Jersey had really been responsible for a seventy-five-thousand-dollar contract on Ferlin's life for failing to get his job done.)

These were not aspects of the case that Kevin Kelly pursued with much enthusiasm. Indeed, he did not pursue them at all. He just let the Greene bridge lie in its state of obvious collapse, and the entire Dew defense consumed less than two hours of trial time.

In truth, Kelly didn't seem to care all that much about convicting Ricky Dew and he didn't have any evidence to work with, anyway. The whole charge against Dew (valid or not) could be seen as just a way to legitimize the plea bargain with L'Heureux. And it had been the plea bargain with L'Heureux that they'd needed to get the man they really wanted—Rob Marshall. Ricky Dew, at this point, was no more than an inconvenient piece of excess baggage.

It had been Rob whom Kelly had been after from the start, with a vengeance he'd never brought into a courtroom before. And it had been Rob whom he'd spattered all over the walls on cross-examination. And, now, it would be Rob upon whom he would focus his energies, and even his venom, during his upcoming closing argument.

The date was Monday, March 3; the day dawned cold and clear, and the Mays Landing courthouse was packed. Two newspaper reporters had to give up their seats so Nathan Baird's wife and daughter could watch him work. Even Kevin Kelly's mother was there. This would be, after all, his final closing argument as a prosecutor. After this, it would be back to Bricktown and real estate closings from dawn till dusk. Kelly badly wanted Rob Marshall's scalp to take back with him. He was all but certain that he'd won it with his cross-exam, but today, with this crowd gathered for

his finale, his adrenaline would not let him lighten
up.

But before he could speak, he had to listen. That
was the way New Jersey worked it. Lawyers for the
defendants spoke first.

Nathan Baird was charming and eloquent. He quoted
the Bible (Deuteronomy 19:15, "One witness is not
enough to convict") and made reference to both his
grandmother and his grandfather, as well as the poet
Robert Burns, and he related an anecdote about beef
stew in which the moral was that one bad piece of beef
ought to make you cast the whole bowl aside, and he
suggested that Ferlin L'Heureux, in his testimony, had
presented the jury with more than just one bad piece
of beef. Then he touched upon burden of proof and
reasonable doubt and suggested that there was far
more evidence that pointed toward L'Heureux as the
killer than toward Dew. Against Dew, he said, there
was not a single shred of evidence, save "the testimony of a man scarcely worthy of belief." Then he sat
down, still slightly radiant from a recent long weekend
in Acapulco.

Carl Seely, whose Caribbean tan had long since
faded into nothingness, but whose heavy gold Rolex
was as shiny as ever, spoke for an hour and fifteen
minutes in a voice so flat and so empty of feeling that
jurors began slouching in their chairs and at least one
appeared to fall asleep momentarily.

He did have some harsh words for L'Heureux: "What
is more dangerous, what is the worst kind of person
that can walk into a courtroom and stink up a courtroom than a cop who's gone bad? And there shouldn't
be a question in anybody's mind that that is what
Ferlin L'Heureux is—a cop who went bad."

The problem was, it wasn't L'Heureux on trial—it
was Rob Marshall, a husband and father who'd gone

bad. And so, when in conclusion Seely perfunctorily asked the jury to "acquit Robert Marshall and send him back to his children," there was at least one member of the audience heard to whisper, "Dear God, haven't they suffered enough?"

Then, after lunch, it was time for Kelly's Last Ride. And he did his best to make it unforgettable. He spent forty-five minutes giving a basic summation of his case. Given the strength of it, and his devastation of Rob on cross-examination, he probably could have stopped there.

But he didn't. Kevin Kelly had come too far to stop there, to stop where the trail of dry fact ended. Instead, he plunged headlong into a final assault upon the tattered shreds of character with which Rob Marshall was vainly trying to clothe himself.

"Ladies and gentlemen of the jury," he said, "you can live an entire lifetime and meet only one Robert Oakley Marshall."

He paused. Business suit, eyeglasses and parochial school manners notwithstanding, he was still a rough-and-tumble Newark street kid, but one who believed in, and would fight for, what was right.

"I'm not going to stand before you and give you reasonable explanations for irrational acts," he said, "and certainly what Marshall had done to his wife goes against every sense of decency and logic known to mankind. But I will tell you that desperation and greed have no limits.

"If every defendant acted rationally, there would be no need for a jury system. If every defendant acted rationally, there would be no need for a criminal justice system, because no defendant would ever get caught."

Kelly walked slowly across the courtroom until he stood directly over Marshall, who was seated at the

defense table, by Seely's side. When he spoke, it was
with measured cadence.

"Don't be fooled by his tears," Kelly said, pointing.
"He cries for no one but himself.

"Don't be fooled by his 'I Love You' signs, because
he loves no one but himself."

He paused again, and took a step back toward the
center of the courtroom. "I'll sit across a table from
Ricky Dew any day, because with Ricky Dew you see
what you get. What you see is what you bargain for.

"But *this* defendant," and now he was pointing again,
and taking that one big step closer to Marshall, and his
voice was as sharp as a handclap, "is a coward, he's
self-centered, he's greedy, he's desperate, he's materialistic, and he's a liar."

He paused for breath, then spoke more slowly. *"He
is a legend in his own mind."* He paused again.

"No one," he shouted, "has the *audacity* to question
Robert Oakley Marshall, as per Robert Oakley Marshall.
He is an outstanding citizen in the community and
no one would dare to point a finger at him. And
if it comes down to Robert Oakley Marshall's testimony
against Ferlin L'Heureux, no juror in his right mind
would accept the testimony of Ferlin L'Heureux over
such an outstanding citizen.

"That," he said, pointing again, "is what is sitting in
that chair. Make no mistake about it. The man was in
dire financial straits, he was desperate, and he's greedy,
and he's a liar. There was no way in the world this
man could maintain his lifestyle and leave his wife.
You know it, and I know it, and he knew it. He was
desperate and he was *greedy*.

"He doesn't wear his wedding band until the day
this trial starts, and then he tells you that 'well, they
wouldn't give it to me in the Ocean County jail.'

That's an *insult!* That was testimony and actions on his part calculated to deceive you."

Now Kelly's anger was burning pure and clear. This was no act designed to sway a jury. This was real. He began to stride more quickly, more aggressively about the courtroom, gesticulating ever more forcefully as he spoke—his voice rising with his cresting emotions.

"On direct examination, 'I miss Maria, I love Maria,' and so forth, and so on. This man carried on *three* separate relationships within a three-month period after his wife died, and misses her so much that her ashes are still sitting in a drawer in a funeral home. *That's* how much he misses her.

"And he gets on this witness stand, after there's an objection at side-bar, after I asked that question, and he's had an opportunity to think about his answer, and he says, 'Well, we were really going to take her to Florida.' "

At full fever pitch, Kelly cried out: "And he has the *audacity* to bring in his three boys to testify. That's *obscene!* To put his boys on that witness stand is obscene, and for that *there's a place in hell for him!*"

An involuntary, collective gasp of shock was heard in the courtroom as Kelly uttered those words. In the front row, John Marshall buried his head in his hands. Roby, his own eyes red with tears, reached up from his second-row seat and squeezed John's shoulders. Sitting next to John, Chris lowered his own head and his shoulders began to shake with sobs.

"He will use anybody, he will say anything, and he will do anything—including using his own family—to get out from under," Kelly said. "And *that's* Robert Oakley Marshall. Make no mistake about it."

Through it all, Marshall sat silently, shaking his head slowly from side to side. With one last, derisive thrust of his arm, Kelly left him and recrossed the

courtroom and took up a position at the very front
row of the jury box.

Now his voice was soft again, his manner solemn. "I
didn't know Maria Marshall," he said, "but I know
and you know that she loved her boys. I know and you
know that she loved her husband. For eight months
that lady knew that his afternoons were spent in the
arms of another woman.

"Yet she continued to cook for him, she continued
to clean his clothes, she continued to keep the house
clean, and she continued to make love with him—
because she loved him.

"She wanted to start all over. She wanted to give
him a second chance. She had the right to live her life
in full. To watch her boys continue to grow. To watch
them graduate from school, to get married, to have
families of their own.

"But he tossed it all away because of his desperation
and his greed. And—*that*—is Robert Oakley Marshall."

For a moment, as Kelly finished—for more than a
moment—there was absolutely no reaction. The jammed
courtroom stayed frozen in silence, while the echoes
of Kelly's diatribe seemed still to reverberate from
wall to wall.

Then the sound of John Marshall's sobbing could be
heard. And, at the same time, a rush of whispers,
mingled with other sobs—these, seemingly, for Maria
and for the life she might have had—swept across the
crowded rows.

John leaned his head against Chris's shoulder and
let himself cry openly, as Chris struggled unsuccess-
fully to hold back his own tears.

Rob twisted in his seat, a grotesque smile on his
face, and looked back toward the boys, apparently still
hoping to see signs of support. There were none.
There was not even eye contact, except, finally, with

Roby, in the second row, and when it came Roby simply shook his head and looked away.

As the deputies led Rob away for the night, none of his sons stepped forward to hug him. Instead, eyes averted, heads down, they turned and filed slowly toward the door.

Back at 884 Crest Ridge Drive for the night, Chris couldn't decide whether he was in a circus or a zoo. Everyone was there and nothing made sense. Tessie McBride, and his father's old college friend Paul Kennedy, and Brenda Dew. (Christ! How *insane* it was to have Brenda Dew living in their house! A couple of days earlier, Roby had said, "Yeah, and when Dad gets off and comes home and finds her here, he'll say, 'Don't worry, boys, she's just like Mom.' ") And now even Brenda Dew's sister!

And all of them acting so goofy now, all of them such a pain in the ass. Tessie McBride cutting up yellow ribbons that she wanted them all to tie around oak trees in the morning, and everybody talking all this *prayer* talk—he felt as if he'd been taken captive and was living in *Jonestown* just before they drank the poisoned Kool-Aid—and Brenda Dew following him around, telling him that no matter what happened, "You got to be law-al to your daddy."

Where had all the good people gone? What had happened to Sal Coccaro, the Rogerses, the Pecks, the Critellis, the Perillis, all the sane, decent, normal friends they used to have?

What had happened, Chris knew, was that the bunker mentality that Tessie McBride had brought with her when she'd moved in—the rudeness, the scorn, the hostility toward anyone who was not "on the team," which meant *everyone* except members of the immediate family—had driven away all the well-intentioned,

caring, loving friends and neighbors who otherwise
might have been there to help.

And Chris knew also that he'd been part of it. And
Roby, too. The decision to show "support" had somehow become a decision not to associate with anyone
unwilling to do the same. It was a trap he wasn't quite
sure how he'd gotten himself into, but as he looked
around the dining room and living room of what had
once seemed the happiest home in the world, and saw
the people by whom he was surrounded, he knew it
was a trap from which somehow, someday, he'd have
to escape.

Then, from the dining room, he heard voices raised.
Tessie's, of course, was raised loudest. She was yelling
at Roby for something he'd said.

"I don't care!" she was saying. "You have *got* to
stay loyal! He's your *father!*" And Brenda Dew was
chiming in with drawls of agreement.

"But, *listen*," Roby said, in a voice that made them
pay attention. "There are some things that just aren't
right. That just don't fit."

"Now, Roby," said Paul Kennedy, "there are some
things that maybe you had just ought to keep to yourself. This night, of all nights, is not a night for negative
emotion. This is a night for faith and prayer."

Paul Kennedy knew, because Roby had already told
him—he was so upset by it that he had to tell *someone*—
how Rob had called him three times to try to get him
to lie. But Paul didn't want anyone else to know. God
forbid the truth should get out. That might make
"support" all the harder to maintain. Though probably not. Nobody seemed to care about the truth
anymore. All they wanted was Rob acquitted. Rob
acquitted could still mean—both Roby and Chris had
come to realize—a lot of insurance money to spread

around, especially when it did not seem that Felice would be there to soak it up.

When he saw Chris standing at the entrance to the dining room, Roby got up and left the table. "Come here," he said, "I've got to talk to you in private."

The two of them stepped into the living room.

"Chris, some things just aren't right," he said. "I know things that other people don't. Chris, Dad tried to get me to lie."

And then he told Chris the whole story. And John came in toward the end, wanting to know what was going on.

"John," Roby said, "we don't want to upset you with the details, but there are just some things that don't work."

"What are you saying?" John asked.

"John," Chris said, "you know we're all hoping for an innocent verdict tomorrow, but if it goes the other way—what we're trying to say—look, if they find him guilty it might not be by mistake."

Coming from his two older brothers—the only substitutes he'd ever have for parents—this was more than John could bear to hear.

"No!" he said. "There's no way. He can't be guilty!"

And John left them and went back to the dining room, to rejoin Tessie and Brenda and Paul and Brenda's sister, who could tell him again how the case against his father was all lies.

Roby and Chris stayed up late that night. Just the two of them, talking. Remembering. Remembering how they'd be playing stickball in the street and their father would be working in his office and he'd hear them and come out and join in. How he'd always shown up at all their games, going way back to third grade—soccer, biddy basketball, things that didn't mean a thing except when you were the kid and it was your father who cared enough to come. And the Christmas mornings, year after year, the pile of presents always higher than the year before, the wrapping paper always a little more expensive, and their father seeming so full of joy and pride as he took the home movies that then were filed away, unwatched for years. And the good times they'd had in Florida, fishing and waterskiing. And the ski trip to Brodie Mountain in the Berkshires. And how happy—how much in love with him—their mother had always seemed. How much in love with each other they'd all seemed. They were such a cliché and they knew it but that didn't stop them from loving every minute of their lives. The All-American family. The American Dream that came true.

And hadn't it been real—any of it?

After a while, they couldn't talk anymore. They just sat on the floor in an upstairs hallway, leaning against a wall, each with one arm over the shoulder of the other. Roby and Chris. Ages twenty and nineteen. With the tears streaming shamelessly down their cheeks.

27

MAYS Landing is a quiet South Jersey town, twelve miles inland and not on a main route to anywhere. If it weren't the county seat, and were not therefore the site of the county courthouse, it is not likely that many travelers passing through would tend to pause, and not much more likely that many travelers would even pass through.

In 1935, in the depths of the Depression, the American Sunbathing Association had opened a nudist colony in Mays Landing. This was considered such a boost to the local economy that not even religious leaders protested. Colony members, it was reported at the time, were "sound-minded and not at all queer."

Almost a half century later, few who had been in attendance in Judge Greenberg's courtroom were willing to bestow such a charitable judgment upon the principals and supporting players in the trial of Rob Marshall and Ricky Dew.

But the town of Mays Landing—unlike Toms River, where the very air was incandescent in anticipation of the verdicts—seemed not to care. The town of Mays Landing, in fact, seemed scarcely to be aware of what had been occurring and of what was about to occur.

There is only one central intersection in Mays Landing, and, except for the courthouse, not much clustered around that: a Rexall drugstore, a gas station, a coffee shop, a real estate agency that is open part-time and a store that sells used Classics Illustrated comic books.

But there is, in fact, the courthouse: a handsome brick building, two stories high and a full block long, if one measures in Mays Landing blocks. At the west end is a small park, which in summer, one can imagine, must be a pleasant place to sit beneath the high shade trees.

Atop the courthouse, rising above its central section, is a tall wooden cupola, painted white. This was the only part of the original eighteenth-century courthouse to be preserved when the new building was constructed in 1972.

Inside the cupola is a bell, a large bell, which can be rung by someone standing one flight below, pulling on a long, heavy rope.

The door leading to the stairway was always kept locked and the key that would open it had years before been tucked away in an obscure drawer in an obscure desk in an obscure corner of one of the more obscure courthouse offices.

No one could remember the last time the bell had been rung. But in its day it had served a purpose.

During the time that the original courthouse had stood, Mays Landing and the area around it had been farm country. In the earliest of those days, the bell at the top of the courthouse tower had been the one way to summon the farmers from their fields and the farm wives from their houses, to call them to the center of town for an announcement of extraordinary importance.

The bell might have been used to signal the start of a war, or one's end, but no one was quite sure of that. The one purpose it did have that was still clearly remembered was to announce to the townspeople of Mays Landing and its environs that a jury in the courthouse had reached a decision in a case where a guilty verdict could mean death.

Had not State Senator John Russo of Toms River brought about the reinstitution of the death penalty in New Jersey four years before, it is entirely possible that the bell atop the Mays Landing courthouse might never have rung again.

But now, at 11:15 on the crystal-blue morning of Wednesday, March 5, for the first time within the memory of most living residents, the sound of the bell was heard across the town and down the back roads that led into the pines. It was a slow, deep, gonglike sound, and it repeated itself again and again as a sheriff's deputy stood at the foot of the stairwell and pulled on the long, heavy rope.

And the courtroom filled, and the judge took his seat, and the prisoners were brought forth from their cells to face the verdict.

Judge Greenberg read first from that portion of the verdict form that applied to Ricky Dew.

"Not guilty," he said.

Dew smiled, just slightly, then shook the hand of Nathan Baird.

"You're free to leave now, if you desire," Judge Greenberg told Dew.

And Dew stood, nodded his thanks to the judge, then walked across to the prosecutor's table and firmly shook Kevin Kelly's hand.

"Take care, Kev," he said, smiling more broadly now.

"Good luck, Ricky," Kelly said, returning the handshake.

This was done in the manner of two professional

athletes congratulating one another after a hard but cleanly fought contest. May the better man win. That sort of thing.

Then Dew stepped through the low, swinging gate that had symbolically separated him from freedom throughout the trial, and walked into the arms of his tearful wife, Brenda.

Next, Judge Greenberg read from that part of the verdict form that applied to Robert Marshall.

"Guilty," he said.

Rob's chest heaved once, but otherwise he showed no emotion. In the front row, directly behind him, Roby and Chris began to sob. John buried his head in Paul Kennedy's shoulder. Kennedy was holding a Bible in his hand.

So it's over, Chris thought. *No technicalities. I always said nothing could be worse than not knowing. I was wrong. This is worse. Why, Dad, why? How could you have?*

And then he thought of the last time he'd ever spoken to his mother: when they'd called him from the table at Harrah's to try to talk him into coming home for the weekend.

You knew, Dad. You knew then, when you got on the phone and said, "Hi, Chris, how are you doing? How's it going so far? Is the work hard?" You knew that when you hung up you were going to take my mother up that dark road and into that dark place and be sure that she didn't come out alive. And you sounded so normal, Dad, you sounded so much like yourself.

Roby's thoughts were less coherent. He just kept asking himself, *Why couldn't they have said, "Not guilty"? That way we'd have him back. That way we'd have a life again. That way it could all have been a mistake. That way he could have been telling the truth.*

That way I would not have been such a fool for keeping faith.

Ricky Dew stepped out into the morning sunshine and held a press conference on the front steps of the courthouse. He said he had no idea why Ferlin L'Heureux had named him as the shooter, "except he knew me well enough, I guess, to know that on any given day I might not know where I was at. I could've been on the lake, fishin'."

He also said he had no idea whether L'Heureux himself had been the shooter. "Everybody knows as much about this as I do. Just what they read about it in the papers and heard about it on the TV. That's all I knew about it from the start and that's all I know about it now."

Then somebody asked him how he liked New Jersey.

"I don't know," he said, grinning. "I ain't seen enough of it to know."

Then he and Brenda and Brenda's sister walked across the street and climbed into his silver Dodge van and he slid behind the wheel and gave a last, cheerful wave to reporters and drove off.

Inside the courthouse, Rob Marshall's sons and a few supporters were gathered behind the closed doors of a witness room, shielded from public view. Some were crying. The boys were red-eyed.

"Now, there's a scripture," Paul Kennedy was saying, as he turned to a page he'd marked in his Bible.

"I don't want to hear your damned proverbs!" Chris shouted. Then he turned to Tessie McBride. "And don't give me any of your sappy little sayings, either. Sometimes I think the whole bunch of you have the mentality of a Hallmark greeting card."

He burst out of the witness room and into a hallway, where, immediately, he saw a dozen reporters and photographers and TV cameramen running toward a rear exit.

"Your father just collapsed!" one of them shouted, running past.

Chris sprinted for the rear door and got to the outside parking lot just in time to see an ambulance pulling away with his father inside it.

He stood there, shouting after it, "Dad . . . Dad . . . Dad . . ." until it turned a corner and disappeared from view.

It did not become apparent until later in the day, but, when he'd reached the Garden State Parkway in his shiny silver van, Ricky Dew had not headed for Louisiana. Instead, he'd driven north up the parkway all the way to Toms River, a town he'd heard a lot about and wanted to see.

His route took him past the Oyster Creek picnic area. Because no one was following him, and because it was just he and Brenda and Brenda's sister in the van, no one can know whether he slowed down, or maybe even stopped—to take a first look, or maybe a last look—at the place where Maria Marshall had died.

But he did continue on to Toms River and, following Brenda's directions, drove to 884 Crest Ridge Drive, the former home of Rob and Maria Marshall.

"Just pickin' up some of my wife's luggage," he explained to a cluster of startled reporters gathered at the curb.

But Ricky stayed on a while, he didn't leave right away. Somewhere inside the house he found a bright red Philadelphia Phillies baseball cap, a souvenir Maria had brought home once from a game. She hadn't been an avid baseball fan, but she was an enthusiast in whatever she did, and so, if she went to a game she'd buy a cap and wear it while she cheered for the home team.

Ricky Dew was wearing it now. It didn't really fit too well, but he'd stuck it on his head anyway—just funnin'—as he stood on the Marshalls' front lawn and had another little chat with the press.

It was a very pleasant afternoon in Toms River, a good day to be outdoors, and Ricky Dew seemed in no hurry to leave. He hadn't been outdoors much for fourteen months and he seemed to be enjoying it. The air was mellow and the sun warm enough to make it seem that an early spring would soon arrive.

Eventually, Tessie McBride and the rest of the Marshall contingent pulled up, and they all milled around on the front lawn for a while—John seemed tearful and Roby seemed stunned, wandering vaguely about, as if he'd been heavily sedated. Ricky, still wearing Maria's Phillies cap, continued to chat with the reporters and the television people.

But Ricky wanted to be on the road before dark, and the others had to go inside to start taking down the Welcome Home, Dad decorations that John had stayed up late the night before putting up, so soon it was goodbye time, with lots of handshakes and embraces all around. Brenda made sure she hugged both Roby and John and reminded them to always stay "law-al" to their dad. Ricky gave each boy a firm handshake and a smile.

Then, with a final wave to the television cameras, he took off the Phillies cap and climbed into his van and was gone.

Chris was not present for Ricky and Brenda's farewell. He, alone among the members of the Marshall family, had stayed behind in Mays Landing to see if his father would be well enough to face the sentencing due to come that afternoon.

Rob had been examined at a nearby emergency room following his fainting spell and nothing was found to be wrong. He was back in the Mays Landing courtroom by 1:30 P.M. and the sentencing phase of the proceedings commenced.

Under New Jersey law, sentencing in a capital punishment case is actually a whole separate trial, before the same jury that delivered the verdict. Each side can even call witnesses. There are only two possible outcomes: a life sentence with eligibility for parole after thirty years, or death by lethal injection.

In this instance, neither side called anyone. Carl Seely—a shellshocked Carl Seely, bereft of the chipperness and suavity with which he'd glided through six weeks of trial—spoke briefly about why Rob should receive the life sentence with parole eligibility after thirty years. He cited two factors: Rob had no prior criminal record and he'd long been active in civic affairs.

When Kevin Kelly spoke, it was if he were an altar boy again. He displayed none of the righteous anger he'd shown during cross-examination or closing argument. He was, in fact, as drained and as unanimated as Seely.

He said simply, "Maria Marshall had no prior criminal history, either. Maria Marshall was civic-minded, too. But Rob Marshall did not give her the option of thirty years. And I really cannot think of any crime more heinous in our society than handing money over to someone to kill your own wife."

The jury went back to deliberate, this time solely on the question of what punishment Rob should receive.

This time, it took them ninety minutes. When they returned with their written decision, it was handed to the judge, as the verdict had been, by the young forewoman who worked as a dealer at Harrah's. Rather an attractive young woman, really—maybe even Rob Marshall's type. She'd even worn a Miami Vice T-shirt to court.

After glancing at the verdict form, Judge Greenberg asked Rob to stand. Then, as he had earlier, the judge spoke in a calm, colorless voice.

"Robert O. Marshall," he said, "I sentence you to death as required by law . . ."

There was more. ". . . delivered to the custody of the commissioner of corrections . . . kept in solitary confinement . . . until such date and time . . . ordered to execute the sentence in the manner provided by law . . ."

But the word "death" was the last one Chris Marshall remembered hearing.

He sat still and alone—beyond tears, at least for the moment—as a phalanx of armed deputies stepped forward, obscuring his father from view.

And he remained there, staring silently, as the brown-shirted officers, guns bulging from their hips, locked arms around Rob and led him out a rear door to the van that would take him to Trenton.

By that night he'd be on death row. And it occurred to Chris then (knowing that death row inmates were permitted no contact visits whatsoever) that no matter how much he might ever want to—not that he was at all sure he ever would—he'd never again be able to hug or to touch his father.

His father was gone, just as surely as his mother. And he was alone now, surrounded by strangers, with the rest of his life left to live.

Wondering if, through some frightful cosmic miscalculation, it was not he and his brothers, rather than their father, who had been relegated to the place in hell.

EPILOGUE

"This whole case is about money.
He didn't do it for love."

—*Ferlin L'Heureux*

ANDREW Myers was tried that June. The prosecutor's office had offered him a deal in which he'd be permitted to go free after pleading guilty to a charge of conspiracy to commit insurance fraud, but he turned it down, apparently hoping that after being tried and acquitted he'd be able to file a large lawsuit against Ocean County for false arrest.

Instead, in a verdict that many even in the prosecutor's office found shocking and disturbing, he was convicted of conspiracy to commit murder and sentenced to life imprisonment. He will not become eligible for parole until after thirty years of the sentence have been served.

Ferlin L'Heureux entered the Federal Witness Protection Program shortly after the Marshall trial but stayed in it for only a few weeks. He said it was overly restrictive and cramped his entrepreneurial style. After testifying in the Myers trial, he was sentenced by Judge Greenberg to five years in prison, but served less than three months before being released on parole, in accordance with his plea agreement. Following his release, he returned to Shreveport and a life of private enterprise.

In formally accepting the L'Heureux plea bargain as valid, Judge Greenberg read from the bench a carefully worded statement that said, in part:

"The acquittal of defendant [Dew] does not lead to the conclusion that the plea agreement should be rejected on the ground that [L'Heureux] did not testify truthfully, as required by the agreement. It must be kept in mind that a finding of not guilty is not the equivalent of a finding of innocence by the jury. The verdict of not guilty as to [Dew] may instead merely reflect the jury's decision that the state's case against him was not proven beyond a reasonable doubt, in view of the fact that [L'Heureux's] testimony as to [Dew's] involvement in the murder was virtually uncorroborated . . .

"In order to reject the agreement for failure of [L'Heureux] to have testified truthfully, there should be clear and convincing evidence of the falsity of his testimony. The testimony of [Dew] and his alibi witnesses does not rise to this level."

It didn't matter to Ricky Dew, though. He returned to Louisiana and he and Brenda filed a $50-million lawsuit against the county prosecutor, investigators Gladstone and O'Brien, and the Ocean County Board of Freeholders. Dew claimed his civil rights had been violated by malicious prosecution and wrongful arrest. He sought $25 million for the personal and emotional injury he suffered as a result, and Brenda sought $25 million to compensate her for the suffering she endured in having been deprived of his company for fourteen months. (In May of 1988, following a two-week trial in Red River Parish, Louisiana, a jury rejected his claims, holding the Ocean County detectives blameless.)

Dew also wrote a letter to John Marshall, telling the

youngest of Rob's three sons that he was welcome at
any time for a visit, or even to live.

And, occasionally, late at night, Dew would pick up
his telephone and call Kevin Kelly. He'd say, "Just
checkin', Kev. Just want to see how you're doin'."
Then he'd laugh a little and hang up.

Kelly left the prosecutor's office, as planned, and began to devote his full time to private practice.

Early in 1987, the county prosecutor was appointed to
a Superior Court judgeship.

Felice Rosenberg remained reunited with her husband,
David, and the couple continued to reside at the beach,
where, in summer, they could occasionally be seen
strolling at water's edge in matching bikini bottoms.
(In Felice's case, there was also a top.)

Her father, Fred Frankel, had died of a heart attack
in October of 1984, only weeks after learning of her
involvement with Rob Marshall.

Maria's father, Dr. Vincent Puszynski, suffered a heart
attack himself during Rob's trial, which he did not
attend. He was stricken after reading in the Philadelphia *Inquirer* that Rob had testified that Dr. Puszynski
was convinced of Rob's innocence and was supporting
him fully.

By late April 1986, Dr. Puszynski had recovered
sufficiently to send a letter to Sal Coccaro, in which he
said:

"Ever since the trial ended, I've been trying to get
the boys together and learn their true feelings and
beliefs regarding their father, although I know that
John will not even admit a possibility of guilt. No
wonder, living in the midst of the pro-Marshall clan.

As long as that snake is alive, he'll keep his fangs in those kids . . . I'll do my utmost to dissuade Roby and Chris from giving in to him. They've been hurt enough."

Not long afterward, however, Dr. Puszynski suffered a second and fatal heart attack. Maria's mother, having slipped deep into senility, was placed in a nursing home.

Settling in for the years-long appeals process that was certain to forestall execution at the least, Rob Marshall remained on death row in Trenton.

"Rob's problem," said one old and well-connected friend in Toms River, "I should say, one of his problems, was that he could not distinguish. He mistook an erection for a vocation. He got grand opera and soap opera mixed up. He saw himself and Felice as star-crossed lovers, daring to challenge the social order. What the rest of us saw was this forty-five-year-old asshole shacking up in cheap motels with Little Miss Hotpants from down the street.

"See, all around Rob, in the eighties, everybody was scoring everything: sex, dope, big-money deals. At least, he thought so. While poor Rob, he was just selling insurance and stuck with an iceberg for a wife. You know, one of those 'you can look but you'd better not touch' ladies. It finally got to him.

He was weak with numbers, he didn't know how to turn a piece of real estate—and around here these are major character flaws—but the one thing he had was a pecker. When Felice seemed to like it he got delusions of grandeur.

"Buy her jewelry, buy her silver, sprinkle rose petals all over the sheets, but then you got to go public—what good is she if you can't show her off? It was as if she wasn't just a broad—David's wife—it was like she was the hottest piece of real estate in town. And Rob had her. He owned her. He'd seen what he wanted and he took it. And he figured he'd never have to listen to that 'Ken and Barbie' snickering behind his back again.

"Trouble was, he got hooked on the casinos at the same time. Nobody knows, nobody will ever know, just how much he pissed away down there, but it was enough to put him in very bad trouble, and I don't mean just socially.

"Listen, in this town—in Brookside anyway, or at the country club—the slightest *whiff* that maybe there's less in the till than there was last year and it's like you got a social disease. In Rob's case, we're not talking social disease, we're talking the equivalent of AIDS. It's fatal.

"Nobody will ever know how bad the trouble was, and who he might have gone to for help—although I can tell you one thing: he was right there on his knees with the rest of them at Gigliotti's funeral, and if you go check a calendar you'll see that Gigliotti's funeral happened to be the day before Rob had his first meet with L'Heureux.

"And something else that never came out: Felice told the prosecutor's office—this was back when she was telling them everything, so they could let her off the hook and keep the right people happy—that Marshall was spending time at the Key West Lounge with Riccio and Gigliotti. It's all down on paper. Not in the official reports, you understand, but it's there.

"What do you think he was doing over there, break-dancing with the teenyboppers? The Key West Lounge was Cocaine City, and there's poor, square Rob Marshall right in the middle of it, with no idea how deep the shit was he was into. And meanwhile, back home, doing the laundry nice and fresh and melting the butter for the pancakes, there's good old reliable gung-ho Maria: without the slightest *clue* about what's happening.

"When she starts to pick up a couple of clues, she can't believe it. This can't be happening to her. This wasn't the way she was brought up. Hey, she's the swim team Mother of the Year. The happy lady waving that big blue finger that says 'We're Number One' and leaving notes in her kids' underwear drawers saying 'Smile, you're a champ.'

"But, hey, that's over now. Things got a little out of whack for a while but everything's back to normal now. No harm done, except, I guess, to Maria.

"And to Rob. You could say, I suppose, that there was harm done to Rob. On the other hand, you could also say he was the one who done it.

"I'll tell you who really got screwed in all this, and everybody says it but that doesn't make it any less true, is the boys. Those poor boys. Those poor boys. I wonder if they'll ever recover.

On April 1, 1987, more than a year after the conviction, Chris Marshall, then a junior at Lehigh University, wrote his father a letter of the kind most sons never have to write.

    Dad,

       The following is a response to your most recent letter and a collection of recent thoughts. There is no particular order to these but I feel the point is clear.

    (1) I think you're guilty.
    (2) I hate you for what *you* did to Mom.
    (3) I hate you for what *you* did to Grandpop.
    (4) I hate you for what *you* did to Grandmom.
    (5) I hate you for what *you* did to our family.
    (6) I hate you for what *you* did to John.

(7) I hate you for what *you* did to Roby.

(8) I hate you for what *you* did to me.

I hate having to talk to you on the phone. In the future, if you want to call, make it person-to-person for John. Otherwise, I will not accept.

I hate getting letters from you. *DO NOT RESPOND TO THIS ONE, I WILL NOT READ IT.* Any letter I receive from you from now on I'm not even going to open. If you *must* contact me, do so through my lawyer: Eugene Leahy.

You were right about one thing, I will do what I want; just like you always did. The difference is I'm not going to kill anybody doing it.

Your son,
Chris

Six weeks later, on Mother's Day 1987, which was a hot and sunny Sunday in Toms River, Roby Marshall sat on a lawn chair in front of a modest home on a well-traveled road in a section of Toms River where the houses were a lot cheaper than in Brookside.

The home belonged to the father of Roby's girlfriend, who was soon to become his fiancée. The small, dirt-covered front yard was filled with tables on top of which were arrayed all that remained of what once had been the possessions of Rob and Maria Marshall.

The house at 884 Crest Ridge Drive had been sold. Now, Roby and his girlfriend, whose name was Michelle DiGiacinto, were holding a tag sale to dispose of its contents. Even Rob's old roulette wheel and blackjack table were up for sale.

"You know," Roby said, "if we'd put up a sign that said 'Last Chance to Grab a Piece of Rob Marshall,' instead of just 'Tag Sale,' I bet we'd do a whole lot better." Then he grinned.

There was about him an air of relaxation and even contentment that came as a surprise to a visitor who

had not seen him since the days of turmoil that had
enveloped his father's conviction. He seemed at peace
with himself and his circumstances.

"It's true," he said. "Going into the trial, I remember saying that once I had everything and now I had
nothing. But the wheel didn't stop there. It kept on
turning, and now I feel—I know this will sound strange,
but it's from the heart—I feel I have everything again.

"The thing is, I've learned what's important and
what's not. Michelle has done that for me. She's taught
me so much. She and her father. The way I used to
be—the values I used to have—I wouldn't even have
known people like this. I wouldn't have bothered with
them, I would have looked down on them, just because they didn't have money.

"Michelle's father used to drive an ice cream truck.
Now he's a handyman. He's the kind of guy we would
have *hired* in the old days, not someone I ever would
have thought could have had anything important to
say.

"But, I swear to God, he's saved me. He and Michelle. I had a hard time, I had a real hard time, after
the trial. I just couldn't accept that my father had
done it. I *knew* it was true, but I couldn't accept it in
my heart.

"It took months. Last summer, I'd go over to the
beach at night all by myself and just sit there under
the boardwalk and watch the ocean and think. I'd sit
there for hours, sometimes all night, and I remember
one night I did that, and there was this tremendous
thunder-and-lightning storm out over the ocean and I
just sat there through it all, watching the sky light up
and hearing the thunder, and when it was all over—I
don't want this to sound too mystical or anything, it's
just the way it happened—when it was over, I suddenly felt like my own head had cleared, like the sky.

"And I realized—I realized—I just didn't believe him anymore and I'd never believe him again. And that was it. It was like this tremendous burden being lifted. Because ever since he'd called me at school and asked me to lie for him I knew, I *knew* he had to be guilty. I knew it but I couldn't accept it.

"Suddenly, as that dawn came, after the storm, I could accept it. I know this may sound like bullshit but it was like all at once there was nothing to fight about anymore. Hey—facts are facts. Lies are lies. It was over. I drove to my friend's house, Keith Wolff's, and I remember waking him up and just telling him, 'Keith, Keith, it's over. I just don't believe him anymore.' And then I cried. And Keith said, 'Thank God, man, now you can rejoin the real world.'

"See, that's what it had been like for so long. This big pretense that Tessie McBride was maintaining and my father was maintaining and we were expected to maintain. I tried to do it—I tried to do it for months, even after the conviction, out of that misguided sense of loyalty.

"Once I stopped fighting it, once I accepted the truth, it was like I was at this point of exact zero, or something. Like this point of nothingness. And what I realize now is that that's what made room in my heart for Michelle.

"She helped me to understand that I was a victim, too. She let me feel the way *I* wanted to feel about all this—not the way people told me I was supposed to feel. I was *right* to feel angry! That was okay. She and her Dad let me know it wasn't my fault. See, I think subconsciously that was part of the problem. Somehow, I was blaming *myself* for Mom's death.

"Michelle and her dad, they both told me: 'Nothing you could have done could have prevented this. And there's nothing you can ever do to change it. Believe what's in your heart, not what your father tells you to believe.'

"It sounds obvious sitting and talking about it now, but it's what has totally transformed my life. It's made me feel like I *have* a life again.

"And it's a life with a completely different set of values. I don't look at a lack of money as being a flaw anymore. Now, I look at it as being an asset, because it can make you a down-to-earth person. Michelle and I, we do things like—*go for walks*. Things that don't cost any money. I mean, I guess it shouldn't have taken me twenty years and the death of my mother to understand this, but you don't have to spend money to have fun. And you don't have to have money to be worth loving. And I love Michelle. And that's what I mean—I feel like I have everything again." He laughed. "Hey, Michelle has even taught me to like *dogs*."

The sun was growing hotter. Occasionally, a car would stop and Roby would get up to make a sale. He wasn't in the mood to drive hard bargains. "How much?" he'd say. "I don't know, what's the tag say, ten bucks? You can have it for five. Three, three, make it three, that's fine."

He walked among the tables, pointing at random. "I'd give this stuff away," he said, "except if you put up a sign that said 'Free Stuff,' nobody would stop because they'd all assume it was junk. Hey, a lot of it probably is. But it's memories. Twenty years of marriage, twenty years of memories. "For sale," he called out. "Right here! While they last! Get 'em cheap!"

Then he sat down in the lawn chair again. "Another thing I've come to accept," he said, "and this one's been harder, is that the loss will never go away. It's like, I used to feel, 'Hey, I should be over this by now.'

"I'm not ever going to be over it. I see a station

wagon drive by that's like Mom's and all of a sudden I'll feel sad. I'll see some woman in a supermarket who just for a minute looks like her, and I get this like *jolt* of sadness and it'll even bring tears to my eyes. Anything can trigger a memory.

"For like a year and a half it was all 'Dad, Dad, Dad, how terrible what's happening to Dad.' That's all I was surrounded by. But it's like Michelle said: 'You've got to stop thinking about your father and start thinking about what happened to your mother. You've got to mourn. Otherwise, you'll never move beyond it.'

"So, I'm mourning. I'm letting myself feel how much I miss Mom, I'm not fighting it. And most of the time it's okay, I can deal. But, Jesus, this past week has been a bitch. All those Mother's Day commercials on TV."

By midafternoon the sun was too hot and no cars were stopping anymore. Roby dragged what hadn't been sold into Michelle's father's garage. Then he drove to the condominium into which he and his brothers had recently moved.

He said some people found it strange that they'd want to remain in Toms River, but, he said, it was the only hometown they'd ever known, and, having lost so much else, they felt they needed something familiar to hang on to.

"Besides," he said, "it's close to the beach. And that's one value that's never gonna change. I love the beach."

Chris Marshall was at the condominium, where the powerful central air-conditioning unit provided a bracing antidote to the heat.

Likewise, Chris's mood seemed in sharp contrast to Roby's. The act of writing such a forceful letter to his father, after two and half years of fighting back his feelings in order to offer support, seemed to have energized him.

Where Roby was newly tranquil, Chris seemed still flush with rebellion.

"Yeah," he said, "my father's written back since I sent him that letter. He's written back about twenty times. But I have no idea what he's saying because I don't even open the envelopes. I just throw them right in the garbage, like he threw Mom.

"I'll never forgive him. There's no way I could forgive him for what he's done.

"Not that he's exactly begging for forgiveness. He's still keeping up the charade. All the bullshit. I reached a point last summer where I just couldn't take it anymore. Tessie McBride called up and said she was setting up a visiting schedule for prison, and I said, 'I'm sick of this shit! I think he's guilty and I'm never going to see him again.'

"I figured it was time for a total break. Time to lay it all out and let my father know just how I felt. And that's it. That's the last communication I'll ever have with him. Philosophically, I haven't really figured out how I feel about the death penalty, but as far as my father goes, if they execute him it's no big deal—to me he's already been dead for a long time.

"And just for what he did to John he should be. By the time this happened, Mom's murder, my personality was already formed. I had already gone to college. *But John was only thirteen years old.* He still had four or five years of mothering coming to him and my father took those away from him. I'm his legal guardian now, big deal. Who's going to make him pancakes in the morning?

"But this is Mother's Day. I don't want to talk about my father. I'm sick of talking about him, hearing about him and thinking about him and nothing but him since the night my mother was killed.

"I'll tell you a story about my mother, although this involves my father, too—maybe there is no escaping it. But this is something I think about a lot. It was three years ago, just about this time of year, maybe a little later in May because Roby had just come home from his freshman year at Villanova.

"To celebrate, we went out to the club for an early supper. We were at this big table in the corner where they usually seated us, and they'd just brought our appetizers to the table. I remember that, because mine was shrimp cocktail and it was nearly inedible.

"Then Tom Kenyon and his wife walked in and were seated very near us. Maybe not right next to us, but pretty close. And I could see that for some reason my mom was getting upset. Then, just as the main courses arrived, she started to cry. She got right up from the table and put her sunglasses on so nobody could see she was crying and left the room.

"She must have been gone for twenty minutes. The waitress asked my father if they should take the food back to the kitchen to keep it warm but he said no, she'd be right back. Finally, he and Roby got up and went outside to look for her. And I remember just sitting there with John, looking down at all this food that suddenly I knew none of us were going to eat, and wondering, *what the hell is going on?*

"We never did eat the meal. She came back in, with her sunglasses still on, but after about five minutes of nobody saying anything we all just got up and left. When I asked her that night what the trouble was, all she said was, 'I've been upset lately, it's been the buildup of a lot of things.'

"It wasn't until all that stuff came out at the trial about my mom going to see Mr. Kenyon and then him telling Felice everything she'd said that I realized that must have been it: here we were, this supposedly perfectly happy family, this *advertisement* for the good life in Toms River, and just as the main course arrives in walks the one man in town who my mom knows is aware that the whole thing is a sham.

"I think she just couldn't take it. She just couldn't take pretending when she knew that ten feet away there was somebody who knew the truth. And I think that might have made her realize that pretty soon all the pretending was going to have to stop.

"Well, it did," Chris said. "Just not quite soon enough."

Roby came into the living room. He was carrying a folded letter on pink stationery.

"Do you remember," he asked, "that my mom and my Uncle Gene were supposed to meet Dad that Monday morning, and lay everything out in front of him? Well, here's the letter she was going to give him at the meeting."

It wasn't long. It took up only one side of the paper. It said:

"The first 20 years."
I hope that you can be whatever you need to be with me.
I hope that you sense enough love from me to feel easy about smiling when you need to smile and crying when you need to cry.
I really hope that you feel secure enough with me to be silent or to show your needs or just ask for a hug.
Feeling that secure is important—I know, because I need that feeling of security from you, too.

All my love, Maria

"Security," Roby said, his eyes suddenly filled with tears. "That's all she wanted from him—security."

"Instead," Chris said, "he gave her a couple of forty-five slugs in the back."

They stared at the note for a few moments without saying anything. Then Chris looked at his watch. It was 4:30 P.M.

"Where's John, upstairs?" he asked.

"Yeah," Roby said.

"Let's go get him. It's time to go to the cemetery."

They brought roses, red roses, just three.

Within days of their father's conviction, the boys had gone to the funeral home in Toms River and had been given their mother's ashes, which had been kept in the cardboard box in the drawer.

They'd buried the ashes in a plot at St. Joseph's Cemetery and had marked the plot with a headstone inscribed with the words Maria had written on the back of Roby's appointment card from Stockton State College a week before she died: "Our Greatest Glory Consists Not in Never Falling but in Rising Every Time We Fall."

The afternoon had turned very warm, as much like July as May. The bright sun gave off a glare. A hot wind blew across the wide expanse of grass, rustling tall trees that were already in full leaf, and setting up a bobbing motion among dozens, maybe hundreds of Mylar balloons that had been affixed to grave sites throughout the cemetery.

This was, apparently, some sort of new tradition in Toms River. Marking special occasions by putting a Mylar balloon on a tombstone instead of flowers.

Roby, Chris and John had only their flowers, one each. They parked on the edge of an asphalt roadway and walked slowly toward their mother's grave.

When they reached it, they knelt together for many long minutes in silent, tearful prayer.

Then each one placed his rose at the base of the tombstone, and together, in fact with their arms around one another, the three sons of Robert and Maria Marshall—two convinced of their father's guilt, the youngest still clinging to his own belief in innocence— walked back toward the roadway, squinting a bit as the sun and the hot breeze dried their tears.